Library of
Davidson College

THE POLITICAL ECONOMY OF SOVIET DEFENCE SPENDING

Also by R.T. Maddock

THE GROWTH OF THE BRITISH ECONOMY, 1918–1968 (*with G.A. Phillips*)

The Political Economy of Soviet Defence Spending

R.T. Maddock

St. Martin's Press   New York

© R.T. Maddock, 1988

All rights reserved. For information, write:
Scholarly & Reference Division,
St. Martin's Press, Inc., 175 Fifth Avenue, New York, NY 10010

First published in the United States of America in 1988

Printed in Hong Kong

ISBN 0–312–01579–8

Library of Congress Cataloging-in-Publication Data
Maddock, R.T. (Rowland Thomas)
The political economy of Soviet defence spending / R.T. Maddock.
p. cm.
Bibliography: p.
Includes index.
ISBN 0–312–01579–8: $30.00 (est.)
1. Soviet Union—Armed Forces—Appropriations and expenditures—
—Economic aspects.   I. Title.
UA770.M29 1988
355.6'22'0947—dc19   87–25075
                                                                  CIP

I Margaret a fy Mam

Contents

Preface ix

1 Estimating the Scale of Soviet Defence Expenditures 1
2 Explaining Soviet Defence Spending 26
3 The Defence Burden 66
4 Economic Growth 95
5 Competing Claims 120
6 External Relations 147
7 Conclusion and Speculation 179

Notes and References 193
Index 217

Preface

Mr Gorbachev's drive for economic modernisation has highlighted to an unusual degree the interrelatedness of military and civilian production in the USSR. The one always was a precondition for the other and the present study seeks to illuminate the nature of the relationship. It is firmly in the interdisciplinary tradition of political economy, which despite its lack of a secure methodology does offer insights complementary to those of the more precisely defined social sciences. Political economy does, however, require the indulgence of those specialists who may be irritated by what they believe to be the casual approach of the generalist to their disciplines. To the economist the analysis lacks rigour and to the political scientist richness of detail. This is the consequence of a study which seeks not so much to push forward but to use existing insights to analyse one particular issue.

I should like to thank those who have assisted with the writing of the book but who for various reasons wish to remain anonymous.

Finally to Mrs Pam Davies grateful thanks for typing so many drafts with her customary and exceptional efficiency and good humour.

R.T. MADDOCK

1 Estimating the Scale of Soviet Defence Expenditures

The Soviet Union has a larger military base and produces a greater array of conventional and nuclear weapons in larger quantities than any other country.[1] It funds a comprehensive military-related space programme, and, with the USA, is one of the two largest armaments exporters.[2] Yet according to its own budgetary data it spent from 17 to 18 billion rubles on defence each year between 1970 and 1984, equivalent to about 3 per cent or so of national income, or just over 2 per cent of the more usual Western measure of gross national product. At existing exchange rates this is equivalent to about 23 bn dollars. In 1984, the USA spent 250 bn dollars in current prices on defence. During that period, the armed forces grew by over 400 000, the stock, the procurement, the technological and operating parameters of weapons systems all increased, as did the fixed and current capital base necessary to sustain a large modern army.

The known physical dimensions of the Soviet military force are clearly quite incompatible with the funds officially allocated for its finance. It is just not possible for the Soviet Union to array such a formidable war machine by spending 17 to 18 bn rubles each year.

The official data, designed to confuse as much as to clarify, must be largely symbolic having a mainly propaganda function.[3] Soviet leaders set out to present the Soviet Union to its own citizens and to those of the non-aligned countries as a peace-seeking nation, reluctantly obliged to arm itself in response to the aggressive armaments expansion of the capitalist nations.[4] Such claims are unlikely to impress if the 'correct' figures were to reveal a level of spending in excess of that of any other country in the world. The published figures (Figure 1.1) must, however, be sufficiently large to explain and justify to the Soviet people their low living standards. Forced spending on military, instead of civilian goods and services, provides a convenient scapegoat for the systemic inefficiencies of the Soviet system, though it is doubtful that Soviet citizens actually believe in the accuracy of the published budget.

Not only do official data conceal the true level of spending, but the

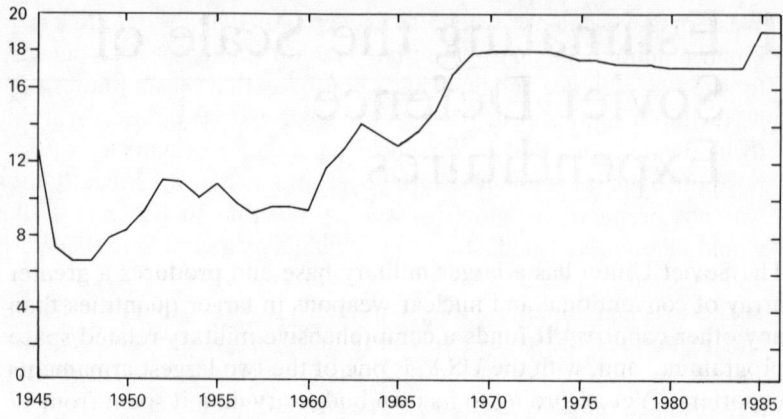

Figure 1.1 Soviet published defence expenditure, 1945–85 (R bn)

degree of concealment has altered over time, probably to meet short-term political objectives.[5] The evidence for this, like much else, is largely inferential. In the 1940s, data were issued on the distribution of the budget between military commissariats, or ministries, and up to 1961 the defence budget contained two entries: an *ex ante* forecast and an *ex post* figure of costs actually incurred. As might be anticipated for a dynamic economy liable to stochastic shocks, the two sets of figures differed, often by a substantial margin. In 1961, for instance, planned spending on military activities, initially set at 9.2 bn rubles, was revised to 12.3 bn rubles, but the sum eventually spent was 11.6 bn rubles.[6] Changes of this magnitude were however exceptional, and in this instance were connected with the Berlin crisis of that year. Subsequently, the difference between the two sets of figures diminished, and after 1963 vanished completely, an unlikely outcome in the absence of a completely inexplicable improvement in planning or budgetary techniques. Furthermore, it is known that sums of money have been periodically transferred between expenditure headings within the overall budget, presumably for reasons of political expediency. In 1959, for instance, some expenditure was shifted from the Defence category to that defined as Financing the National Economy (FNE) which finances, amongst other things, investment for industry and construction. In 1962, the reverse transfer occurred from FNE to Defence.[7] It is more than likely that further transfers, so far undetected by Western analysts, have occurred as circumstances warrant. This explains the largely passive response by

Western governments when, in November 1984, the Minister of Finance announced an apparently enormous increase of 12 per cent for the 1985 defence budget. This is not to say that the announcement was without significance. It was more than likely a political warning to its own citizens that increased living standards might have to be postponed again, and to Western governments that the Soviet Union was not prepared to allow its security position to be eroded, but would take, undisclosed, steps to match higher spending in the West, and especially in the USA.

There is agreement amongst Western experts that the budget underestimates the true level of military spending. There is less agreement, however, on what that true level is, and on what military activities are officially financed through the budget.

In view of disagreement over both methodology and data, it may be wondered whether the effort by intelligence services, private organizations and individuals to devise economic estimates of Soviet defence spending is worthwhile. War, after all, is not mainly an economic activity. The physical dimensions of the defence programme are well known, and knowledge of how much it costs in dollars or rubles to finance a given array of weapons does not assist the military strategists and planners. Even so, good estimates of the economic dimension of the military programme are useful.

The physical parameters of armed forces are varied and complex, and it is not possible to devise a consolidated index of aggregate military power in terms of purely operational criteria. Comparisons of military potential between different periods in one country, and, in the absence of war, between different countries at a point of, and over, time are especially difficult given that the numbers, the mix and the design and performance characteristics of weapons vary so considerably. Summary indices of pairs or groups of countries are feasible only by constructing synthetic measures which define the total array of parameters in terms of a common denominator. The simplest, most comprehensive and useful synthetic measure is value which, through the price system, gives an overall assessment of the dimension of defence programmes and allows an aggregated comparison of equivalent military worth.[8] Value estimates (Table 1.1) are, however, no more than analytic tools which enable useful economic judgements to be made about, for instance, the defence burden, and hence society's assessment of military versus civilian objectives which might otherwise be difficult to make. In addition the different items which constitute a defence budget can be aggregated

Table 1.1 Estimates of Soviet defence expenditure

	1955	1960	1965	1966	1970	1975	1980	1982	1983	1984
CIA (bn 1970 rubles)[1]	24–23	23–31	35–43		45–53	53–65	62–79		70–86	
CIA (bn 1979$)[2]					131	150	171			
DIA (bn current $)[3]								93	213	252
SIPRI (1980 $)[4]							122	131		142
French (bn current rubles)[5]					34	42				
British (bn current rubles)[6]							81–86			
Chinese (bn current rubles)[7]		19.0	29.2		49.6	69.4				
Lee (bn 1970 rubles)[8]		27–31	41–52			100–125				

[1] *Measures of Economic Growth and Development, 1950–1980*, studies prepared for the use of the Joint Economic Committee, Congress of the United States (Washington, DC) 1982.
[2] *Soviet and US Defence Activities, 1970–1979. SR80–10005* (Washington, DC: National Foreign Assessment Centre) 1980.
[3] *World Military Expenditure and Arms Transfers, 1972–1982* (Washington, DC: US Arms Control and Disarmament Agency) 1984.
[4] *World Armaments and Disarmament*. SIPRI Yearbook (London) 1985.
[5] *Combien de Rubles pour la Defense* (Paris: Defense National) 1976.
[6] *Statement on Defence Expenditures* (London: HMSO) 1981.
[7] *Peking Review*, 28 November 1975.
[8] *Hearings before the Subcommittee on Oversight of the Permanent Select Committee on Intelligence* (Washington, DC) 1980.

and disaggregated into useful or convenient subcategories, to reveal trends or turning points in the priorities given to competing services or missions, and thereby provide a supplementary source of information on military doctrine or strategic and tactical planning. It must be emphasised, however, that the major benefits are politico-economic rather than military.

Value figures may be calculated in a variety of forms and there is no *a priori* way of determining which is optimal, which must be a judgemental decision depending on the purpose for which the estimates are obtained. If the objective is to compare the level of spending between a pair of countries such as the USSR and the USA, or alliances such as the Warsaw Pact and NATO, data in local currencies must be converted to a common base. This is the justification for Western efforts to calculate Soviet military spending in dollars, though converting American data to rubles is equally valid, as indeed would be the conversion of both into a third currency.

Dollar estimates of Soviet spending are politically important inputs into Western, and in particular American, decisions on how much to spend on its own armaments.[9] To the extent that estimates of Soviet spending are used for political purposes in the USA, for good or bad, it is obviously sensible that they be available in a form easily understood, though the inherent conceptual and statistical limitations should also be known by the polity. For instance, comparison of Soviet and American spending in dollars will lead to quite different interpretations over the relative quantity of resources each country allocates for defence purposes, compared with estimates of exactly the same physical dimension measured in rubles. Countries tend to show an inverse relationship between price and quantities of goods and services, producing relatively more of the cheaper and less of the more expensive goods, models or brands. Due to systemic and policy-induced factors, and to the level of economic development which each country has attained, the Soviet price system differs quite markedly from that in the USA. Many goods which are relatively cheap in the USSR tend to be expensive in the USA, and vice versa, a phenomenon which exists in the military, quite as much as in the civilian sector. The Soviet Union will therefore produce in greater quantities those military goods which are cheap in rubles but expensive in American dollars, and vice versa. Since Soviet conscripted military personnel are comparatively cheap, and technologically sophisticated weaponry expensive, and the reverse true of the USA, a statistical device which weighs the Soviet array of weapons in American prices gives a high weight (price) to quantitatively abundant inputs (labour), and so exaggerate the level of Soviet defence spending compared with that of the USA. The reverse procedure, weighting American weapons in Soviet rubles, will tend to exaggerate American spending compared with that of the Soviet Union.[10] The value disparity between the two estimates will be larger the greater is the structural and price difference between the two countries. If Soviet prices were, in fact, similar to those which prevail in the USA, the Soviet quantity mix would differ from what it is in reality. Dollar estimates of Soviet military spending have one additional limitation; they do not, and cannot represent actual Soviet expenditures. These, of course, are always priced in rubles, so that if Western economists or politicians seek a representation of the sort of economic information available to Soviet leaders, the estimates must be constructed in rubles.

Ruble data can be calculated in fixed or current prices, and as with the choice of currency there is no reason in principle to prefer one measure over the other. If Western analysts seek to measure the growth of real spending on armaments over a period of time, fixed price indices which exclude inflationary increases are most useful. If, however, the objective is to assess the political and economic pressures on Soviet policy-makers in the light of competing demands for scarce resources, the measure of burden will be more usefully calculated in current rubles.

Since all synthetic measures are artificial constructs of more or less limited usefulness, they should ideally be available in both rubles and dollars, and in current and fixed prices such as to maximise the amount of information which they reveal.

Value estimates of economic activity, be they civilian or military, are necessarily based on prices and are valid only to the extent that price relatives provide a reasonable approximation of the valuation by society of the prevailing array of goods and services. That is, prices must fairly represent the opportunity cost of production and consumption possibilities foregone at the margin. Despite obvious market imperfections, capitalist economies are in general sufficiently competitive to generate prices which are reasonable approximations of economic worth. There can be no presumption that this is the case in the Soviet Union, however, where prices are passive, and play no role in the allocation decisions. Military and civilian outputs are planned in real terms, and prices, though not arbitrary in terms of objectives, are largely administered, and are not responsive to economic forces as in capitalist societies. They do not reflect the real cost at which commodities can be technically substituted for one another, nor, by the same token, can they be assumed to be a fair approximation of society's evaluation of the existing array of goods and services. Since goods and services are not politically neutral, prices are manipulated to reflect planners' preferences. Some goods, for instance, housing, are subsidised, others, such as vodka, bear a heavy tax. Furthermore in the machine sector fully 30 per cent of the existing types of goods are at any point of time allocated temporary prices which exceed, sometimes by considerable margins, the permanent prices at which they will eventually be transacted. Low capital and rental charges do not measure the real cost of capital, land and raw materials. Of particular relevance to the present discussion is the presumption that prices are not independent of the structure of output. Defence goods have high status and are likely to be underpriced, so that the efficiency requirement that the same category of goods in the defence and the civilian sectors bear the same price is unlikely to be met. Since armaments production is a capital intensive activity, the lack of a proper capital charge understates the true cost of production. Overheads which in military production may account for 45 per cent of total costs[11] are usually disproportionately borne by the civilian section in plants which produce both military and civilian goods,[12] and defence plants may also obtain top level scientific and managerial talent at less than the true opportunity cost to society. The extent of military underpricing is difficult to assess however. They are expected to follow economic accounting (khozraschet) procedures, and though some Soviet plants are planned to operate at a loss, it is not known how many of these produce military outputs.

Value estimates provide useful information on a range of inputs which go towards producing the final 'good' or objective, that of national security; they are not however a measure of the good itself. Nor do the data measure the narrower concept of military security, which economic statistics alone cannot quantify. The estimates provide no information on the effectiveness with which the allocations achieve the objectives, and do not in themselves measure defence capabilities. A nation's security is very considerably influenced by non-economic factors such as the effectiveness of military doctrine, the morale of troops and citizens, the appropriateness of the array of outputs in terms of strategy and tactics,[13] and in the event of long drawn out hostilities, the ease with which civilian facilities can be transferred to the production of military outputs. For instance, though the USSR has more soldiers under arms, the investment in each individual soldier is less, and they tend to operate at a lower degree of readiness than in the USA, quick response being sacrificed for size and endurance. Military security is also, of course, influenced by how much other countries, both allies and foes, spend on defence. Moreover data on current expenditures do not necessarily provide good approximation of military force potential, described as the ability to apply force consistently against an external aggressor, [14] which depends upon the stock of armaments in being that has been built up over a period of years. Current output data provide information on gross additions at a point of time, to which withdrawals from stock each year due to destruction, physical or technological obsolescence must be subtracted, data for which are difficult to obtain, though Soviet forces tend to retain major weapons systems for long periods. The stock must also be adjusted for exports which, for many types of Soviet weapons systems, are quite large, and by some imports from Eastern Europe. Net additions normally account for only a small proportion of existing inventory, so that the longer the period of time for which data are available, the more useful will they be as surrogates for military force potential.

Each year the national budget contains monetary expenditures which are not specifically itemised. Since the Defence heading in the budget clearly understates the true level of spending for this purpose, it is reasonable to assume that the shortfall is at least partly made up from the unidentified monies. Logically therefore it should be possible to compute those unidentified expenditures which finance military activities as budgetary residuals. That is, the difference between total allocations and identified spending for each major head of civilian expenditures are presumed to finance military activities. The aggregate sum of such residuals plus the overall budget surplus may then be assumed to complete total spending on military goods and services. Since the official Ministry of Defence definition of its activities does not correspond to that of the civilian budget, research workers must determine their own assessment of precisely what the Soviet headings actually finance. The narrow definition of military spending, corresponding to that employed by the American Department of Defence, includes pay and subsistence, operations and maintenance, procurement and military construction, and military research and development. An alternative, broader, definition includes in addition expenditures on internal security and border guards, military stockpiling, foreign military assistance and that portion of the space programme operated by and on behalf of the military establishment. These additional expenditures may add around 9 per cent to the narrow definition.

In 1940, personnel costs amounted to 7 to 8 billion rubles, equivalent then to 40 per cent or so of the total defence budget of 17 billion rubles. It is unlikely that the 10 billion rubles residual could have financed procurement, maintenance, investment and research. It is even more unlikely in the modern period. Some activities are clearly wholly or partly excluded. There is general agreement that R&D expenditures must be entirely excluded, and are funded under other headings or even from sources outside the official budget altogether. Military procurement clearly cannot be wholly, but it may be partially, included.

It has been argued that, based on direct investigation of output and manpower trends, it is correct to assume that, since the Korean War, procurement has been totally excluded from the official figure,[15] for the budget figure has varied in a manner consistent with the known expansion in personnel and other costs required to service the growth of the strategic and general purpose forces. However, the trend in the published outlays since the mid 1970s has decisively undermined such a supposition. William Lee has argued that published work on the principles of Soviet public finance indicates that the Defence entry contains the same subcategories as those for such expenditure heads as Health and Education, which are known to exclude procurement. Therefore, by implication, so does defence. The budget Defence figure therefore includes current operating costs only; pay, allowances, current repairs, food/non-food quartermaster expenses. If current expenditure alone amounts to over 17 billion rubles per annum, the total defence activities, including procurement, investment and R&D must exceed the published figure many times over. Lee argues that in 1980 total expenditure in 1970 rubles was 100–120 billion rubles, equivalent to 18 per cent or so of GNP.[16] While the scale of known physical parameters of the military programme makes it abundantly clear that procurement cannot be not wholly included, evidence that it is wholly excluded is less than compelling, especially since it may be the case that Lee has misinterpreted one key Soviet source,[17] which was in any case a tenuous base on which to build such a powerful argument.

A modelling exercise designed to test the hypothesis that budget data have consistently excluded procurement offers inconclusive results. From 1960 to 1970 the hypothesis was supported, but not between 1970 and 1975.[18] Until further information is obtained, it is prudent to assume that a certain, probably large, but not necessarily complete, portion of procurement spending is excluded from the budget data. In any case, coverage is unlikely to remain constant, for Soviet planners manipulate the residuals, sometimes increasing, and other times decreasing them for political purposes. It is this practice of transferring funds from unidentified to identified heads which explains how the apparently giant increase of 12 per cent could so easily be accommodated in 1985.

The two categories which are most likely, because of their size, to contain the concealed defence expenditures, are the overall budget residual – that is, the difference between total outlays and the sum of expenditures on all listed items – and Financing the National Economy (FNE). Since the FNE total is too large for the economic activities which it is claimed to finance, there is a strong presumption that certain components, in particular the Industry and Construction residual plus, possibly, the overall budget deficit, either directly funds defence activities or indirectly subsidises those enterprises which supply material to the military branches, though it is not possible, given present information, to isolate these activities within FNE. The other major expenditure head, Social and Cultural Measures (SCM), probably includes some expenditure for military-related, health or education provision, military pensions and some military R&D. It may also in principle be possible to calculate defence outlays as the difference between public sector income and civilian public sector expenditure.

The method of residuals is intuitively appealing and has the advantage of using published Soviet statistics. It does, however, have very serious drawbacks. Because the budgetary items are not defined, researchers have to ensure that the statistics do cover the activities claimed for them. Since the FNE surplus may, in any one year, account for up to 50 per cent of the total, the room for error in interpreting the data is clearly very large. The method also requires that prices correspond correctly to the economic activities to which they refer, which in practice may not be the case given the strong presumption that defence activities are subsidised so that even if and when they are properly identified the true cost is understated. Furthermore, while it is almost certainly the case that the various deficits do budget for military spending, it cannot be assumed that they are exclusively for that purpose. Thus although the method of residuals has highlighted some major issues of identification and interpretation, the methodological and data problems associated with using budgetary information invalidate it as a wholly satisfactory method of obtaining the true figure, though it may serve a useful supplementary purpose.

Although our limited understanding of Soviet public finance principles makes the residual method only partially useful, the technique is intrinsically sound, and has been used to estimate specific components of total defence spending, in particular, military procurement. Most military production is located in the Machine Building and Metal Working (MBMW) sector, so that, using published industrial and manpower statistics, it is in principle possible to identify military procurement as a residual from published data of gross output, intermediate and final demand. Given published information on Gross Value Output (GVO) in the MBMW sector, and subtracting all known civilian designated activities, the residual should provide an estimate of the proportion of total production of durable goods allocated to defence.

A hardware residual can be estimated as follows:

Residual = Gross Value Output (GVO) of the Machine Building and Metal Working industries *minus* intra-industry sales within the MBMW industries *minus* value of components allocated to capital repair of machinery *minus* net output of MBMW industry *minus* sales to other industries *minus* sales to the consumer sector *minus* stock changes *minus* exports *plus* imports

Although statistics on the value of output are not available, Soviet economic handbooks do provide an index of the growth of output in real terms which can be converted to a current basis. Intermediary flows between sectors are obtained from the official input–output tables. The advantage of this method is that it yields a direct calculation of the trade-off between civilian and military deployment of industrial machinery and hardware, and hence a good measure of one of the key burdens to the economy. In practice, however, the problems are similar to those for the budget, and the proponents of the hardware residuals themselves admit to a large margin of error.[19]

The official budget has been variously defined to finance non-capital procurement,[20] the personal material of troops and the net accumulation of weapons,[21] and personnel operations and maintenance – the latter partly funded from the increasingly profitable activities of defence plants and military personnel. Quantitative and qualitative problems of data and technique dog these as they do the other interpretations of the budget. Until more evidence becomes available, it is prudent to assume that the Soviet Union determines the size of the published defence budget to meet domestic and international political objectives. That is, it funds some, but an unknown and probably variable proportion of total military spending, and that expenditure heads may be easily transferred to or from other unidentified areas of the civilian budget.

The methodological and data problems of using published data have led research workers to seek techniques which bypass such an unreliable information source. The most well known estimates publicly available are those offered by the CIA, which are a hybrid of different techniques.[22] The unique characteristic of the CIA method is that military procurement is based on direct observation of Soviet weapons production, while other components are valued from different budgetary and non-budgetary data sources. Although the CIA estimates are not free of criticism, they provide the touchstone compared with which other estimates, both inside and outside the intelligence community, may be evaluated. The Agency has published dollar and ruble data, and has claimed to be most confident of its dollar calculations.

The CIA calculates Soviet military procurement and investment on the basis of the so-called building block approach. Using surveillance and other intelligence sources, it obtains information on the gross additions to the Soviet stock of arms for over 1000 individual components of the armed forces. From its information on the Soviet order of battle it allocates the new weapons to the appropriate service or force and so builds up a picture of the gross accretions each year. Although it can identify the physical items which enter service each year, the agency cannot observe directly the cost of production or price. Monetary values must therefore be calculated directly. After allowing for what is known of Soviet production techniques, the CIA estimates what it would cost in the USA to produce the Soviet array of weapons.[23] Some information is obtained directly from American defence contractors, even though no weapons are actually manufactured,[24] while other information is calculated from parametric cost-estimating relationships. It is important to emphasise that despite allowances for Soviet practice the dollar estimates are based on American technology and production techniques, and hence, most importantly, reflect American prices. Where the CIA finds it difficult to obtain information on operating characteristics it 'Sovietises' its own weapons stock, that is, adjusts the most similar of its own weapons to known Soviet design concepts. Some ruble outlays are estimated directly from intelligence information on the domestic cost of Soviet expenditures, mainly personnel, R&D and operations and maintenance. Most weapons costs are, however, initially priced in dollars, which are then converted to rubles, using RAND derived conversion ratios, partly for civilian machinery and partly for weapons. Until 1986 the ruble estimates were based on 1970 prices, but they have recently been recalculated to a 1982 price base.[25]

Military construction and procurement, which together make up military investment, is the cost of modernising and expanding Soviet forces, and accounts for 30 per cent of total defence expenditure measured in dollars,[26] but 50 per cent measured in rubles.[27]

Procurement of new weapons accounts for 90 per cent of the total investment category and provides the dynamic drive behind the long, steady expansion in expenditure since 1960. The cost of modernising the weapons stock as Soviet defence planners introduced new and more costly armaments, sustained growth at an annual average rate of 4 to 5 per cent,[28] with a degree of variance as major procurement programmes were phased in or out.

The building block method is appropriate only for those items of expenditure which can be physically identified. The activities which cannot be identified must be directly estimated. Operations and Maintenance, defined as the cost of sustaining current force levels, is directly related to the size of the force, its level of activity, and reflects the cost of day to day functioning of the military; pay, allowances, food, health, maintenance, fuel, etc. The dollar estimates calculate the cost in the USA of servicing and manning a military force of the same size with the same weapons' inventory as that of the Soviet Union and operating that force as the Soviets are known to do. The ruble calculations are first made in dollars and then converted to rubles using specially constructed dollar/ruble ratios. This category accounts for 25 per cent of total expenditure measured in rubles,[29] but 35 per cent in dollars.[30] Because it is, measured in dollars, the slowest growing category, its importance is slowly diminishing. By far the largest item is that of personnel, which accounts for 60 per cent of total operations, and has grown at around 2 to 3 per cent p.a. The ruble estimates are calculated from direct information of Soviet pay rates and rank structure. The dollar manpower estimates are calculated by evaluating in the American army the equivalent rank required to perform a specific function, and then multiplying numbers of personnel by American rates of pay and allowances. This technique distorts the dollar estimates very considerably, for American personnel are paid far more than their conscripted counterparts in the Soviet army, which explains the very substantial difference in the ratios of operating to total costs when measured in dollars and rubles. The non-personnel items such as food and clothing are obtained by direct observation of Soviet practice, or by comparison with American practice if direct information is not available.

The final major category of expenditure is that of Research and Development (R&D), the cost of exploring new technologies, developing and improving new and existing weapons. Since there is no discernible output from R&D activity other than that embodied in technologically more advanced weapons, direct observation is not possible, and CIA estimates of military R&D outlays have depended upon published Soviet statistics, statements by Soviet authorities on the financing of research and evidence from specific programmes. The R&D activities are funded from the Science budget, but the Soviet definition excludes many of the activities and hence costs associated with developing and testing prototype weapons which are typically included in the West. The defence-related science expenditures are therefore likely to underestimate the correct figure. The total 'Science' budget is far too large to finance known civilian research and development activity, and it must be assumed that it contains some, though not necessarily all, military-related R&D. The dated, though still most influential, investigation by Nancy Nimitz, concluded that in 1968 between 39 per cent and 55 per cent of Soviet R&D outlays were allocated for Defence and Space activities.[31] The CIA calculates that in addition to the official 'Science' budget, between 40 and 50 per cent of non-budgetary sources of finance, most probably from investment in industry and construction, are also allocated for defence-related development. Another investigation estimated that 60 per cent of Soviet scientists and engineers were employed on defence and space programmes.[32] Although precise monetary data are lacking, the CIA believes that, based on its knowledge of the scale and complexity of Soviet weapons production and the range of activities known to be under way at Soviet design bureau and testing facilities, R&D has recently been the fastest growing defence category. In 1970 and 1976, R&D accounted for 20 per cent or so of total military spending. By 1980 it had increased to between 20 per cent and 25 per cent, a sum of around 30 billion dollars at 1979 prices.[33]

Many of its civilian critics believe that CIA assumptions regarding the derivation of R&D expenditures and the figures obtained from them are defective. Based on detailed investigation of manpower statistics, Lee argues that since the early 1960s the official 'Science' category falls far short of the true figure, and that only a small proportion is in fact for defence purposes.[34]

In view of the conceptual and data problems inherent in the building block technique, the CIA periodically reviews its estimates, which are often revised, sometimes drastically, which undermines confidence in the usefulness of those extant at a point of time. In 1976 the Agency increased its estimates of the proportion of gross national product allocated to defence in rubles, from 6 per cent to 12–13 per cent, and growth rates from 3 per cent p.a. to 4–5 per cent p.a. However, 90 per cent of the revision was purely monetary brought about by a better understanding of Soviet ruble prices.[35] The CIA insisted that the physical dimensions of the Soviet programme had not increased, merely that the cost of producing a given quantity of weapons had grown. That is the CIA had previously overestimated the efficiency of defence sector production. Less dramatic changes occur periodically, to reflect inflationary price movements. For instance, the estimates for 1978 calculated at 1980 prices were 9 per cent higher than at 1979 prices.[36]

Defence expenditures measured in constant 1970 rubles grew by 4–5 per cent p.a., and by 1980 amounted to 62–79 billion rubles.[37] For most of the period the rate approximated that of GNP, so the proportion of the nation's resources allocated to defence remained steady, at around 11–13 per cent of GNP. During the eleventh Five Year Plan period, however, as growth of GNP declined, the share of defence increased to 12–14 per cent. Military spending measured in dollars grew at 3 per cent p.a., and by 1980 reached 165 billion dollars in 1979 prices.[38]

One of the advantages claimed for the building block method is that because procurement data are based on detailed investigation of single items which are individually priced, they can be aggregated or disaggregated as desired, by service, activity or force, such as to illustrate trends in the composition and balance of defence activities over time.

Over the past fifteen years or so the fastest growing service has been the Air Force, which grew at around three times the average rate of military spending, increasing from 20 per cent of the total expenditure in 1970, to 25 per cent in 1980. By far the largest expenditure category was procurement, which accounted for over 70 per cent of total following the deployment of new fighter bomber and transport planes. The largest expansion occurred in Frontal Aviation, where the number of tactical aircraft increased by 50 per cent, and meant that by the late 1970s fully 60 per cent of aircraft had entered production since 1969.

In the Ground Forces, manpower increased from 1.2 million in 1967 to 1.7 million in 1977. Investment accounts for 50 per cent of expenditure, 90 per cent of which is procurement of tanks, armoured personnel carriers and tactical ground to air missiles.

The third largest spending service was the Navy, with 20 per cent of the defence total, and as with the Air Force, procurement accounted for over 70 per cent of total expenditures. Then, in descending order of expenditure magnitudes are the National Air Defence, with 12 per cent of total, and finally the Strategic Rocket Force, the relative importance of which varies according to the phasing of ICBM deployment cycles.

Value figures can also highlight trends in force expansion. Until 1974 for instance ballistic missile submarine expenditure grew faster than general purpose Navy spending, after which the trend was reversed. Procurement data indicate that over the long period more importance was given to strategic attack, and open ocean anti-ship and anti-submarine missiles, the latter in particular showing a marked rate of expansion. The estimates also illustrate the geographical distribution of men and material. Expenditures for the NATO Guidelines Area grew at twice the rate of defence as a whole, as indeed did the accretion of forces along the China border, which absorb between 10 and 25 per cent of total expenditures.

The data also facilitates comparisons between the USSR and any other country, particularly the USA, of course, in terms of military mission. According to American definitions the Strategic Forces are those assigned to intercontinental attack, strategic defence and control and surveillance and excludes all R&D expenditures. In 1980, 35 per cent of total strategic force expenditure was accounted for by intercontinental attack, compared with 65 per cent for the USA. Fifty per cent of the intercontinental outlays were spent on ICBMs. Strategic defence accounted for 50 per cent of the Soviet total, compared with only 25 per cent for the USA.[39] The General Purpose forces are defined as all land, tactical air, naval and mobility forces, and in the USSR, as in the USA, absorbed the largest share of the total budget.

Estimating the Scale of Soviet Defence Expenditures

The sole justification for assessing Soviet expenditures in currencies other than rubles is that they facilitate comparisons with other countries. The data show that Soviet military spending grew at a steady, though not especially spectacular rate, of 3 per cent p.a. in dollars, with comparatively small adjustments to major procurement cycles. In the USA, on the other hand, expenditures varied quite substantially over time, with a variance of between − 30 per cent and + 60 per cent.[40] Because American spending was initially so large, not until 1971 did Soviet expenditures for the first time exceed those of the USA. Since then, and up to the end of the decade or so, the gap progressively widened, but narrowed again following the priority given to military spending under President Reagan. Although the differential has narrowed since 1980, it has not disappeared. In 1980 as measured in rubles, Soviet expenditure was estimated by the CIA to exceed the USA by 30 per cent. Measured in dollars, however, the Soviet excess was 50 per cent, 165 billion dollars, compared to 108 billion dollars.[41] In 1985, Soviet military investment in dollars more or less equalled that of the USA, general force expenditures exceeded the USA by $16 billion, and R&D by 50 per cent. American procurement expenditures exceeded the USSR by $8 billion, though the cumulative Soviet total still exceeds the American.[42] Over the longer period, however, both countries have spent a roughly similar figure on defence, the USSR 3.5 trillion dollars, and the USA 3.7 trillion dollars, and as has been pointed out, the longer the time period the more useful the data.

Given the many and obvious limitations associated with the CIA methodology and data, it is not surprising that both have been heavily criticised even to the degree that CIA dollar estimates are worthless for international comparison.[43] Some problems are inherent in any statistical exercise of the type attempted by the CIA. Others, it is argued, derive from deliberate manipulation of method and data, some of its critics accusing the CIA of consciously understating the true figure, while others of exaggeration.

The building block method has two major problems. First, the physical items may be incorrectly observed, and secondly, the monetary transformations do not correctly measure the real value of the variables which have been identified.

Although the CIA has access to a vast intelligence network, the very nature of the exercise makes it unlikely that all gross additions to the weapons stock are actually observed. Indeed, Stephen Rosefielde argues that its man and weapons count consistently understates the physical dimension of the Soviet armed services by as much as 15 per cent,[44] though he offers no evidence for this claim. A more reasoned assessment concludes however that Soviet physical capability is known with some certainty.[45]

The greater dispute arises over the value aspects of the estimates. The divergence between dollar and ruble data already noted is caused by the index number problem, which has the effect of exaggerating Soviet expenditures in dollars compared with the USA. Measured in rubles American spending is exaggerated.

The difference derives from the previously noted fact that both prices and quantities differ in the two countries and that there normally exists an inverse relationship between the two variables. Since Soviet soldiers are cheap, the Soviet military force is more labour intensive than the American. Machinery and equipment, on the other hand, are comparatively cheap in the USA, but expensive in the USSR. Thus weighing Soviet forces by dollars (American prices), is equivalent to allocating a high price to the most abundant input, and vice versa, quite contrary to rational economic behaviour. Formally the comparison between the two sets of data may be calculated as an index number.

$$L = \frac{\sum_{i=1}^{n} P_{US_i} Q_{USSR_i}}{\sum_{i=1}^{n} P_{USSR_i} Q_{US_i}}$$

$$P = \frac{\sum_{i=1}^{n} P_{US_i} Q_{US_i}}{\sum P_{USSR_i} Q_{US_i}}$$

where
- P = defence goods prices
- Q = defence goods quantities
- US = USA data
- USSR = Soviet data
- L = Laspeyeres index
- P = Paasche index

To provide a comprehensive comparison, estimates obtained from both the Laspeyeres and the Paasche index should be published, plus the geometric mean of the two. The CIA, however, is unable to provide acceptable ruble estimates of American defence spending, since it lacks sufficient data on Soviet production and costs.

Comparing growth rates over a period of time also shows different trends when measured in dollars as opposed to rubles; 3.0 per cent in the former currency, and 4.5 per cent in the latter up to the mid to late 1970s. This phenomenon is also common to all index number measurements. The explanation, though similar, is the reverse of that for absolute quantities. International competition is forcing Soviet military production to become more like that of the USA, showing a comparatively high rate of growth of technologically advanced aircraft, missiles, ships, etc. That is, the pattern of growth forced upon the USSR increases the relative importance of those goods which are expensive to produce in its own currency. The opposite tendency would, of course, be true of growth rates measured in dollars, which give a high weight to the comparatively cheap but slower growing military inputs such as manpower. Therefore, if dollar data overestimate the true excess of Soviet spending over that in the USA at a point of time, they underestimate the difference in growth over a period of time. Price indices using Soviet data are analagous to those which formally compare two periods in terms of base year prices, and those using American data to indices which use end period prices.

The index number problem identifies a further source of statistical uncertainty, even if no comparison between rubles and dollars is involved. Whatever the currency in which measurement is made, prices as well as quantities change over time. Although it is true that the longer the period of time over which data are available, the more useful they are as surrogates for force potential, the more likely is it that relative prices at the terminal date will differ from those at the outset. Analysts must therefore choose a Paasche (base year) or a Laspeyeres (end year) price index. The Paasche index will tend to exaggerate the perceived growth rates, for by an exact analogy with using Soviet weights for international comparison, it tends to give higher weights (prices) to those items which are scarce in the early period but which grow in relative importance over time, and which therefore exaggerate the growth rate. The opposite is, of course, true of measuring in late period Laspeyeres weights. The difference in the perceived growth can be very considerable. Measured by the Laspeyeres index, procurement in the Soviet Union between 1960 and 1975 grew at an annual average rate of 0.4 per cent, compared with 4.0 per cent p.a. as measured by the Paasche index. It was in part the use of an inappropriate index that led the CIA to underestimate the true spending on military procurement from the 'correct' figure of 17–18 billion rubles in 1970 to its own figure of 5.5 billion rubles,[46] and total expenditure from 40–50 billion rubles to 24 billion rubles.

The building block technique requires data in one currency to be converted to that of the other country. For procurement the conversion is normally made from dollars to rubles, for research and development from rubles to dollars. The rate of exchange at which the conversions are calculated obviously influences the final figures. Even in trade between capitalist countries the prevailing rate of exchange need not exactly reflect purchasing power parities. They are, however, sufficiently approximate to provide an acceptable basis for comparison. There can be no such presumption for Soviet prices and exchange rates. As has already been noted, Soviet domestic prices are largely administered and do not reflect real transformations at the margin. The official exchange rate between rubles and dollars is fixed by the Soviet authorities for their own purposes, and is generally regarded as having scant relationship to the true purchasing power of the two currencies in international markets, and is therefore inappropriate for international comparisons.[47]

The conversion rate can, in principle, be calculated by expressing the purchasing power parity of the ruble in the defence sector as a ratio of the purchasing power of the dollar through a representative sample of defence goods costed in both dollars and rubles, the totals being expressed as a ratio. In practice, however, since weapons and armaments are not traded in world markets, only limited information on relative prices is available. Where prices of roughly equivalent military equipment are known, it is relatively straightforward to obtain a conversion ratio for that category of weapons. Where Soviet prices are not known, they must be estimated on the basis of civilian machinery and equipment whose specifications most closely correspond with those for weapons, on the assumption that the technology required to produce civilian and military goods are not too dissimilar.[48] The most relevant metric is the output of the MBMW branches, which produce investment goods for both civilian and military output. Even so, the degree of overlap is limited, due not only to different specifications of American and Soviet equipment, but also to the many qualitative components in machinery, such as reliability, service life, etc., which cannot be easily incorporated in a simple price comparison.[49] Furthermore, dollar–ruble ratios change over time because

Estimating the Scale of Soviet Defence Expenditures 21

of differing inflation rates. They also, of course, vary between different weapons systems. In the West a variety of calculations have been offered over the years ranging from 0.2 rubles to 1 dollar, to 0.5 rubles to 1 dollar for defence equipment, and up to 0.8 rubles per dollar for R&D activity.[50]

Many of its critics argue that the Agency compounds the inevitable statistical and interpretation problems by deliberate manipulation to meet political objectives. One problem derives from the higher average levels of productivity and technology attained in the USA. The CIA seeks to adjust for the lower level of Soviet technology by 'Sovietising' equivalent American weapons. If, however, because of lack of data, it is unable to 'Sovietise' it must base its calculation on American methods of production, which inevitably overstate the Soviet cost of production in dollars. In 1980 this was described as being 'probably the general case',[51] though as more information on costs, prices and production technologies are obtained by covert and open means this source of exaggeration will diminish. Although the Soviet Union manufactures more weapons than the USA, the latter can and does produce some weapons systems which are technologically too advanced for the USSR. Since these cannot be replicated in the Soviet Union, it is obviously not possible to devise a ruble estimate for their performance parameters. To compensate for this gap in knowledge, the CIA, in its reverse 'Sovietising' process costs the technologically nearest, but obviously inferior, Soviet weapon, which understates the value of the technologically advanced American weapons, and hence American spending, in ruble prices. Some estimates suggest that up to 30 per cent of American procurement by value may be in this category which, as Franklin Holzman argues, undervalues that aspect of American defence spending where it has the greatest comparative and absolute advantage.[52] Other investigators suggest that the range of weapons which the Soviet Union cannot technologically achieve and whose characteristics must be seriously undervalued is most likely small.[53]

Holzman also argues that the CIA data are further exaggerated. Although conscription pay understates the marginal productivity of Soviet military personnel, to price soldiers in dollar wages, as the Agency does is to grossly overstate their true cost. It makes no effort to adjust for the lower productivity of Soviet soldiers, even though labor adjustment ratios have been calculated for other sectors of the economy. Western estimates for health, education, etc., discount Soviet wages by fully 20 per cent to account for this factor. Given that

American soldiers are, on average, better educated and better trained, Holzman believes that a discount factor similar to that used in estimating dollar costs of Soviet health and education manpower might well be appropriate for defence.[54] On the basis of his calculations, Holzman estimates that the CIA may overestimate Soviet spending in dollars by between 20 and 25 per cent.[55]

For the USA, product improvement in weapons has occurred at a long-term annual average rate of around 5 per cent or so. Although precise figures are not publicly available for the USSR, the known large expenditures on military R&D, plus the observable improvements in the operating characteristics of Soviet weapons, suggests that technological improvement is also substantial in the USSR. Improved performance of the type and at the rate achieved by the Soviet forces is extremely costly, and it is argued that one of the most severe tests of the CIA method is how it incorporates technological progress into its data. Steven Rosefielde, a persistent critic of the CIA, argues that it uses fixed vintage parametric estimates, which are strictly valid only for the year they were obtained, or at least so long as no major changes in technology occur. Thus the dollar estimates of modern vintage weapons are lower than they really cost, for improvement costs are excluded. If, he argues, variable vintage CERs are applied to CIA physical data, the annual increase in costs would lead to expenditures far in excess of those actually calculated by the CIA. In 1980, for instance, Soviet procurement cost would double, growing at 12.9 per cent p.a.[56] implying a great addition to the Soviet stock of armaments. Since Rosefielde also argues that inflation in machinery inputs has been quite small,[57] the higher costs are largely due to real improvement in performance. Although the CIA itself has not directly responded to these allegations, a retired chief of its Military Economic Analysis Center has defended its methodology, insisting that technological improvements are systematically incorporated in its CER estimation,[58] which yield a cost factor growth for Soviet weapons consistent with that experienced in the USA. Burton gives the example of tactical aircraft whose costs, according to CIA techniques, grew at an annual average rate of 7 per cent p.a., which increased their relative price from around 66 per cent in 1950 to more than 100 per cent of their American equivalent in 1982.[59] The increase in the relative price probably reflects the Soviet Union's effort to catch up technologically with the USA, but having to incur higher costs to do so. It is also the case that few Western specialists accept, as does Rosefielde, that Soviet machine prices fell during the 1970s.

Estimating the Scale of Soviet Defence Expenditures 23

The other major American producer of Soviet expenditure data is the Defence Intelligence Agency, a unit in the Defence Department. The Defence Intelligence Agency, though it does offer dollar data, professes a higher degree of confidence in its ruble estimates. Since it seeks to replicate the type of information which is most likely to be available to Soviet leaders, the DIA argues that current price rubles are more useful for assessing policy. Based on information on 200 weapons systems and on what it claims are well-placed sources, the DIA makes the simplifying assumption that defence accounts for a constant 31 to 34 per cent share of the All-Union budget. On this basis, military spending in 1970–81 increased at an annual rate of 6 to 7 per cent p.a., much higher than the real growth estimated by the CIA and, which, since it exceeded nominal growth of GNP, implied, unlike the CIA data, that defence absorbed a higher proportion of the nation's resources. By 1981 this had increased to $220 billion.[60] It does, however, admit to an enormous 33 per cent confidence error. DIA data are compromised however by a reluctance to publish its estimating procedures and its practice of deliberately distorting its data for overtly political purposes.[61]

The sole European organisation to issue regular data based on its own research efforts is the Stockholm-based SIPRI, which has been consistently critical of both the methodology and the data offered by the CIA. SIPRI has used a number of approaches. Till 1973 it accepted the official budget figure as being a reasonable approximation of total military spending. When, after that date, it became abundantly clear that could not be the case, it followed a simple stratagem of adding 30 per cent to the published figure, which showed defence expenditure levels well below those of the CIA. Recently, however, the methodology was changed again, described as a compromise corresponding to neither the official Soviet figure nor the CIA estimates. It has not yet disclosed the precise nature of its new methodology, which yields a surprisingly constant annual rise in outlays of 0.6 or 0.7 billion rubles since 1970, and also a declining defence burden.

In 1983, the CIA announced a further revision of its estimates for the level and rate of expansion of defence spending in the USSR. Based on what it claims was evidence from its intelligence sources, especially its spy planes, it announced a substantial downward revision in the ruble rate of growth of Soviet defence expansion from its previously announced figure of 4 to 5 per cent p.a., to 2 per cent p.a. In dollars, the revision amounted to a much smaller fall of from 3 per cent to just under 2 per cent.⁶² Unlike its previous revision, which was largely monetary in nature, the reasons for the decline since 1976 are very real. The key explanation is that military procurement, which had long been a dynamic sector in overall defence expansion, grew scarcely at all between 1977 and 1981, and beyond. An independent count of weapons production shows that of 25 classes of weapons produced for Soviet forces between 1977 and 1981, the level of production decreased in 13, remained much the same in 5, and increased in only 7 categories.⁶³ The DIA, however, argue that, though procurement growth, which in the first half of the decade was 9 to 11 per cent p.a., had declined in real terms, the cost of developing and deploying new weapons had increased such that monetary spending, though less than in the first half of the decade, still grew at 6 to 9 per cent in nominal terms, which had the effect of sustaining total defence expenditures at a rate of 6 to 7 per cent measured in current rubles.⁶⁴

A real criticisms which had come to be levied against the CIA ruble estimates was that the 1970 fixed price base, upon which they were calculated, had become increasingly remote from current prices in the Soviet Union.⁶⁵ In 1986 the CIA, in conjunction with the DIA, published the initial results of its efforts at recalculating the physical and monetary data into 1982 prices. The consequent revision, though not as dramatic in its implication as that which had been made in 1983, none the less shows a significant increase in the military economic indices. The two agencies, though less divergent than they had been, still disagreed over the trend for real procurement. Both agreed that for a period real growth had been negligible. The CIA argues that the real trend was maintained into the mid-decade, whereas the DIA argues that real growth was resumed again.⁶⁶ In 1985, the two agencies disagreed over the dimensions of the defence burden, which the CIA calculated at 13 per cent to 14 per cent of GNP and the DIA at 15 per cent to 17 per cent.⁶⁷ As a result of the recalculation to 1982 prices both now agree that the burden is from 15 per cent to 17 per cent of GNP.⁶⁸ Because the new measure was calculated in end year prices, the real growth rate was reduced slightly from that measured in 1970 prices to 3 per cent p.a. Prices increased at an annual average rate of 3 per cent, and the increase of the defence burden in 1982, as compared to 1970 prices, suggests that on average the price of defence goods has increased faster than of civilian goods.

Since dollar estimates of Soviet defence outlays are amongst the most frequently cited influences on American spending decisions, it is not surprising that allegations have been made that they are deliberately manipulated to justify politically or ideologically determined objectives.

The CIA it is argued has an implicit asymmetric loss function,[69] consistent with its practice of assuming a worst case scenario, that the cost of underestimating Soviet spending on defence far exceeds that of overestimation. Western assumptions about Soviet expenditures are ideologically loaded reflecting what has been described as an autistic perspective on the USSR, the consequences of which have been explored elsewhere.[70] In 1976 a second group of appraisers was created to oversee the CIA estimates with, it is argued, the objective of increasing the total, where possible, for domestic political purposes,[71] though there is some doubt that the so called 'B' team was politically inspired. Estimates which are deliberately pitched too high increase the virulence of the arms race.

There are also those who argue that CIA data are too low because the Agency deliberately chooses conversion coefficients which consistently understate the correct figure,[72] though it is not explained why the CIA should wish to underestimate its data, however. Estimates which deliberately understate Soviet spending increase American vulnerability to Soviet military power.

The CIA itself is confident that its estimates are to within 10 per cent or so of the correct figure, and argue that while many uncertainties exist over the original data and their conversion to the form in which they are published, there is no systematic bias upwards or downwards in its estimates. As of 1985 however it has refused to publish its dollar estimates on the grounds that they are systematically mis-used for political purposes,[73] though even this decision might not be entirely free of political motivation.[74]

It is clear that the problems associated with obtaining accurate statistics from a country which deliberately seeks to confuse inquisitive and potentially hostile investigators have not fully been resolved. Those that exist do offer useful approximations of Soviet defence spending, so long as the limitations are borne in mind. The prudent conclusion must be to accept each set of data with a, and probably varying, degree of scepticism.

2 Explaining Soviet Defence Spending

The Bolsheviks viewed the capitalist dynamic as one of inevitable collapse in societies rent by their own internal contradictions. If the indigenous proletariat was in a position to exploit the socio-economic contradictions, revolution need have no adverse impact on the international community, and hence on the socialist states already in being. However, no timetable could be established for the resolution of the proletarian struggle in any one capitalist country, nor in capitalism as a socio-economic system. Until that time the capitalist class would seek to mitigate internal discord by aggressive attacks on those states which had made the successful transition to socialism. Thus even in socialist states, which were by definition harmonious, military expenditures were a regrettable necessity. War, if and when it came, would inevitably be the decisive phase in the competition between the capitalist and socialist states, from which the USSR, as the only exponent of socialism, must emerge victorious. It was not enough that the Soviet Union match capitalist spending on armaments, it had to ensure superiority in the production and deployment of personnel and those armaments which were likely to prove crucial in war. Thus although Bolshevik intellectuals had argued that socialist states had no need of a standing army, Socialism in One Country forced and/or justified to political leaders a more practical assessment of the role of the military. Even in the midst of severe economic difficulties in the 1920s, the Bolshevik party set out to establish the organisational basis for the expansion of the Red Army. In 1927, the Party published a Five Year Plan which outlined proposals to bring the armed forces up to requisite numerical strength and technological level. Party leaders understood that armaments production was feasible only on the basis of a secure economic, and especially industrial, foundation, and from the outset, the objective of catching up and overtaking capitalism inextricably conjoined the economic and the military dimensions of socialist development.[1] This crucial requirement for a coordinated and systematic expansion of military and economic production gave a powerful rationale for centralised economic planning, and in 1928 the first economic Five Year Plan was accompanied by a Five Year Plan for the development of the Red

Army, a symbiosis which has characterised the Soviet Union since that time.

The Soviet growth strategy, later characterised as extensive, was based on mobilising massive quantities of underutilised, mainly agricultural, factor inputs, with only a secondary role for economic efficiency as conventionally understood in the West. Although it is not possible to identify exact and explicit causal correlations between economic and military strategy, there did emerge a broad based synergising relationship between the two, as planning for national security reflected the basic parameters of the economic model. The overriding objective of rapid growth plus the shortage of technically competent planners and managers rationalised quantity planning in terms of targets which were easily understood and monitored. At much the same time Soviet strategists rejected the then favoured Western strategy of a small highly mechanised force using technologically sophisticated weapons, in favour of one which emphasised a large standing army.[2] It would, under the circumstances, be quite inconsistent and inefficient to plan for the production of small quantities of technologically advanced weapons. From the outset, therefore, Soviet armaments factories produced large numbers of relatively simple but sturdy and high quality artillery, tanks and aircraft,[3] a principle of weapons production which has been sustained by and large to the present day.

Khrushchev announced that war was not fatalistically inevitable, but this did not mean that the Soviet Union could relax its war efforts. Quite the reverse, for armed conflict was avoidable only if the correlation of forces between the socialist and the capitalist states could be so weighted in favour of the Soviet Union and its allies that the cost of waging all-out war would prove too prohibitive to the capitalist nations. Although war was not therefore inevitable, it was always possible, and the Soviet Union and its allies had to be prepared to fight and win. Nuclear armaments increased the cost of military preparation, and the Soviet Union had to match the capitalist states and allocate resource for nuclear research, production and deployment. Even in the nuclear age, however, wars would be waged by mass armies, so that resources for nuclear weaponry could not be obtained by reducing outlays on conventional weapons. The Soviet Union had to plan for and finance a balanced array of armaments, and after China turned from being an ally to an ideological foe, to deploy on both the Western and Eastern fronts. Soviet assessment of what it understood to be the aggressive ambitions of ideological enemies, which was given empirical justification by military spending in the USA and its NATO allies, created what many believe to be an excessive preoccupation with national security.[4] That being the case, it is reasonable to assume that the level of Soviet defence spending shows a purposeful response to that of the USA in particular, or the NATO alliance in general.

Economic analyses of the arms race, and hence by implication of the level of Soviet defence expenditures, have been largely based on models derived from Lewis Richardson.[5] Although his original intention was to explain American spending, the methodology is valid for countries other than the USA. In the generalised model it is assumed that countries are motivated to spend money on defence, which in the absence of threat is implicitly assumed to yield less utility than equivalent civilian expenditures, by feelings of fear or hostility towards known or anticipated enemies. The incentive to spend money for military purposes is positively correlated with the degree of uncertainty about enemy intention. Defence expenditures are, however, costly in terms of civilian goods foregone, especially in economies such as the Soviet Union, where resources are constantly fully employed. Distrust or hostility is affected by such considerations as territorial disagreements or ideology antipathy, which in the short term are unlikely to change very greatly. Fear on the other hand is related to the perceived intensity of aggressive intent of the enemy. It is assumed in the model that the different behavioural characteristics can be usefully encapsulated by the single variable of how much of the enemy's resources are spent on military production. As enemy spending increases, fear is increased, provoking a defensive response. However, as more resources are allocated to meet the security objectives, the social opportunity cost increases, and demands from domestic political constituencies to restrain additional spending for this purpose become more intense.

The model is typically formalised as:

$$\frac{dx}{dt} = ky - ax + g$$

$$\frac{dy}{dt} = lx - by + h$$

where

$\frac{dx}{dt}$ = increase in defence expenditures in country X over time

$\dfrac{dy}{dt}$ = increase in defence expenditures in country Y over time

ky = defence or reaction coefficient in country X, that is, the response in country X to spending on defence in country Y;

lx = the coefficient of response in country Y to defence spending in country X;

ax = the coefficient of response in country X to prior expenditure in country X;

by = the coefficient of response in country Y to prior expenditure in country Y;

g = distrust factor in country X;

h = distrust factor in country Y.

Military spending in one country is positively correlated with the distrust factor and the level of spending in the other country, and is negatively correlated with the level of expenditures already incurred in its own defence. Although the model is intuitively plausible, a number of conceptual and empirical problems have to be overcome.

The theoretical concepts of thrift, hostility and fear must be made operational and compatible with the available statistical data. The distrust factor is so diffuse that it is not possible to devise an appropriate operational metric for it. Some models totally exclude the variable from their calculations, while others include distrust as a dummy variable, a sort of residual which captures all those forces not explained by the specifically modelled thrift and fear. This is rationalised on the grounds that since mistrust between nations is influenced by factors which are largely unchanging in the short run, it is unlikely to be important in explaining changes in defence spending from one year to the next. Over time the distrust factor does change in both socialist and capitalist countries. It is unlikely, for instance, that the death of a hard line ideologue such as Suslov has no impact on how the Soviet Union views the outside world, in which case the degree of grievance is transformed into a dynamic variable which may affect not only the level, but also short-term changes in Soviet defence spending.

It is also a simplification to suppose that agressive intent can be encapsulated by the single variable of how much is spent on armaments. This assumes that the military and non-military foreign policy parameters are rationally coordinated to meet well-defined objectives, whereas in fact countries often send out conflicting signals, about their intentions, deliberately or otherwise, which their enemies must evaluate as a total package. It is not necessarily the case that a constant level or constant rate of increase of military spending has the same foreign policy message, if other things do not remain equal. The real or monetary cost of producing weapons may increase, yielding less weapons per ruble. In contrast, the efficiency of the manufacturing process may have increased due to improved productivity or technological progress which increases the number of weapons available per dollar or ruble, a real source of disagreement between the CIA and some of its critics. The message of intent which can be drawn from a given level or growth of outlays will also differ as to whether GNP and hence the defence burden is growing quickly or slowly. It has in any case been emphasised that the sum spent on armaments cannot be equated to military force potential, which is presumably what countries seek protection against.

As the economic circumstances of nations differ so, other things being equal, do their evaluation of the exhaustion factor. In societies where material living standards are low and/or resources are always fully employed, the burden of a given volume or percentage of resources allocated to non-civilian objectives is likely to be higher than in societies where those characteristics do not prevail. Both elements exist to a stronger degree in the USSR than in the USA, where, *a fortiori* it might be anticipated that the opportunity cost is higher and therefore the signal to be read from a given allocation more powerful than in capitalist countries where defence spending may offer positive economic and political returns in postponing economic crisis.[6]

Even if appropriate data can be obtained they may be correlated in diverse ways. The level of defence spending in one country, say the USSR, in a particular year, may be related to the level of spending in another country, the USA, in that year, in the previous year or large number of years. The independent variable may be the long-run average rate of increase or it may be significant departures from trend. Since our understanding of the precise Soviet perceptions of the capitalist system and the organisational framework within which military operational decisions are made is limited, there is no way of determining *a priori* which parameters are most important. It may also be the case that positive correlation between defence expenditures in a pair of countries are more influenced by circumstances in the international community which impinge equally on both.

There remains one final problem, that of data availability. For the Soviet Union official budgetary data are not appropriate and Western estimates must be used. If purposeful behaviour by Soviet political and military leaders is assumed, the most useful data are those which most nearly replicate the sort of information available to them in determining allocations between the civilian and the military sectors. Ruble estimates are therefore more appropriate than dollars. Constant rubles measure the real trend in armaments production and deployment, but current rubles measure the defence burden. There is no reason to believe *a priori* that one ruble evaluation is intrinsically superior to another.

Given the conceptual and empirical problems of making the model operational, no more than broad indications of the relative importance of international competition on the level or the rate of growth of Soviet defence spending can be anticipated.

In the simplest models the variables show a temporal sequence between the USSR and the USA, the grievance term is removed, and a term is introduced to allow for possible random fluctuations in Soviet expenditure. It is also often assumed that the USA is the leader and the USSR the follower country.[7]

The structural form of the equation is transformed to:

$$Y_{Rt+1} = a_{11}Y_{At} + b_{12}Y_{Rt} + U_{Rt+1}$$

$$Y_{At+1} = a_{12}Y_{Rt+1} + b_{22}Y_{At} + U_{At+1}$$

where:

R = USSR, $\quad A$ = USA

Y_{Rt+1} = expenditure by USSR in period $t+1$, i.e., the current period.

Y_{At+1} = expenditure by the USA in the current period.

$a_{11}Y_{At}$ = the defence coefficient for the USSR which indicates that current Soviet spending is correlated with American defence spending in the previous period.

$a_{12}Y_{Rt+1}$ = the defence coefficient for the USA which indicates that current American spending is correlated with current Soviet spending.

b_{12}, b_{22} = the fatigue factor in both countries.

U_{Rt+1}, U_{At+1} = the random distribution term.

The statistical tests on this model show, perhaps surprisingly, that enemy behaviour has 'little impact'[8] on the defence expenditures of either country and offers little support for the hypothesis that Soviet defence spending is systematically related to that in the USA.

The hypothesis is so inherently plausible, however, that various attempts have been made to rescue the model by changing the functional relationships in different ways, for instance that Soviet expenditures are related not to the level of American spending but to the difference between its own spending and that by the USA.[9] A further modification requires Soviet outlays to respond to change in American spending only after a lag because of the bureaucratic nature of the Soviet decision-making process. Since resources are always fully committed, more for one sector implies less for another, unless growth rates are adequate, and a reordering of expenditures priorities is politically time-consuming. Even with a sophisticated function which allows variation to the speed with which some procurement programmes may be altered compared with others, the lags add little to the explanatory power of the model.[10] Additional modifications to incorporate expectations show only modest improvement,[11] and tests which initially show significant statistical relationships[12] are subsequently observed to be flawed in one way or another.[13] Simple econometric testing thus fails to establish a statistical relationship between the level and the rate of growth of Soviet and American arms spending, contrary to what might reasonably have been anticipated, and also contrary to what Soviet leaders claim to be what motivates them.

The failure to obtain a statistical correlation does not of itself mean that American defence decisions are irrelevant for Soviet decision-makers. Military planners presumably seek to maximise military force potential, which is determined by the stock of the weapons in being rather than the flow of those newly produced. This will be particularly important if at the outset of the relevant period the stock in one country, the USSR, lags so far behind that of the other, that catching up provides a rationale for steady expansion irrespective of the variance in American production from year to year. Although expenditures over time approximate to stock, information on technological obsolescence, which may be high, attrition and also on net exports, since the USSR exports a high proportion of total production of some weapon categories, are needed to complete the real data. A proportion, usually high, of total expenditures each year are overheads, manpower, operations and maintenance, some military construction and research and development, which is unlikely to respond in a systematic manner to short term fluctuations in expenditures elsewhere. The defence item which might be anticipated to show greater variance is procurement, and there are well-documented instances of Soviet procurement decisions designed to narrow and eventually close a gap which had been opened up by American superiority.[14] It might also be the case that in a technologically dynamic arms race countries anticipate spending by their enemies.

In a planned economy, allocations between competing sectors eventually tend to atrophy into a bureaucratic process in which constant ratios or constant rates of increase offer the simplest political solution to political disagreements over disbursements. The bureaucratic model forecasts constant rates of expansion of spending for each major budgetary head so that it is departures from trend which must be explained as a response to American spending. In log form this is shown as:

$$\ln D_{USSR} = \ln a + b \ln D_{USA} + c \ln Y_{USSR}$$

where

D_{USSR} = Soviet defence expenditures

Y_{USSR} = Soviet national income

D_{USA} = American defence expenditures

a = Absolute magnitude.

Investigation of one such model in 1974 showed a high and significant coefficient of multiple determination, whereby a 1 per cent increase in American defence spending provokes a 0.6 per cent response by the Soviet Union.[15] However, as the author points out, there exists a high likelihood of autocorrelation, that both sets of data are simultaneously influenced by an exogenous trend which might be the true explanation for the correlation between the two variables. After eliminating the trend, the correlation of variance is still positive and significant. Even so, certain problems remain. Both countries are likely to interpret and respond to events in the international community in a similar manner, and the test ignores whatever impact China might have on Soviet spending. Furthermore, the test uses dollar estimates of Soviet spending derived from the method of residuals which cannot be assumed to yield a fair estimate of the true figure for defence spending in the Soviet Union.

Defence expenditures clearly cannot be explained solely as a purposive response to international competition, for though long-term American and NATO armaments policies must in some way impinge on Soviet expenditures, the interpretation of these policies is very considerably influenced by domestic, economic and political factors. The Soviet Union is a supply constrained economy in that aggregate demand for economic resources always exceeds supply, and planners cannot ignore the domestic burden of defence spending for not even in the USSR is the military claim unlimited or uncontested. On the one hand, the USSR cannot lag militarily too far behind its enemies, and American spending provides a floor below which the USSR cannot fall without provoking protest from the military and its associated industrial ministries. On the other hand, defence spending cannot be allowed to increase to a level which could cause an unacceptable degree of economic inefficiency, or even serious political or social unrest. The final outcome reflects a political and bureaucratic compromise between international security and domestic economic well-being. There exists a zone of uncertainty within which the political claimants compete, which does not, however, remain constant, but shifts in response to changes in the domestic and international environment. Higher spending by the USA will squeeze from the one end, while industrial or agricultural failure of a particularly severe order will squeeze from the other end. Low growth increases the likelihood of an enervating political battle between the military and civilian claimants.

Some evidence of competition between the military and civilian claimants is given by the apparently cyclical pattern of budgetary expenditures between defence and civilian items over the five year planning cycle.[16] Though high growth rates reduce the intensity of competition between resource claimants,[17] variations in economic growth around the long-term trend have lesser impact, implying perhaps a reluctance to make allocations which might take on the characteristic of a policy-induced departure from norm.

The Soviet political process has been described as institutional pluralism,[18] where specialised bureaucratic élites compete within the official institutional framework for political support. Bureaucratic politics offers satisficing solutions to problems of resource allocation, whereby organisational conflict is contained by standardised procedures and tacit agreement on rules of the game which satisfy the aspirations of different groups, without necessarily maximising the preferences of any one. A minimum requirement for each bureaucratic group is that allocations in one period do not fall below those of the previous period, which is a public expression of failing power and status. This requirement necessarily reduces the amount of 'free' resources to be allocated. In a rapidly growing economy the residual might in absolute terms be substantial, but in relative terms is likely to be small, so that from year to year allocative decisions take on the character of small steady accretions to stock without excessive discontinuities, for significant departures from trend imply a change in priorities. It is not necessarily the case that such solutions are inherently irrational, for they allow reasonably efficient management of difficult economic and technological choices which require stable and predictable environments.[19] Such a solution is, however, inimical to change, yielding a conservative solution to social and economic problems.[20] Unrepresented groups have limited opportunities to exploit new circumstances or opportunities, while within the defence sector itself it tends to lead to the practice of allocating sizeable budget shares to each service[21] which contains the intensity of inter-service rivalry. Western models of the political market predict that bureaucratic spending will exceed a competitive optimum,[22] though the implications for a society in which all allocations are so ordered is unclear.

Econometric investigation of end use allocations in the post-Stalinist period reveals the incremental characteristic of the bureaucratic solution with, up to the mid 1970s and possibly beyond, relatively small departures from trend, though its precise significance as an explanation for the level and change in defence expenditure remains unclear.[23] It is likely that the relative weighting of the bureaucratic variable alters, being less important during or after periods of international tension or rapid technological change, when new circumstances, problems, and hence solutions, make historical procedures less useful. The current distribution of bureaucratic power reflects historical circumstances, when society was more fluid, and bureaucracies justify the forward momentum of distributions which had been politically agreed in some past period. They do not explain why the proportionate distributions are as they are, nor do they necessarily illuminate the political choices which determined those outcomes in previous periods. This is true of military production in the USSR.

Production statistics for the 1930s (Table 2.1) show a clear and, perhaps after 1934, a decisive preference for military production,[24] which profoundly influenced the pace and pattern of civilian economic expansion.

Table 2.1 Soviet arms production 1930–40

	1930	1933	1936	1940
Aircraft	899	2992	3770	10 555
Tanks	170	3509	4800	2794
Artillery pieces	952	4368	4324	15 300
Rifles (thous.)	126	241	403	1461

Source: M. Harrison, *Soviet Planning in Peace and War 1938–45* (Cambridge University Press, 1985) p. 8.

Quantitative data alone fail to measure the full weight of the military resource claims, for in addition to multiplying the number of weapons, their overall quality, and hence cost, increased, as did the investment in material and human capital necessary to sustain production and technological momentum over the long period. After 1935, for instance, production of heavy tanks replaced the existing light models, so that the numerical decrease after 1936 in fact represented an effective increase of 80 per cent over 1937.[25] In 1938 military related activities absorbed fully 26 per cent of total industrial production and 16 per cent of transportation freight turnover.[26]

Lev Shanin had argued in the 1920s that though some provision had to be made for military production, too large or too rapid an allocation for this purpose would distort the pattern of industrialisation and postpone the transition to socialism.[27] Other Bolsheviks, more acutely influenced by the experience of capitalist invasion during the Civil War, argued that the cost of failing to invest against what Marxism–Leninism predicted would be the inevitable counter-revolutionary onslaught from the conservative capitalist forces, would far exceed those of unbalanced growth and socialism postponed.

The latter group won the political argument, but since there was no coherent theory of military economic planning in being, the administration of military, as of civilian, production grew by a process of trial and error as an empirical learning-by-doing response to problems of practical management. By the beginning of the Second World War the organisational structure was largely in place, the dominant, though far from uniform, principle being increased specialisation along functional lines but controlled ultimately by the civilian political authorities.[28]

Although artillery pieces and ammunition had been manufactured in a military economic combine (voenprom) under the guidance of the Supreme Council of National Economy, aircraft and ship production were manufactured in the civilian Glavmetall (section). In 1926, a drastic reform of the administration of military planning was carried through, when, after establishing a special war committee, the combine was divided into four separate trusts for the production of rifles and machine-guns, small arms, military related chemicals and ammunition. At about the same time, aircraft production was transferred from the civilian Glavmetall into the military voenprom. Shipbuilding was also moved out of Glavmetall but into another civilian-based machine-building trust.

In 1930 functional specialisation was carried a stage further by the formation of a separate association (obedinenie) for aircraft. In 1936 the process was briefly interrupted by the creation of an independent defence industry commissariat, consisting of four sections (glavk), for aircraft, armaments, ammunition and shipbuilding, which was at this time transferred from the civilian to the military sector. In 1939 the trend towards specialisation was reasserted when the commissariat was dissolved and its functions taken over by four independent glavk based on those which had made up the defence industry commissariat.

At the same time, the engineering and metal-working industries were producing increasing proportions of their output for military end use, and in 1939 three commissariats of heavy machine building, medium machine building and general machine building were established, which were eventually to be absorbed into the Defence Industry. This process did not cease with the war. In 1953 the Ministry of Medium Machine Building was established, that for the Radio Industry in 1954, and the Ministry of General Machine Building in 1965.

From the beginning, Soviet economists understood that planning military production was bound up with that of the civilian economy, and as early as 1927 the Party Congress was informed that a Five Year Plan for the development of the armament industry was being worked out, and in 1928 the government formally approved the first

Five Year Plan for the development and reconstruction of the armed forces in conjunction with that for industrial and economic development. In 1937 Stalin created a Committee of Defence, a subcommittee of the Politburo to coordinate the scientific, economic and military aspects of military production,[29] and in 1940 a Defence Industry Council composed of leading representatives of the military industrial commissariat, its chairman being N.A. Voznesenskii, chairman of GOSPLAN. Meanwhile, in 1938, a Military Industrial Commission attached to the Committee of Defence had been brought into being to ensure that priority assignments to the military-related manufacturing plants were fulfilled and that economic resources for military production be effectively subsidised.

Planning for 'armaments in depth'[30] required, in addition to current outputs, contingency plans for mobilisation during wartime, for Soviet strategy conceived of war as a long drawn out struggle in which armaments in being would have to be supplemented by wartime production. Although buffer capacity was built in to military plants, this was an obviously expensive method of meeting peak wartime requirements. In 1926 the Politburo, as a means of resolving the conflicting claims between military and civilian industries, urged that new and reconstituted civilian enterprises should be planned and constructed such that they could be easily converted to military production during war or in periods of high international tension.[31] During the 1930s the principle was formalised by the practice of creating special sections and branches in civilian enterprises. In 1940 fully 43 per cent of the output of the Heavy Industry Commissariat was despatched to military producers, and many enterprises initially producing for civilian markets were taken over almost entirely for military production. Tractor and locomotive plants in particular were planned for possible conversion to tank production.[32] The process was not one way, however, for Defence Industry plants manufactured 17 to 20 per cent of steel output and up to 20 per cent of machine tools.

Weapons, unlike civilian goods, had to meet exogenously determined minimum quality standards, and given the high level of civilian–military transactions the General Staff had to devise ways of ensuring a higher degree of quality control than normally prevailed in civilian enterprises. In 1932 a number of specialist military academies were formed with the objective of improving the management of weapons production.[33] Many of the graduates of these specialist academies provided a core of professional managers for the defence industry, and also the cadre of military inspectors who had the responsibility of mobilising economic resources for military production in the face of competing claims and to ensure that plants produced high quality outputs. Furthermore each industrial commissariat was headed by a deputy minister to coordinate production.

Because the capital stock was so small, even the exceptionally high rates of economic expansion and structural change which were achieved could not meet the combined demands of civilian consumption and investment as well as military output. Aggregate demand exceeded supply, and since the price mechanism as a means of allocating resources had been rejected, political priorities had to be explicitly identified, so that organisation alone cannot explain inter-war economic outcomes which were, however, not always in accord with initial objectives. Resource allocation was ultimately a matter of political choice, and defence was one, perhaps the major beneficiary of that process. Consistent balance was not for Soviet theoreticians and planners a desirable outcome in itself, the objective being less to manage than to create industry. The planning style embraced the virtual inevitability of excess demand, which though it meant that balance at a point of time was unattainable, did create a dynamic impetus to relieve the shortfalls, usually by increasing supply. This planning principle was less appropriate for armaments production, however, where potential confrontation in battle required that the planned stock of weapons was in being, for failure to meet targets based on, and related to, strategic requirements might compromise the very rationale of that strategy and jeopardise the existence of the State. Military production had therefore to be shielded from the more destabilising outcomes of Soviet mobilisation planning. In the event of excess demand, which was the norm, defence plants claimed priority for material and human resources. If military demands were still unfulfilled, supplies were rerouted from their original civilian destinations, especially from those branches which were not themselves important suppliers of military-related raw and semi-manufactured material inputs. The defence branches were allocated better quality materials and machinery,[34] and workers enjoyed better pay and conditions of work.

The ambivalent relationship with the civilian sector which exists to the present day derives from the mode of organisation which evolved during the 1930s, for the armaments industries were at one and the same time part of the civilian economy, but also protected from it. They were subject to the same system of centralised planning by civilian organisations such as GOSPLAN and GOSSNAB,[35] working through a hierarchical ministerial system which reflected the ultimate political control of the Party. Their managers and workers faced the same structure of incentives and constraints as their civilian counterparts and responded to them in similar fashion. However, barriers to shield the defence sector from the debilitating consequences of central planning were systematically incorporated into military economic production and management.

The 1930s outcome was the result of a dynamic political process and within its own terms successful. Since that period, however, the organisations and habit of mind that accompany them have atrophied into a conservative mode of production which remains to this day, but which appears to be increasingly ill-suited to the demands and requirements of modern armies.

Apart from a brief interruption between 1957 and 1965, when Soviet planning was organised on territorial principles, the functional ministerial system of military production has remained intact. Production of armaments and military-related machinery and equipment is mainly concentrated in eight ministries which make up the Defence Industry and which are omitted from the list of plan fulfillment industries.[36] Some military-related production also occurs in the quasi-military industrial ministries of Tractor and Agriculture, Chemicals, Automobiles and Instrument-Making, which are not however formal members of the Defence Industry.

Table 2.2 Ministries in the Defence Industry Group

Ministry	Output
Aviation	Aircraft parts
Defence	Conventional army material
Shipbuilding	Ships
Electronics }	Electronic equipment and components
Radio	
Medium Machine Building	Nuclear weapons
General Machine Building	Strategic missiles
Machine Building	Ammunition

Source: D. Holloway, *The Soviet Union and the Arms Race* (Yale University Press, 1984) p. 120.

Formally the eight ministries form an administratively separate sector of the Soviet economy, directly answerable to a Deputy

Chairman of the USSR Council of Ministers, who is also a member of the Presidium of the Council. In reality, the lines of command are confused and blurred because of the active involvement of the Party in weapons selection and procurement. For such a crucial activity there naturally exists a considerable degree of overlap between Party and State, as, for instance, on the Defence Council. Soviet leaders, it is argued, have a collective knowledge of armaments technology and procurement which far surpasses that of most political leaders,[37] and the Politburo takes an active, and in some cases decisive, role in weapons development. Even so, its expertise can in no way comprehend the entire technical and strategic requirements of modern armies, and it and the Council of Ministers are advised by professional staff officers and military administrators from the various organisations that together make up the military economic sector. It is widely believed that high level coordination of the political, military and economic elements occurs via the Military/Industrial Commission, in all probability an executive arm of the Defence Council,[38] and which also undertakes some inter-branch R&D, which might otherwise slip through the vertical planning and organisational fissures. An alternative interpretation views the MIC as no more than coordinating supply and that the high level authority usually attributed to it is in fact weilded by the Defence Council itself.[39]

The consequence of the prevailing organisational mode is inevitably a highly centralised military planning, production and research control and command structure.[40] Nominally the Ministry of Defence, within the political guidelines laid down by the Politburo, initiates and approves proposals for weapons procurement and development.[41] Military officers work out the force requirements for different strategies and identify performance specifications, guidelines, etc. These must, in turn, be coordinated with civilian targets within the overall economic potential, and a special department at GOSSNAB coordinates with the Ministry of Defence to quantify and if necessary modify the economic supply implications of weapons procurement and development targets. In reality the complex interrelationship between doctrine and technology makes the decision making process more complex and confused.[42]

Despite disagreements within and between the civilian and the military components of the military industrial sector, the political leaders empathise to an unusually high degree with the objectives of the military planners.[43] Until the very recent creation of military-style inter-ministerial bodies in agriculture and machine tools, defence production organisation was uniquely different from civilian planning in that there exists no single department in the Central Council of Ministers to oversee the work of the Ministry of Defence and the General Staff, which therefore have direct access to the key political bodies.

The political priority which is given to military objectives is reflected in the high proportion of the nation's resources which are allocated to defence purposes, and also by the *ad hoc* and formal procedures which allow military producers to by-pass some of the more debilitating characteristics of central planning.

The Ministry of Defence initiates proposals for military procurement and expenditures, which are assessed in terms of military need and economic potential. These by their very nature however, are elastic concepts. In the Soviet Union military need as defined by the General Staff is virtually impossible to challenge because it claims a monopoly of professional military-related information,[44] the quality of which gives it a bargaining edge over other state bureaucacies. Despite the existence of national bodies such as the All Union Institute of Interbranch Information designed to disseminate the flow of technological information throughout the defence economy,[45] the highly structured Ministerial planning tends to compartmentalise and limit the lateral flow of information, to which the security implications of military information give added weight. Military information is limited to those whose business it is to know, and since the political system gives little weight to those interests which are excluded from the bureaucratic pluralism, there were until recently no public or private organisations interested in limiting defence expenditures. The disarmament process has recently created a corps of diplomats and scholars, expert on military affairs who have opposed the entrenched military positions.[46] The representatives of the military-related complex have generally been well able to deflect attempts by other bureaucratic élites to limit their claims on the nation's resources, though the slowdown since 1976 suggests that in view of mounting economic difficulties this may no longer be so easily achieved.

Superior planning and organisation is reflected at the enterprise level, where military producers lay prior claim to scarce resources. Since, other than wages, prices have no allocative function, better quality materials and quicker supply is a function of superior political or bureaucratic bargaining power. Where, as in the labour market, prices do have a role, generous funding enables defence plant managers to pay higher wages to their workers which may exceed those in the civilian branches by up to 20 per cent or so,[47] and which, other things being equal, improves recruitment and employment patterns.

In planning and allocation terms, manufacturing plants are generally categorised by how large a proportion of output is supplied to the armament manufacturers. Those plants which produce entirely or mainly for the arms manufacturers are formally included in the first round of planning, and their supplies of funded or scarce commodities are incorporated into the material balances. They possess a systematic buffer capacity, which may currently amount to 25 per cent or so,[48] which is not only indicative of soft production targets and but also allows them to increase production in times of international tension, to meet especially heavy export orders, and builds in a degree of flexibility to be more innovative than their civilian equivalents. Normally part of the buffer capacity is used for the production of civilian, usually consumer, goods, which are often of higher quality than the civilian norm.[49] Plants which produce mainly or entirely for the civilian industries are less favourably treated. They are residual claimants, whose demands for inputs are treated at a second or even lower stage of the planning process and which are therefore much less secure.[50] If unanticipated bottle-necks in the supply of raw materials or semi-manufactured goods occur, allocations initially destined for the civilian plants may be rerouted to the priority sectors, leaving the former to fend as best they can. Association with defence production is not an unmitigated benefit, however, for, given a customer which has the political authority and the will to refuse inputs which do not measure up to demand, the quality of output must be higher and delivery dates more binding than normal. Quality control is maintained by a cadre of military inspectors, a system first introduced in the inter-war period, which ensures that supply problems are resolved and coordinates military and civilian production in the enterprises. The inspectors (voyenpred) are usually high ranking military officers, in some plants of equal status with the nominal manager, and since they draw an army salary, they have no material interest in the plant's performance in relation to its targets. They have the incentive and, since they represent a high priority sector, the authority to insist that enterprises meet the exacting requirements of the army. Given the generally low quality of Soviet goods, this they achieve by the effective but inefficient method of rejecting a high proportion of inputs.[51]

Furthermore, defence plants have a greater degree of lateral freedom, for they often possess independent sources of finance, and therefore are less dependent on the State Bank for their hiring and procurement policies.[52] Though the military inspectors screen armaments producers from many of the inefficiencies and delays characteristic of Soviet planning, they cannot do so completely, and Defence Industry ministries, like many in the civilian economy but to a greater degree, protect themselves against unanticipated delays of low quality supplies by 'in-house' production of semi-manufactured material products. The aviation industry, for instance, owns plants for producing steel, aluminium, manganesium and other raw materials, as well as machine tools. One Soviet investigator reported that GOSSNAB, the formal supply organisation, allocated only 33 per cent or so of the inputs used in the aircraft industry.[53] Autarchy, though it protects producers against unanticipated supply bottlenecks or inferior quality products, does reduce the dynamic economies of scale which are potentially available to specialised production.

Representatives of the military industrial complex are influential in the highest organs of the State and the Party. In participatory bureaucracies, shared interests and organisation with identifiable groups are essential prerequisites for exercising power, and the military and supplier industries have communal interests in maximising production and research on weapons technology.[54] They have also closer regular contact than tends to be the case for many other common-interest groups. The system of military inspectors cements relations between the military and the defence industry, which is, in any case, organically tighter because of the powerful customer–supplier relationship and the insistence on certain quality standards which, though not unique, are more deeply embedded in the military–industrial nexus. In practical terms this is reflected by superior representation on the highest decision bodies. The Defence Industry is disproportionately represented on the Central Committee of the CPSU, for not only is it the only economic sector whose ministers are uniformly accorded full membership, but they are elected as representatives of an economic interest and not as individuals. It is the only identifiable group whose ministers have more or less automatic full membership of the Central Committee of CPSU, and whose secretary usually has Politburo status.[55]

The military industrial representatives are not, however, a formally integrated and exclusive interest structure.[56] In addition to their obvious collective objectives, the military community does have interests different from the economic, and within each community as well there are conflicting individual as well as supportive mutual obligations and interests.[57] Even in the most co-ordinated planning system, the customer–supplier relationship is partly adversarial, producers wanting to sell low quality goods expensively and buyers to receive high quality goods cheaply.

Despite the entrenched power of the military-industrial complex, the Party, because of its deep involvement in military/economic affairs, and also because it makes the ultimate allocations between and within the defence and civilian sectors, the Party retains final control[58] over the broad parameters of defence spending. The complex retains its special status only to the extent that its objectives coincide with those of the political leadership. In practice this has been very considerable.

Although the Party has ultimate authority over the direction and dimension of military spending, it only partially controls the environment within which it functions. It cannot be indifferent to the domestic consequences of military spending, especially when growth rates are low, competing demands are more insistent and the coercive apparatus of the Stalinist state largely dismantled. By the same token, it cannot ignore the international environment, neither the level of military spending by the USA or NATO, nor the rate of technological change embodied in new weapon parameters consequent on the large sums of money spent by the capitalist countries on military R&D. Technologically advanced weapons in one country do not necessarily have to be matched by countervailing systems of a similar degree of technological sophistication, and the traditional Soviet response has been to offset quality with weight of numbers. One country cannot however lag too far behind the other, for technological expansion has a cumulative consequence on force potential which requires proportionally greater quantities of offsetting, lower-quality armaments. Even in the Soviet Union that response eventually ceases to be viable, especially in the light of the quantitative diminution in the growth of factor inputs. Therefore, even though Soviet doctrine typically lays emphasis on large quantities of men and on armaments of comparatively simple design and performance, it must, by and large, given the average level of technological attainment, match the USA in the quantity of resources it allocates for military research and new weapons development.

The Second World War demonstrated clearly the great and growing importance of science and technology to defensive and offensive capabilities, and though countries had engaged in armaments-related R&D before 1939, the war proved to be a watershed in the systematic exploitation of science and technology for military progress.[59] In the inter-war period, R&D absorbed less than 1 per cent of the military budget of the major powers. By the end of the 1970s Soviet defence chiefs spent over 20 per cent of the armed forces' budget on R&D, amounting to around $30 billion. Competition in this aspect of the arms race grossly distorts the balance of military spending such that whereas between them, the USA and the USSR account for 50 per cent of total world defence expenditures; they account for over 80 per cent of those on military R&D. Although both undertake research over the entire armaments spectrum, the average level of technological attainmnent in the USSR falls short of that in the USA,[60] and it is generally the follower in the technological arms race, constantly in the position of trying to catch up with the USA.

Military R&D may be understood as the array of skills and techniques which are applied to military production with the intention of creating more effective weapons, more effective means of using weapons or of making some weapons ineffective, thereby accomplishing objectives which were previously unattainable more cheaply or efficiently. The activity relates not only to the manufacture of weapons themselves, but also to the entire range of communication, reconnaissance, command and control equipment, which are inputs into modern armies. The increase in post-war spending on defence has been due, not so much to the larger number of new weapons produced, but rather to the increase in their overall technological parameters, and hence costs.[61] Hard information on development costs in the USSR is limited, but they are generally presumed not to depart too greatly from the American norm. Soviet modernisation programmes take on average between eight and fifteen years to come to fruition, a time-scale not too dissimilar to that achieved in the USA.[62] In the USA, the comparative ratio of costs to performance parameters are shown in Table 2.3, and it is widely assumed that in view of the similarity in time-scale, development costs are unlikely to differ too greatly in the USSR.

Despite its importance for economic growth, the basic dynamics of technological progress are relatively little understood, and has indeed been described as a measure of our ignorance.[63] In particular, it is not known with any degree of certainty whether technological change is essentially demand or supply determined. On the one hand, it is argued that the protean nature of basic science allows potential expansion in any direction. Therefore the factors which at a point of time determine the pattern and pace of change are essentially econ-

Table 2.3 Increase in cost and technical performance of American military aircraft in the 1980s (factor increase)

R&D	Unit	Payload or endurance	Range	Speed	Avionics	Delivery or navigational accuracy
5.4	4.7	2.3	1.9	1.8	3	3

Source: *World Armaments and Disarmament.* SIPRI Yearbook 1982, p. 125.

omic, i.e. demand determined. There is, however, a view which argues that the commercial exploitation of basic science does not depend solely on demand but also on the innate nature of scientific knowledge and understanding. That is, it is sometimes scientifically easier to expand in some areas than others.[64] Although attention tends to be focused on discontinuities created by weapons which are 'new in principle' or which dramatically change the parameters of existing weapons, technological progress which occurs on a more incremental basis, can be quite as effective and expensive in changing the performance characteristics of weapons, as for instance, has been the case with precision-guided munitions.

The development of new armaments from basic research to the stage which they can be effectively deployed is a long and complex process. The lead times on new fighter aircraft, for instance, may be up to ten years and, in common with all technological activity, involves a number of stages, from basic research, through prototype construction and development, series production to deployment by the armed forces. At each stage, appropriate bodies must evaluate progress to date and undertake a cost-benefit calculation of proceeding to the next, which involves a combination of technical and economic judgements. The effectiveness of the overall process depends on the quantity of resources allocated for the activity and on the efficiency of the institutions which exist to promote, evaluate and control at each stage.

The concept of military need which provides the rationale for R&D is elastic, especially in view of the long lead times typical of research and development activity. Military planners who lack information, especially on the early stages of weapons development in enemy countries, must anticipate the likely consequence of research and development in advance of actual outcomes being known, so that the fundamental question of how much is enough is particularly difficult to evaluate for R&D. It is highly judgemental, based as much on ideological perceptions of enemy intent as on objective scientific criteria. Since the cost of underestimating enemy intentions is likely to be large but immeasurable, military planners work to asymmetric functions planning for worst case outcomes, which, deliberately or otherwise, has the effect of sustaining demands for existing weapons and generating research for new.

High levels of, and growth in, spending increase the range and diversity of real research activity and therefore the probability that new avenues will be identified as fruitful areas for further research and development, and also increases the rate of technological obsolescence of existing weapons stock. The internal logic of the military R&D cycle makes it virtually inevitable that new scientific insights will attract funds for additional basic or development research. Once new areas of research are identified and applied to weapons production in one country, it becomes rational for planners to assume that the enemy will sooner or later obtain the same or similar scientific knowledge, which will lead to improved characteristics of its own weapons, or to effective counterweights. Military planners fear above all being taken by surprise and guard against the adverse consequences of that by spending to defend not so much against known weapons in being, but against those which do not exist but which can be anticipated.[65] A high degree of ignorance over the pace and direction of military progress in the enemy country adds to the inducement to guard against surprise, increases the range of possible advances which must be anticipated, and therefore the amount of money to be spent. The ultimate logic of such a process of competition is that countries compete against themselves,[66] until eventually military R&D in one country may come to have only a tenuous link with that undertaken in the enemy country.

Technological research has come to assume such importance that the process itself, irrespective of current performance or utility, must be nurtured to yield maximum long-term return. R&D work is complex and expensive, often requiring a large stock of physical and human capital which needs to be nurtured to maximise the economic and military returns. Technological progress is most effectively embodied in personnel, and there are strong incentives to maintain at maximum operational efficiency research teams of skilled scientists, engineers and operatives and their complementary inputs of expensive specific and general capital. Overhead expenses, both material and intellectual, are reduced by continuous research and development, and new work, if it follows on from existing contracts, using resources in being and working within established parameters reduce learning costs. The dispersion of human capital which follows from the break-up of a research team can be costly to replace or reassemble at some future time period, and it is often cheaper to keep the team together by funding new contracts. Major R&D establishments which have made significant contributions to military progress may be accorded the status of national assets not to be broken up, but which does, however, create an inexorable follow-on dynamic. As existing research or production comes to an end, new contracts are offered and the pattern of expenditure is maintained.

Both the USSR and the USA allocate fully 50 per cent of total R&D expenditure for military purposes, and the research intensity, as measured by the percentage value of R&D to output exceeds that of the civilian sector by a ratio of 20 to 1.[67]

Because of the systemic rewards of free enterprise and a dynamic resource base, the USA is comparatively more efficient in the production and diffusion of complex technology. The opportunity cost of R&D is lower than in the USSR, which gives it every incentive where possible to switch international competition to that area of military activity where it has the greatest comparative advantage, and which is assuming greater absolute and relative importance in the defence planning of all countries irrespective of their comparative status as technological powers. The trend of spending is therefore in directions in which the USSR is comparatively less efficient than the USA, which puts it in the position of constantly seeking to catch up and at the same time increases the defence burden. Thus even though its particular institutional structure allows it at one level to screen out élitist pressure and so avoid the 'mad momentum' which characterises military R&D in the USA,[68] there exist powerful exogenous forces which propel the Soviet Union to by and large match the USA in the quantity and direction of research and development, though within its own distinctive style.

The Soviet Union publishes minimal data on the dimensions of its military R&D expenditures and the CIA is least confident over the accuracy of its estimates for Soviet military R&D expenditures. The 3 per cent of scientists and engineers which is officially acknowledged to work in military R&D[69] clearly understates the true number. Numerous methods have been proposed to estimate the current output, but they are all conceptually or empirically limited.[70] One method is to estimate ratios from information on total Soviet defence spending, assuming the ratios between end use categories do not depart too far from Western practice. This technique requires the gross figure itself to be reasonably accurate, which incorporates a degree of circular reasoning in that the component which is being estimated is itself part, and in this instance probably a large part of the total sum from which it is being calculated. It is also assumed that the percentage of total expenditures which is allocated to R&D is similar to that which exists in other similar countries. Since the USSR and the USA are the only two which finance research over the entire range of weapons development, Soviet allocations are assumed to replicate those which prevail in the USA. However, American circumstances differ from those in the USSR in many, often conflicting, ways. Because of its disadvantaged position on the learning curve it is likely that, per unit of output, the real personnel and material costs in the USSR will exceed those of the USA, and that technologically more complex research and development will be relatively more expensive. For instance, Soviet design shops are highly labour intensive, requiring almost four auxiliary workers per scientist or engineer more than their American counterpart. On the other hand, Soviet military strategy aims for a different technological mix from that of the USA. By following evolutionary design principles based on known and easily assimilable precepts, and where necessary compensating for lower achievements by increasing physical parameters, it probably can avoid some of the expensive costs which the technological leader must incur. Since the basic information is not available, there is no way of calculating how or to what extent these conflicting factors cancel out.

A second method is to infer from an examination of the performance characteristics of newly deployed weapons the rough order of magnitude of the technological inputs which must have been incurred to produce the observed characteristics. This procedure also is based on a direct comparison with American practice and costs which are unlikely to be fully relevant to the different economic and technological conditions which exist in the USSR.

The third is a variant of the residuals method already encountered in military procurement and possesses the limitations which attend all budgetary techniques. R&D expenditures are estimated as those budgetary and other expenditures which cannot be otherwise identified in Soviet budgets. The budget allocations most likely to include military R&D must be identified, together with unspecified residuals in other expenditure heads. In the All-Union Budget this is probably 'Science'. Detailed investigation using this procedure yields the following information (Table 2.4).

Table 2.4 Estimated structure of Soviet R&D outlays

	1960	1965	1968
	(billion current rubles)		
Total outlays	3.3	5.9	7.8
Defence/Space	1.6–2.0	2.6–3.4	3.0–4.5
Other R&D	1.7–1.3	3.3–2.6	4.7–3.6
	(per cent of total)		
Defence/Space	48–62	45–57	39–55
Other R&D	52–38	55–43	61–45

Source: N. Nimitz, *The Structure of Soviet Outlays on R&D in 1960 and 1968* (Rand R-1207 – DDRE, 1974) p. vii.

William Lee, however, argues that very little of 'Science' expenditures is for military research, the real value of which considerably exceeds budgetary outlays on this activity.[71]

The final method estimates numbers engaged on military R&D work from an examination of employment trends, especially of engineers and scientists. The information on likely R&D workers is consolidated by their field of training and then supplemented by American data on industrial sector ratios of R&D to production workers to obtain a sectoral distribution of specialised R&D organisations. Since American practice differs from that in the Soviet Union, the Soviet figures must be adjusted, to incorporate estimates on capital and current non-personnel expenditures, information on which is usually scanty. Sixty per cent of Soviet engineers and scientists are estimated to work on military research and development programmes.

In view of the problems with data and methodology, precise estimates for military R&D must be considered highly tentative, though from what is known of physical investment in plant and machinery, employment trends and the deployment of new weapons systems, it cannot be other than considerable.

Assessments of the level of technological attainment or the rate of technological progress are intrinsically problematic because they involve judgements about qualitative parameters which lack a theoretical and empirical basis. Nevertheless, there is a wide measure of agreement that the Soviet military research production cycle is in general more effective than that in the civilian sector, and that as a consequence the rate of technological improvement in the defence industry exceeds by a substantial margin that on average attained in the civilian economy. Investigation of weapons development, for instance, indicates that, though the technological relationship between the USA and the USSR fluctuates, advanced weapons such as ICBMs, lag behind American best practice by smaller margins than do comparable advanced scientific machinery and equipment such as computers.[72]

On the other hand, most indices of international comparison show that on average Soviet weapons embody lower levels of technology than comparable American weapons, and that in some key areas the gap may be widening.[73] It is also claimed that a Soviet lead, where it exists, is often due to the USA choosing not to compete rather than a technical inability to do so.[74] In 1972 a Pentagon study of 167 'areas' of weapons technology found the USSR to be superior to the USA in 28 areas of knowledge, and 37 in application, equal in 72 areas of knowledge, and 57 in application and behind the USA in 67 areas of knowledge and 75 in application.[75] A more recent assessment of deployed military systems (Table 2.5) shows an overall American superiority that is only being marginally eroded in some areas.

Research into twenty basic technologies that are predicted to have the greatest potential for significant increase in military capabilities in the next ten to twenty years show that the USSR leads in none and is equal to the USA in only five (Table 2.6).

In order to assess the Soviet achievement, both phenomena need to be explained.

The military R&D cycle replicates and draws upon the civilian science economy in crucial ways and the characteristic innovation culture which prevails in the society at large bounds the effectiveness and the efficiency of military related R&D. Despite abundant funding, the economic returns to civilian related technological progress has by and large been disappointing, and has been so acknowledged by one Soviet leader after another. The various reasons which have been offered in explanation may be categorised as those inherent to the systemic inefficiencies of central planning, those associated with the policies and objectives pursued by the Party leadership, and finally those which derive from the Soviet Union's particular geographical, social and historical environment.[76] Although the specific

Table 2.5 Relative US/USSR technological level in deployed military systems

	USA Superior	USA/USSR Equal	USSR Superior
Strategic			
ICBM		X→	
SSBN	X		
SLBM	X		
Bomber	X		
SAM			X
Ballistic missile defence			X
Anti satellite			X
Cruise	X		
Tactical			
Land forces			
SAM		X	
Tanks		X	
Artillery		X	
Infantry combat vehicles		X	
Anti-tank guided missiles		X	
Attack helicopters		X	
Chemical warfare			X
Ballistic missiles		X	
Air Force			
Fighter attack aircraft	X→		
Air to Air Missiles	X		
PGM	X→		
Air Lift	X		
Naval			
SSN	X→		
Anti-submarine warfare	X→		
Sea-based air	X		
Surface combatants	X→		
Naval Cruise Missiles		X	
Mine warfare		X	
Amphibious warfare	X→		
Command, control communication & intelligence			
Communication	X→		
Electronic counter-measures	X		
Early warning	X		
Training simulators	X		

→ = Direction of change.   *Source overleaf*

Source: *The FY 1985 Department of Defence Programme for Research, Development and Acquisitions*. Statement by the Hon. R.D. De-Lauer (Washington, DC: 1984) pp. 11–33.

Table 2.6 Relative USA/USSR standing in the twenty most important basic technological areas

	US Superior	US/USSR Equal	USSR Superior
Aerodynamics/Fluid dynamics		X	
Computer and software	←X		
Conventional warheads		X	
Directed energy (laser)			X
Electro optimal sensor	X→		
Guidance and navigation	X→		
Life sciences	X		
Materials	X→		
Microelectric material	X		
Nuclear warheads		X	
Optics	X→		
Power sources			X
Production/Manufacture	X		
Propulsion	X→		
Radar sensors	X→		
Robotics	X		
Signal processing	X		
Signal reduction	X		
Submarine detectors	X		
Telecommunications	X		

→ Direction of change
Source: *The FY 1985 Department of Defence Programme for Research, Development and Acquisitions*. Statement by the Hon. R.D. De-Lauer (Washington, DC: 1984) pp. 11–32.

explanations cannot be explored in detail, because the national technological style has an impact on military outcomes, a brief summary of those most immediately relevant is necessary.

Western economists view innovation as essentially entrepreneurial,[77] an activity where the rigid procedures and cast of mind brought about by central planning are especially inimical of progress and advance. Civilian R&D is mainly undertaken in research bureaus and design shops which are largely financed by non-competitive budgetary grants.[78] Since finance is assured, there is little incentive to compete for business for personal or commercial gain. Indeed, quite the reverse, for individual scientists and establishments may not retain control of their patents and sell or license them for personal financial reward.

Production enterprises, where possible, avoid real innovation because of its disruptive effect on the rhythm of established work practice. Retooling, often a necessary part of investing for innovation, may require managers and workers to learn new work patterns or new skills, which take time to assimilate and increase the likelihood of equipment breakdown. New supply routes often require different suppliers, new and uncertain administrative contacts and therefore higher probability of raw materials and semi-finished inputs arriving late or not at all or in inadequate quantities or qualities. In the crucial machine tool industry enterprises may require up to four years to make up for the disruption to output, and hence lower rewards brought about by retooling for innovation and technological progress.[79] Even after the new techniques have been successfully assimilated, higher targets consonant with enhanced productive capacity may not yield rewards sufficient to justify the risk of interruption to existing work practices.

On the other hand, there are some compensating features. Enterprises pay little for licenses to use technologies developed elsewhere, and the existence of national bodies such as the State Committee for Science and Technology should in theory speed the diffusion of new knowledge throughout the scientific and economic communities. Recent reforms in organisation have improved the economic links between customer and supplier, and in the economic mechanism, the incentive to meet customer requirement more effectively. There is some evidence that the research cycle has improved, the throughput of patents has increased, and lead times have been reduced. However, the weight of evidence suggests that the level of technological attainment and the rate of technological progress in the civilian community still falls short of best Western practice, and that the gap is in general not being reduced.

The overlap between the civilian and military research cycles inevitably means the transfer, though in perhaps less virulent form, of many of the outcomes characteristic of civilian R&D to the military branches. The distinction between the two areas of research is especially blurred at the early stages of the research cycle, where practical applications of ongoing research can be only dimly identified. Indeed, one of the abiding objectives of military planners is to identify as early as possible those scientific and technological developments which occur in civilian funded research enterprises and which may have military applications. At the early stages the distinction between civilian and military research is arbitrary, but even in the later stages, where it may be more meaningful, scientists and engineers in both communities work within civilian planning structures and to similar constraints and incentives.

Military related R&D is undertaken at three levels. That under the aegis of the Academy of Sciences concentrates on the early stages of the research cycle where the military return may at best be only dimly discerned. The increasing importance of 'science' to military power blurs the distinction between the early and later stages of the cycle, and that between military and civilian objectives and research undertaken by the Academy of Sciences is likely to assume greater importance for defence than has hitherto been the case. The Ministry of Defence owns its own R&D facilities for research, with a more operational or military significance. Most research and development work of overtly military purposes occurs in specialised shops and bureaus which are organically linked to specific services or weapons areas. Such contract research as does occur tends to be limited to comparatively unimportant areas of development, and most of the funds are obtained from non-competitive budgetary sources in the form of non-repayable grants. In conjunction with their grants the research organisations are set developmental targets and bonuses are paid on the degree to which the exogenously determined schedules are attained rather than for genuinely innovative progress.[80] Target planning gives a powerful impetus to achieve predetermined specific milestones, and since it is administratively easier to plan and monitor progress in terms of quantitative criteria, there exists a chronic tendency to neglect or to relegate to secondary importance qualitative parameters of progress. Since the R&D organisations have little economic incentive to pursue innovative developments for commercial reward, the effectiveness of the research cycle depends very critically on the success of the military planners in identifying targets and devising reward mechanisms to stimulate the innovative energies of Soviet scientists and engineers.

Organisationally, improved performance is obtained by allowing research shops and design bureaus some latitude from the constricting procedures which characterise the civilian research cycles. In the technologically dynamic aircraft and missile sectors they have considerable autonomy from the production enterprises,[81] and are freer to experiment and take risks without loss of economic reward. In the Defence Ministry, on the other hand, which produces conventional army equipment and where innovative change is less rapid, the R&D shops are tightly controlled by the production enterprises and have only limited lateral freedom. Even so the latitude is relative.

Although the precise relationship between Soviet military doctrine and emerging technology is complex and confusing, to a greater degree than is normal in the West doctrine determines the pace and pattern weapons development.[82] The military professional, though politically subservient, is thus crucial, especially given the monopoly of information which is claimed by the General Staff. It and the Ministry of Defence have the major roles in delineating the broad parameters of military progress,[83] and weapons development has traditionally been largely demand determined. Military officers initiate or approve proposals for research programmes and lay down the performance criteria which the R&D institutions must meet. The Ministry of Defence, in conjunction with the Military Industrial Commission, monitors progress, and eventually orders the new weapons which embody the final outcome of the research programme. The high degree of political control which is implicit in such procedures is consonant with a user orientated philosophy,[84] ruggedness, interoperability, ease of handling and repair. Professional and political control holds in check, though does not abolish, the internal dynamic which characterises weapons development in societies where the constraints on technological progress are more often commercial than administrative.

The particular combination of the Soviet economic incentive mechanism and user orientation have over the years decisively directed the style of the armed forces towards a conservative philosophy of technological development.[85] Soviet design principles emphasise evolutionary changes and individual weapons, though often of high quality, tend towards simplicity of design with a high ratio of common and interchangeable parts. The current T72 tank, for instance, was initially developed in the 1960s, and itself derived from the earlier vintage T62 and even the T34 tank, which was initially designed in the inter-war period.[86]

Commonality and conservatism are not inherently irrational, and it is not the case that military worth is always best served by innovative departures from the orthodox.

Western analysis of military technological progress suggest that developments which do not depart too dramatically from existing engineering parameters and are within the intellectual competence of planners and designers are more likely to be successfully completed than those which are new in principle. In the USA cost overruns and time delays are sytematically related to the degree of technological advance which the designers seek.[87] A Pentagon study in 1976 found Soviet jet engines to be cheaper than comparable American engines by 33 per cent to 50 per cent due to design, maintenance and specification differences even if built by American personnel in American factories with American costs.[88] Soviet officers prefer more frequent though smaller design changes and the Soviet weapons stock has a greater range and number of weapons systems. Although the follower country cannot fall too far behind the technological leader there are circumstances in which a larger array of slightly inferior weapons are militarily preferable to a smaller number of superior weapons. The Soviet style is also well suited to the management of large well articulated development programmes and the defence industry has often surprised Western politicians (though less often Western scientists) by the speed with which it completes large R&D projects.

In a technologically lagging society, a weapons design philosophy which gives weight to the known and the predictable is an effective means of economising on those resources which are in real terms most expensive, and is moreover consistent with the broad parameters of military and economic strategy. The extensive growth model, traditionally geared to injecting large quantities of labour and capital, is consonant with a military doctrine which even in the nuclear age gives weight to a large standing army of often comparatively poorly educated and ill-trained personnel. A philosophy based on rapid change in weapons technology of high and increasing complexity is clearly not compatible with the other components of economic military power. Moreover, a change in one element cannot effectively occur without corresponding changes elsewhere. Intellectual, as well as organisational and economic adaptation to new circumstances, is not easily achieved,[89] and the improbability of achieving one without change elsewhere must be one entirely rational explanation for always postponing fundamental reform. Since a thoroughgoing shift to a new and rapidly changing technological style holds the possibility of great risk as well as great rewards, the cost of failure to achieve a mutually consistent economic, military and technological style may exceed that of civilian wealth foregone by keeping to a less efficient but known design philosophy.

Technological change, is by its very nature dynamic, and, the USSR cannot fall too far behind the USA. The resource cost of matching quality with quantity increases more than proportionally as the gap widens, and there eventually comes a time when no reasonable quantity of technologically inferior weapons will compensate. The greater the technological lag, the larger are the required quantitative indices of compensation, and as Soviet growth declines, conservative design choices become increasingly expensive and inappropriate.

If conservative solutions and evolutionary design precepts are not consciously chosen but are imposed by the bureaucratic command structure, or the failure of R&D communities to produce more imaginative solutions within acceptable time periods, these characteristic features of the Soviet military R&D cycle are even more indicative of inefficiency.[90]

The weapons sector has achieved a notable degree of success in matching American weapons, especially in those areas of technology where the Soviet military has chosen to compete most vigorously, and as the American data shows, in some areas the Soviet Union is ahead. Located as it is in a comparatively inefficient civilian sector, the military performance must be considered highly effective, explained only by the special circumstances which prevail in the military sector and which therefore distinguish it to a greater or lesser extent from the civilian norm.

Better performance may simply reflect generous funding. Around 50 per cent of the total R&D budget is for military purposes. An estimated 60 per cent of scientifically related workers are employed in defence-related enterprises, and of the scientists and engineers working in the civilian sector, about 71 per cent are concentrated in the Machine Building and Metal Working branches,[91] a large percentage of whose output is destined for military end use. Superior funding enables defence managers to claim top quality factor inputs, the most skilled and best educated manpower, special quality raw materials and semi-finished products, and the most advanced machines and equipment. They control their own extensive production and testing facilities which facilitate the comparatively rapid transformation of scientific ideas into prototype weapons and, if successful, to series production. Since enterprise targets normally fall short of capacity, they are able to experiment with new ideas without jeopardising current production, which so inhibits civilian innovation.

The real resource claim is greater than the data suggest. Military

R&D organisations do not pay the full burden of their research activities. In those institutions which undertake scientific work for both the civilian and the military sectors, accounting devices tend to shift overhead costs systematically to the civilian component. Institutions in the military sector do not have to pay a capital charge and, because of Soviet policy to reduce socially unacceptable income distribution, and therefore wage spreads, do not pay the full opportunity cost of their highly skilled and trained engineers and scientists.

The superior performance of the military scientific community is however greater than can be explained solely by generous funding, and for a given level of expenditures military output exceeds that in the civilian branches.

For all its many theoretical and practical benefits, central planning is particularly inimical to rapid technological progress. Planning most effectively deals with routine and predictable outcomes which facilitate quantitative calculation of costs and benefits. Effective innovation, by its very nature, is often a departure from the orthodox, which requires an unstructured response to new risks and opportunities. Since there is no private sector seeking to exploit new opportunities for financial gain, there is no commercial counterweight to the innate conservatism of the planning bureaucracy, and hence no automatic system of harnessing the benefits of new scientific developments. It must be the case, therefore, that the superior performance of the military R&D cycle is due to particular circumstances which exist only, or to a significantly greater degree in military-related R&D, and which enable military research institutions to avoid the most debilitating consequences of the formal system.

Many of the inhibitions which are placed on civilian institutions have been removed or lessened, resulting in less pressure to meet short-term deadlines and inducing a rather more risk-taking pattern of behaviour. Major development programmes are planned to overlap, and each important design bureau works on about three large projects simultaneously. As one cycle is completed, resources are routinely transferred to new research programmes which sustain constant employment of men and material and encourage follow-on finance which is in any case powerfully present. If research projects in the civilian sector are shown to have military implications, the civilian elements are relegated from the project and, on occassion, the enterprise organisation may be absorbed into the military branch.

The military insistence on quality controls higher than generally exist in the civilian economy further encourages departmental autarchy. The R&D organisations produce 'in-house' a proportion, often high, of semi-finished materials, equipment and machinery, a practice which has prevailed since the early 1930s, and is especially powerful in those branches which routinely achieve high rates of technical progress.

Such benefits are largely policy induced, and reflect the political priority of military production. A change in that priority would erode the special flexibility which currently exists, and therefore to a degree in the superior performance of military R&D.

Policy alone does not account for the higher rate of technological achievement, for the defence sector is structurally different in that it uniquely faces demands for a more exacting technological and economic performance than is generally the case in the civilian branches.[92]

In the civilian economy, customer bargaining power is weak, being both systemically and policy constrained. Supplies of raw materials, equipment and machinery are allocated via central planning organisations, which link supplier and recipient. Although the unofficial Tolchaki system gives some flexibility, formally producers must dispatch to, and recipients receive from, designated enterprises. There exists little horizontal latitude to seek alternative outlets or supplies. Rigid supply routes, though inflexible, might yet be allocatively efficient if customers had incentives to reject supplies which for one reason or another were unacceptable. This tends not to be the case, however, for enterprise output plans are predicated on the assumption that supply plans will have been fulfilled and that recipient plants will have received the designated raw materials, semi-finished products or machinery. Failure to meet production targets can result in financial penalties, and recipient plants have little effective power to reject inferior products. Suppliers know this, and since better quality outputs are more costly, and troublesome to produce but yield little extra reward, there is no mechanism to maximise quality production and customer satisfaction spontaneously. This, however, is not the case in the defence sector.

International competition with a technologically dynamic enemy imposes minimum standards on the Soviet armed forces, which if they are not met, must seriously compromise the survival of the State in its existing form. Although there is no necessity to match American technology exactly, there is clearly a level below which weapons quality cannot be allowed to fall. The military customer therefore requires and insists upon minimum standards from its suppliers. The political importance of national security is made manifest in the bargaining strength of the General Staff, which can and does reject outputs which do not meet the standards determined for it by international competition. Since the Politburo is so deeply involved in weapons development, the power of the military customer is enhanced. Though military R&D is well funded, the research and development process is expensive, and institutions do not have access to unlimited funds, especially since the Politburo is so closely aware of the social opportunity cost of the level of, and growth in, military spending. The squeeze, on the one hand, of limited resources and, on the other hand, of having to meet externally determined quality levels, forces the military customer more than any other in the Soviet Union to economise on the resources allocated to it, leading to a preference for what has been described as an austere technological style.[93] Soviet weapons possess a high degree of commonality, so that equipment and sub-components may be used for more than one purpose and on more than one occasion. Pressures to reduce weight and economise on fuel and raw material intensity are greater than exist elsewhere in the economy.

It is also the case that the management of weapons research and production is in a sense simpler. In a civilian economy which from the 1930s has preferred a policy of autarchy, international competition is only marginally important in imposing quality standards. Civilian planners and managers have the dual task of establishing *ex ante* quality parameters, as well as minimising cost of production. For military producers, however, the first decision is determined for them by international competition. Because the Soviet Union is the technological follower, quality parameters are, by and large, fixed for it. Military planners are thus faced with the conceptually simpler task of meeting the exogenously determined parameters most effectively.[94]

Soviet procedures to screen out élitist and commercial pressures on weapons innovation, have been largely successful, but at the expense of sustaining the Soviet Union's technological lag *vis-à vis* the USA. Soviet military authorities acknowledge that science has become the basic catalyst in military technological progress,[95] and hence a key resource in the East–West strategic balance. Protean science opens up outcomes which are difficult to predict as the military consequences of scientific technological choice shift progressively to the early stages of the research, development, production cycle, and where the barriers erected to separate the military and the civilian research communities are increasingly onerous. The secrecy and the inhibitions of the lateral flow of knowledge, information and ideas which characterise the Soviet Union in general and the defence sector in particular are especially inhibiting to the imaginative matching of different and often disparate building blocks which in many key areas of military science has replaced the linear progression more appropriate to a constricted hierarchical command structure.[96]

Despite the expertise of the Politburo and the Party in general, a weapons selection process which is as much political as scientific is haphazard and arbitrary. It is also expensive. The traditional Soviet model was not only effective but was also perfectly consistent with the overall economic strategy of extensive growth pursued since the first Five Year Plan. Gorbachev has made clear his belief that the solution to the Soviet Union's economic problems lies in the intensification of production in which growth is more dependent on increased productivity and technological progress than was the case in the extensive growth model. His modernisation programme coincided with and was in part a response to economic shortage and scarcity, and is predicated on an upsurge of embodied and disembodied technological progress, the replacement of obsolete machinery and equipment and an improved incentive mechanism. Defence claims around 50 per cent or so of the nation's R&D resources and 60 per cent of scientists and engineers. In the light of slower growth and more insistent competing claimants the R&D burden grows more onerous and the spill-in effects to the civilian community are limited. Thus in addition to systematising the weapon selection process, Soviet leaders also seek to minimise the real cost of development and deployment once the choices have been made. These are not independent of one another of course. They have introduced optimising techniques which allow competent officers to scan in a systematic and ongoing manner the entire array of scientific and technological choices and to identify the appropriate cost–benefit calculus at each decision stage.[97]

The economic debate coincides with an equally portentous disputation within the strategic community over the most apposite doctrine for the Soviet Union in the light of revised thinking about the defensive role of strategic nuclear weapons.[98] A group of officers following the logical consequences of the view articulated by ex-Chief of the General Staff, Ogarkov, that nuclear weapons have lost much of their utility argue that the Soviet Union should lean less on its stock of nuclear weapons and develop an array of non-nuclear alternatives which however are technologically advanced and therefore expensive to produce. One consequence of the new thinking is that the Soviets cannot lag behind the Americans in such weapons but must match them at every stage in the range and level of their technological characteristics. The military scientific community must therefore transform itself into being truly innovative and imaginative.

This is more so since the Americans under the Reagan presidency have pushed international military competition into areas in which the Soviet Union is at a comparative disadvantage. Since 1980 R&D as a proportion of military spending has increased to 13 per cent, and in a well-publicised leak the Pentagon has argued that the USA should develop weapons that are difficult for the Soviets to counter, impose disproportionate costs, open up new areas of major military competition and obsolesce previous Soviet investment.[99] Despite doubts over the eventual strategic usefulness of such ambitious programmes as the SDI Soviet leaders are sufficiently in awe of American scientific and technological capability to take seriously the possibility of a degree of success which would leave them vulnerable unless compensated by a responsive Soviet programme of matching scale and expertise.

The traditional Soviet military technological model is under pressure from a variety of sources to modernise. The reality is that in the Soviet Union, as in any society, the scientific community is not static and unchanging, and the likelihood of a successful response to the new challenges should not be underestimated. The new multipurpose Flogger series fighter planes and the SA10 SAM missile show a range and level of technology consonant with the new doctrine. Nevertheless there exist powerful barriers to the quick and easy adoption of a new and more innovative technological style. More autonomous technological progress is likely to conflict at key points with traditional Party control over military as all other affairs of the State, although the commercial motivation for innovative change so potent in capitalist societies is still largely absent. It is thus a matter of speculation how far change in one dimension can provide the necessary stimulus without corresponding change elsewhere. The industrial sector has little motivation to change from traditional procedures which yield little prospect of gain but a high probability of more difficult targets. One possible compromise might be to build in excess capacity to industrial plants by giving them targets which are easy to reach, and which might stimulate them to use excess capacity for truly innovative change. The modernisation programme requires, however, that obsolescent equipment be replaced as rapidly as possible to improve productivity, so that capacity is fully and sometimes over-fully used to meet immediate targets. The leadership, as so often in the past, is faced with an acute dilemma between short and long objectives. It is not possible to anticipate whether modernisation of defence R&D can occur independently of fundamental reform of the civilian sector. To date Gorbachev's modernisation has been on the whole cautious and the response of the military in supporting or opposing economic reform will clearly depend on how they assess the benefits and costs of the status quo.

Although some officers argue for a change in doctrinal emphasis on nuclear and non-nuclear weapons the debate has not been resolved. Traditionalists insist that the Soviet Union has been well served with the traditional model. The Soviet Union has not been notably successful in meeting the type of challenge implicit in the new doctrine and it should not hasten to a mode of allocation in which the likelihood of failure is high, and the benefits uncertain and delayed.

3 The Defence Burden

Estimates of Soviet defence outlays calculated in rubles, more than in any other currency, replicate the sort of economic infomation available to ministers and planners when they decide on the allocation of resources between competing claimants. In conjunction with other ruble data, they provide a metric of the dimensions of the burden which military spending imposes on society, and the relative social priority of end use allocations. Western estimates suggest that by 1985 the Soviet Union directly allocated 15 per cent to 17 per cent of the nation's resources to military-related activities, proportionately far greater than for that of any other developed country. If the output of the industrial branches which are related to military production are also included, defence, widely defined, may appropriate up to 30 to 40 per cent of Soviet GNP.[1]

The proportion of the nation's resources allocated to military spending is not a complete measure of the defence burden which should also incorporate the numerous indirect consequences on economic growth, efficiency and welfare. However, the usage is so well established that it would be unnecessarily pedantic to seek an alternative terminology. It might, however, be useful to distinguish between the concept as measured by the defence-GNP quotient and a more diffuse but wider conception of burden. The static burden is a measure of the share of the nation's resources allocated to defence and is a metric of civilian production foregone at a point in time. The dynamic burden measures the cumulative effect on civilian investment and consumption goods foregone over a period of time,[2] which in dynamic societies usually means that the marginal measurement of cost differs from the average. Economic expansion has a potent effect on economic welfare, and current growth rates influence the quantity of resources available for investment in plant and machinery and hence the pace of technological progress in future time periods,[3] so that the growth inhibiting consequences of current military spending cumulate and multiply. Statistical analysis of a group of industrially mature countries shows there exists a statistically significant and strongly negative correlation between defence spending and, respectively, economic growth, investment and productivity growth.[4] Hence the possible reconciliation of the fact that only a minority of the nation's resources are normally allocated for defence purposes with the, admittedly rather extreme, assertion that 'the civilian sector has been bled to support the Soviet military machine'.[5]

Implicit in the concept of burden is the view that the activity for which the expenditures are incurred is intrinsically value-less, or at the very least adds less to social welfare than other activities for which the resources could be used. In the particular case of defence it implies that military spending is essentially unproductive,[6] consistent with the economic view that society's objectives are the maximisation of current consumption, or the means to maximise future consumption. If material resources have diminishing utility, societies rich in material wealth should accept with greater equanimity the real burden occasioned by the diversion of resources from the creation of current or future consumption. In fact, of course, that is seldom the case.

The weight of burden is related to the degree of uncertainty which habitually prevails in the international community. If countries know with certainty that enemy countries will or will not attack, as the case may be, the social evaluation of defence spending and hence the perception of burden is more easily assessed. Since, during peacetime, uncertainty prevails,[7] the subjective assessment of the degree of threat and its consequences leads to an equally subjective assessment of the utility of and political solution to the problem of burden. Security is a valid component in society's preference functions, if only as a prerequisite for the enjoyment of the more conventional measures of welfare, though of course there remain disagreements over its relative weighting and how it can be most effectively attained.

Defence spending is an economic burden to the extent that resources employed in the production of military goods both could and would be used to meet civilian objectives, if released from their current employment. If military resources were, in the light of changed objectives to remain unemployed, the burden of current expenditures is thereby reduced. The weight of burden thus depends on the flexibility of the market or planning mechanism, in particular the ease with which resources can move or be directed from one activity to the other. The greater the degree of flexibility, the more onerous is the opportunity cost and hence the burden of allocating resources for defence, for resources released from military activity will not long remain idle, but will be quickly brought into alternative civilian employment. Economic flexibility also requires resources to be quickly substitutable in the other direction, from civilian to military employment. It might therefore be presumed that, other things being equal, less resources will be allocated on a permanent basis to military production in economically flexible societies, but that the burden of a given quantity is high. The weight of burden also depends, of course, on the relative efficiency with which given resources are used in the civilian and the military sectors.

Despite its manifest microeconomic deficiencies, the Soviet economy has many characteristics which should in principle increase the flexibility of the transfer mechanism. Planners have the political and economic authority to allocate resources between competing ends. Centralisation of power is a strategic device to mobilise and to concentrate resources in those areas which are deemed to have priority,[8] thereby bypassing what Marxists claim to be the anarchic and slow outcomes of markets. All planned economies possess to a greater or lesser degree characteristics which should increase flexibility. Firstly, resources are fully though often inefficiently employed at the macroeconomic level. The problem for planners is one of excess demand rather than excess supply, so there is not, as is often the case in capitalist economies, insufficient aggregate demand which might lead to unemployed human and material resources. In the Soviet Union economic flexibility is additionally enhanced by the common practice of manufacturing civilian and military goods in the same plant, using a similar inventory of capital, manpower and techniques. It is often the case that the civilian goods which are produced in joint civilian–military enterprises are consumer durable goods which have a high income elasticity of demand in Soviet society, additional production of which could have a disproportionate effect on material incentive rewards, and hence on the transformation to intensive growth. This illustrates the point that the quantity of resources alone may be an inadequate measure of cost or benefit. The release of particular bottle-necks or shortages in the economy could have non-marginal consequences on the civilian parameters, as, for instance, may be true of human or material resources currently employed in military research. If as a consequence of reduced military spending economic resources do become available, planners should have knowledge of where in the economy they might be effectively deployed and the power to allocate them quickly and directly, without, as is the case in market systems, having to respond to price adjustment which will occur only after a transition period which could be long. Thus the economic transfer between the military and civilian sector should be effective, and is so argued by Soviet economists.[9]

However, the practice of Soviet management vitiates many of the presumed advantages.

Much of the industrial capital in defence plants, even in the Soviet Union, is specific to military production, while the microeconomic parameters of Soviet central planning reduces the efficiency of given transfers between sectors and branches. Since the Soviet price system offers limited guidance to social opportunity costs, the alternative distributive outcome between competing sectors, while not necessarily arbitrary in terms of planners' preferences, may yet fail to maximise economic returns. Soviets in practice trade off the macro benefits of full, though underemployment (unofficial unemployment may in fact be substantial) against the micro cost of not knowing whether a particular allocation is consistent and efficient, even within the known objectives of the planners who have incomplete information.

Even if all military activities are correctly identified, the defence quotient underestimates the true cost to Soviet society, for the structure of prices is not independent of the sectoral distribution of resources,[10] and military activities are incompletely costed. Prices lack a full interest component which reduces the relative cost of such capital intensive goods as weapons and military equipment. Low pay below their marginal productivities for scientists in military R&D, and for recruits, and the allocation of overhead costs in those plants which supply both civilian and military goods to the civilian component further reduce the nominal burden below its true level.

Despite its relative inability to achieve high rates of technological progress, the Soviet Union has matched to a considerable degree the technological attainments of American weapons.[11] This well-established fact has led many Western analysts to the conclusion that the defence sector is on average a more efficient user of resources than is the civilian sector.[12] The defence burden obviously depends on exactly how efficiently military goods are produced and on the source of that efficiency, especially if burden is measured as the additional civilian output produced by a marginal adjustment of spending from military to civilian objectives. It has already been argued that superior performance cannot be explained solely as a consequence of better funding, but is much more likely to be due to the specific features which are unique to, or are more deeply embedded in, the armaments sector. These have been categorised in Table 3.1 by Nancy Nimitz as follows:

Table 3.1 Characteristics of the Soviet civilian and defence space sectors

	Civilian	Defence/Space
1. Experimental production and testing facilities	Poor	Good
2. Series production plant	No slack	Excess capacity
3. Vertical integration (ministerial autarchy)	Low	High
4. Design commonality (use of off-the-shelf components)	Low	High
5. New product cycle (research to production)	Long	Short
6. Foreign and domestic competition	Low	High
7. Style of output	Heavy, expensive	Spare, simple, cost-effective
8. Bargaining power of customer	Low	High
9. Target production price at beginning of design	No	Yes
10. R&D costs considered in weighing alternative designs	No	Yes

Source: N. Nimitz, *The Structure of Soviet Outlays on R&D in 1960 and 1968* (Rand R-1207 – DDRE (Santa Monica, 1974) p. 43.

In both military and civilian sectors enterprises are induced to maximize technical efficiency, though the systemic consequences of central planning induces a high degree of X-inefficiency. The key issue is the degree to which the special advantages enjoyed by military producers are policy inspired, and hence ultimately transferable to the civilian economy in the event of a change in policy objective, and the extent to which they are structural and uniquely characteristic of the defence sector and therefore not at all, or only partially, transferable. The weight of burden, in the sense of benefit to the civilian economy of a transfer of economic resource to it from defence production, depends to a considerable degree on which type of explanation is the more significant.[13] Most of the advantages which accrue to military products it is argued, are policy induced, resulting from the priority status of defence and of the special procedures which have been devised to protect it from the most debilitating characteristics of civilian planning. Defence production does therefore impose a real burden on the civilian economy.

It is also the case, however, that perhaps the single most important explanation is largely unique to defence, in that military producers face a powerful and discriminating customer which is forced to economise because of the existence of an effective international competitor, the USA.[14] International competition creates absolute quantity/quality standards, and although the Soviet Union has traditionally offset higher quality with weight of numbers such substitutability is limited over the entire range of armaments over time, and the Soviet Union cannot lag too far behind the technological leader without compromising the very survival of the State. Such absolute requirements exist, if at all, to a much lesser extent in the civilian economy, protected as it is by the autarchic policies preferred by the political leaders. If resources were transferred to civilian branches where pressures for austere production are less, their efficiency might well be below that in military production, and the real burden thereby reduced.

Furthermore the special flexibility of military procurement and R&D may be obtained only by shifting the costs of inflexible planning to those civilian sectors excluded from special treatment.[15] If, following a policy-induced transfer of real resources to the civilian sector, these also were relaxed, the additional increase in civilian output brought about by disembodied technological progress suggests that the burden is doubly onerous.

It is possible, however, that the defence sector is not more, but less, efficient.[16] The fact that armament producers face a powerful international competitor need not of itself induce economy. If resources are always abundantly available, desired technological levels may be attained by means which are effective, but inefficient. It has been argued, for instance, that military inspectors ensure quality control by rejecting a high proportion of finished outputs, which is wasteful not only of raw material resources and manpower, but also hastens the depreciation of capital. A number of planning characteristics, though endemic to the Soviet economy, exist to a more virulent degree in defence production. Soviet vertical style planning induces a high level of departmentalism which inhibits the lateral flow of resources, technology and information. Efficient research is particularly influenced by how quickly human beings and information can move across organisational barriers. New ideas and modes of investigation often require new organisational solutions, and hence a degree of flexibility which appears lacking in the bureaucratic supplier–customer relationship which, despite some modification in the direction of contract research and interagency competition, are still hierarchical and rigid. This is magnified by the high degree of secrecy[17] by which the military and associated economic groups defend their special status in Soviet society. The General Staff insists on monopolising military information, military producers are reluctant to share with other ministries their best machinery and equipment, and despite such bodies as the All-Union Institute of Interbranch Information, the systematic pooling of scientific and technological information is ill-developed. Scientists who seek a national or international scientific reputation may be hesitant to undertake research or development which will have to remain secret.[18] However, the higher pay, better research facilities, more intellectually interesting work and the high social standing which some designers attain may more than compensate.

It might be argued that in a rationally organised society the concept of burden is either irrelevant or has to be extended to include the entire array of goods and services. All goods have an opportunity cost and if security is properly internalised in the welfare preferences of the society's decision-makers, there is no logical reason to believe that it should count for any less than its civilian counterpart. Only if defence yields no utility to society, or there is reason to believe that its weighting in the set of social preferences is deliberately manipulated for domestic political or ideological purposes, is it possible to speak of a uniquely defence burden. It is clear that for the Soviet Union, or at least its leaders, the assumption that military spending has no utility is not correct,[19] and the evaluation of the burden must be balanced by the degree to which it adds positively to society's welfare as interpreted by the key decision-makers. Indeed, some Western critics argue that not only does military output possess positive utility, but it is the single most desirable outcome of planning. The Soviet objective is to maximise economic–military power, in which the military component, though not exclusive, has a high weight.[20] Taken to its logical conclusion, this requires that planners seek not to maximise consumer welfare, but to provide only that minimum level which is consistent with and required for the attainment of the power objectives. Under Stalin such might have been the case, but does not reflect current Soviet priorities.

Although it is not necessary to adopt a *gestalt* view of Soviet society, it is highly militaristic,[21] nurturing the Army through a civilian leadership which empathises to a high degree with the values and goals of the military establishment,[22] which is articulated through an aggressive ideology. The Party is the final arbiter in the political competition for resources, and the sympathy of the civilian leadership is attested by the consistently high proportion of the nation's resources being allocated for defence, and by the civilian costs which are endured.

Military education is highly pervasive and in technical and vocational institutes the subject matter is often quite deliberately oriented towards military or military-related disciplines.[23] Military education has traditionally had a quite explicit role in the socialisation of Soviet citizens. Even as consumer living standards were held down, an improvement in education was perceived as being useful in increasing the nation's economic potential. Educational resources were limited, however, and one economising solution was to centralise their provision. For a long time the military was the sole point of assembly where young people from different cultural backgrounds might be effectively nurtured in civic as well as military virtues, for it was axiomatic of Soviet ideology that training the good soldier was inseparable from creating the virtuous citizen.[24] Although an efficient programme of public education has lessened this social role, the army is still an important provider of technical and vocational training. Conscripts are taught secretarial skills, truck driving, electrical repair, etc., which they can and do retain in civilian employment.[25] At the top end of the skill level, spin-off effects to the civilian economy are limited by the pervasive secrecy; though there have been some benefits of management and organisation.[26] The armed forces also provide some health and social services which would otherwise have to be financed from the civilian budget.

In addition to increasing the economic and technical skills of young recruits, the Army, along with other State and Party organs, has the important but delicate task of making Soviet citizens more receptive to the social and moral obligations of Marxist–Leninist ideology. Economic performance has been only moderately successful in meeting the political and economic aspirations of the Soviet people, and the Army, with its emphasis on the traditional virtues of discipline, respect for order and authority and submission to the precepts of the official ideology, may be a necessary counterweight to what is alleged to be a growing mood of pessimism and even nihilism.[27]

The politicising function of the Army is likely to be particularly important to Moscow's policy to Russify the different Soviet nationalities. Many of the richest non-Russian people, such as those living in the Baltic states, are resentful of what they perceive to be heavy-handed centralisation from Moscow,[28] while the rural and largely Muslim population of the Asian Republics accept only imperfectly the values which are identified with Greater Russia.[29] They reject many of the conventional mechanisms to integrate them into the wider Soviet economy, and since they provide a growing proportion of the Soviet population, Russian authoritarianism, through the armed forces, may be a useful device to keep them within the Soviet polity.[30] Russian is the sole language of instruction in the Army and provides perhaps the only common bond between the young people of all the Soviet nations.

At a more practical level, the construction units of the armed services provide, at minimum cost, assistance in the form of a mobile labour force which can be moved to meet specific objectives as required. Construction troops have been employed to complete capital projects, such as the BAM railway in Siberia where, despite high economic incentives, labour shortages often cause delays in meeting targets. They have been employed throughout the country to build roads, bridges, schools, etc., and even to help with the harvests, when the indigenous workforce cannot cope with peak demands.[31] Although marginal, such assistance, if concentrated on high priority tasks such as gathering the harvest, may have an impact out of all proportion to their numbers and skill level. The Ministry of Defence also earns revenue from military farms and some other such economic activities.

Soviet foreign policy is informed by an aggressive Russian nationalism and an ideology which has a view of history consistent with Russian experience, and is reflected in an extraordinary concern with the security and survival of the State.[32] Russian consciousness of its long land barriers and vulnerability to invasion by stronger nations East and West, often brought to a high pitch of consciousness by Slavic writers,[33] projected itself externally in an aggressive policy of imperialism and alliances. Russian preoccupation with the defence of the homeland and its people was given theoretical substance by Marxist-–Leninist ideology, which divides the world into two warring camps engaged in a constant struggle for supremacy.[34] The Soviet people must be constantly vigilant, and though ideological fervour has waxed and waned, the basic view that capitalist countries are continuously seeking to crush the revolutionary impulse, prevails.

The greater the degree of internal contradiction in advanced capitalist states, the more likely are they to seek its resolution through aggressive warlike actions, which is what accounts for the continuous intensification of the arms race.[35] The reason why the capitalist nations have so far failed in their counter-revolutionary objective is due in large part to the correlation of forces which inhibits their capacity for aggressive action. Moreover the Socialist states have a more positive role in world affairs, for they cannot stand idly by and acquiesce in the exploitation of the working classes in capitalist societies. The Soviet Union, as the leading Socialist State, must therefore support and inspire revolutionary movements throughout the world.[36] Soviet leaders, like the Russian Czars before them, have responded to actual or perceived threats and obligations by allocating a large portion of the nation's resources for security purposes, and current ratios are historically modest.[37] As the changing technology of war reduces the utility of the traditional strategy of buying time by space, the need for superior forces in being increases as, *ceteris paribus*, does the economic impact on the civilian economy.

Although in practice the distinction is not consistently clear, governments typically deploy an array of domestic and foreign goals and instruments. Since for most Soviet citizens the domestic material rewards of socialism have been modest, Soviet leaders seek compensating spectacular successes abroad to legitimise the leading role of the Party,[38] in which sphere Soviet status as a superpower is based to a substantial degree on its military power, the only area in which it has been able to compete on equal terms with the most advanced capitalist countries.[39] Soviet ideological fervour has settled into a cautious orthodoxy often supportive of conservative governments,[40] while economic aid has consistently been secondary to armaments sales and military aid as a mechanism for increasing Soviet penetration and influence in the Third World.[41] The importance of military power as a surrogate for a more widely based influence in the international community has conflicting implications for Soviet leaders. So long as the Soviet Union fails to rediscover its economic or ideological dynamism, the military components will remain preeminent, but so long as military objectives have priority, economic prosperity and revolutionary élan will be more difficult to rekindle. The positive rewards for military power exist precisely because of the civilian economic costs created by exceptionally high military outlays.

It is clearly inappropriate to assume that for the Soviet State, as indeed to a greater or lesser extent is true of all countries, defence expenditures are perceived solely as a drain from more useful expenditures. It is equally clear that spending on military objectives does have opportunity costs and, if only in the most general terms, a clear assessment of the relative utility of defence spending might be feasible if what is forgone could be ascertained. Since we know little of the subjective *a priori* preferences of Soviet leaders or the technical rates of transformation between the different sectors of the economy, the analysis must of necessity be inferential.

Throughout Soviet history, the material requirements of the armaments industry have decisively influenced the rate and pattern of economic expansion.[42] For Soviet leaders, the security of the home base and defence of the Soviet empire have assumed absolute priority. Even when international opportunity coincided with powerful domestic incentives to ease the defence burden, as in the mid to late 1970s, Soviet leaders were reluctant to institute a decisive re-ordering of priorities, preferring instead to reduce the rate of civilian capital formation, spreading the burden of adjustment and avoiding a damaging confrontation with entrenched power centres.[43]

An observed cyclical pattern of expenditures between civilian and military budgetary heads in the five year planning cycle suggests that once the basic allocations have been determined between competing end uses, there ensues a political struggle at the margin between the civilian and the military claimants. The precise pattern of the cycle may reflect the fact that at the margin civilian items have priority and that only when they ease can the military representatives mount an effective claim to marginal additions to their allocations. Budgetary data, though incomplete, indicate that on average civilian expenditures peak in the initial and terminal years of the Five Year Plan, which may reflect a political calculation by planners to increase welfare in these important periods. In the middle years, civilian demands ease, at which point the defence representatives find it politically expedient to pursue their own claims, which in the nature of political compromises are granted. In the succeeding Five Year Plan the process commences again. Though suggestive of a political process, the argument's validity depends critically on the assumption that the budget heading measures a real military component, and is partly vitiated by the fact that military procurement, that element of military spending most likely to be immediately and directly competitive with civilian material spending, is probably largely excluded.

The economic costs of defence are of two kinds: the priority allocation of resources to military spending within the prevailing mode of production, given chronic excess demand, necessarily reduces the quantities available for civilian purposes. In addition the mode of production is itself not independent of the policy objectives of the leaders. Since the attainment and, subsequently, the maintenance of military power was a crucial policy objective from the outset, this was an important determinant of the mode of production. Military power on the desired scale and pace could not have been achieved via the market mechanism, and had therefore to be replaced by a system of economic planning which centralised the power to allocate economic resources. Central economic planning is itself a source of systemic inefficiency which must in part be due to the priority of military objectives.

In the first few years of the Republic, arms production was relatively neglected as the Bolshevik leaders struggled with the crippling economic and social consequences of war and civil war. By the middle of the decade, however, the Soviet planners were giving serious consideration to how best to integrate civilian and military output, and within a short period of time, the rhythm of military production came to influence to a high degree the pace and pattern of economic industrialisation. Although the turbulence of the 1920s makes conclusive judgement difficult, it is likely that even in this early period the growth of defence production capacity had deleterious consequences on the civilian economy.[44]

The economic dimensions of military production grew phenomenally during the 1930s (Table 3.2), but even so, the budgetary data may underestimate the true spending on defence by as much as 70 per cent in some years.[45] Growth at such a rapid pace inevitably imposed a heavy cost on the civilian sectors. In 1935, defence took 15 per cent of the funds available for working capital and investment. By 1939 this had increased to fully 50 per cent.[46] The defence sector absorbed 20 per cent of the output of the machine tool branches, and by 1938 between 33 and 40 per cent of steel output and 10 per cent of the output of the chemical industries.[47] Investment in material resources demanded complementary employment of skilled workers in the defence plants, and the armaments' commissariats competed directly with civilian industries for the output of the metal, engineering, machinery and machine tools branches, which were at the heart of the industrialisation programme. The headlong pace of military procurement, especially after 1934, decisively influenced the pattern of industrial investment. In 1937, when the country began to re-arm, the supply of machinery for civilian investment actually declined, as

Table 3.2 Allocations to defence in the state budget (expenditures)

	Total budget expenditure	Expenditure on defence	Defence as % of total	Annual increase of expenditure on defence (Previous year = 100)
1st 5 Yr. Plan				
1928–29	8105	880	10.5	115
1929–30	12 329	1046	8.5	119
1930	4635	434	9.4	
1931	23 069	1288	5.6	123
1932	30 740	1296	4.2	101
All FYP	78 878	4944	6.3	
2nd 5 Yr. Plan				
1933	40 153	1421	3.5	110
1934	50 795	5019	9.9	353
1935	66 391	8186	12.3	163
1936	81 827	14883	18.2	182
1937	93 921	17481	18.6	117
All FYP	333 087	46990	14.1	
3rd 5 Yr. Plan				
1938	124 039	23 151	18.7	132
1939	153 299	39 181	25.6	169
1940	174 350	56 752	32.6	145
1941	216 052	70 866	32.8	125
All FYP	451 688	119 084	26.4	

Source: J. Cooper, 'Defence Production and the Soviet Economy', in CREES Discussion Paper, SIPS No. 3 (University of Birmingham Centre for Russian and East European Studies, 1976) pp. 35–6.

within four years defence as a proportion of total industrial production doubled.[48] The pattern of industrial development was permanently distorted. Lower quality steels and metallurgical products useful mainly for the civilian branches were relatively neglected, which reduced long-term productive potential as well as current output. In the period 1928–52 funds earmarked for military production increased twenty-sixfold in real terms, a rate of expansion twice as rapid as those for civilian-based heavy industry. Rapid and disjointed growth were especially demanding of managerial skills, perhaps at that time the scarcest of all resources.

Production statistics show a broadly inverse relationship between military and civilian growth. When, in 1932–3, military production increased particularly rapidly, growth of measured GNP declined, and when in 1934–6 the pace of military expansion abated, civilian growth picked up.[49] Although it cannot be proven that one variable was entirely or even mainly responsible for the other, there does exist a strong presumption of a causal relationship.

Investment in and production of military outputs distorted the allocation of investment goods between competing sectors, but the major burden was borne by the consumer, for conflicting resource claims could only be reconciled by forcing consumers to the status of residual claimants.[50] The measured increase in total personal income of around 33 per cent or so represented in actuality a large decrease in *per capita* consumption of between 25 per cent for wage earners, and 40 per cent for the farm workers. The priority provision of food, clothing and shoes to the military sector meant that in some years civilian *per capita* income was little more than one half of that attained in 1928. Indeed, so effective was the policy of suppressing civilian consumption that it almost attained the status of a policy objective.[51]

The sectoral distributions described in this brief account could not have been attained in an economy responsive to market signals and incentives, for consumers would not willingly sanction such a level of sacrifice. Soviet leaders recognised that if military production was to grow at the rate and attain the level which they envisaged, the market, which the Bolsheviks in any case rejected as an allocating device, would have to be replaced by a mechanism which would give the Party effective political control of economic resources.

In 1922, the Soviet Union was a poor and technologically backward society. The short-term Bolshevik objective was economic recovery from the depradations of war and civil conflict, which the NEP, with its relatively high degree of economic freedom, achieved to a substantial degree. The long-term objective was nothing less than to catch up with and surpass the level of economic development attained by the capitalist countries. The participants in the great intellectual debates of the 1920s were agreed that only through a policy of deliberate industrialisation could that objective be attained within a reasonable period of time. (The conduct of the debate has been expertly analysed elsewhere. See, for instance, A. Ehrlich, *The Soviet Industrialization Debate 1924–28*, Cambridge, Mass.: Harvard University Press, 1960, but a brief overview is necessary to put the events of the 1930s in perspective.)

The dispute between the Right and the Left factions centred on the pace at which industrialisation could be forced. Following Marx, both sides understood that the dynamo for growth was investment, in particular Category I goods. The two factions disagreed on the overall pace of investment and on the relative contribution of different economic sectors to the growth process. The Rightist faction, led by Bukharin and Shanin, argued that so long as the Soviet Union remained largely agrarian, overall economic expansion was limited by the pace of growth in agriculture. Capital and consumption goods had to be made available to the agrarian sector to increase production and productivity, to grow more food and industrial crops to feed the growing urban proletariat and to provide the exports to finance imports of foreign capital and technology. This strategy would unfortunately hold back the pace of industrialisation but would lay the foundation for the political alliance between the peasants and the workers, necessary to secure the revolution. Shanin recognised that military requirements would hasten the industrialisation process, but argued that too rapid expansion of defence would distort the pattern of development and impair economic efficiency.

The Left, led by Preobrazhenski, insisted that the socialist society could and should break free from the constraints of a backward agricultural sector. Material and human resources had to be transferred, forcibly if necessary, to the manufacturing sector to create the industrial infrastructure which alone would guarantee the desired rapid growth and transformation. This would inevitably mean an insufficient supply of consumer goods, the so-called goods famine, and would be fiercely resisted by the peasants, who would have little incentive to deliver to the State the required quantities of food and industrial crops. Therefore, the economic link between production and consumption, and between the rural, agricultural and the urban, manufacturing classes had to be broken. Food procurement had to be centralised and the peasants forced to yield a surplus to be expropriated by the State. At the same time, peasant demand would be held back, thereby freeing a high proportion of expropriated resources to be allocated for investment, especially of Category I goods.

By the end of the decade, both sides had modified their initial stance. Bukharin acknowledged the inevitability of discontinuous growth, while Preobrazhenski warned about the risks of too rapid expansion. In the event, Stalin, by a series of manoeuvres, crushed first the Rightist and then the Leftist factions, and after consolidating his supremacy imposed his own preferences on the Party, which were for a rate of industrialisation and a degree of coercion that not even the superindustrialists of the Left faction had contemplated. Stalin accepted the Left view that to bring about the transformations which he sought, voluntary exchange, the basis of the market mechanism, had to be destroyed. This objective was made more immediate by a drop in grain procurement in 1927–8 of over 30 per cent, which seemed to justify the widely held belief that reliance on the market would make the State too dependent on the rich peasants whose loyalty to the Revolution could not be guaranteed. A high level of open and disguised unemployment exacerbated the economic problem, the most effective solution to which was to increase complementary capital investment.

In theory, planning can involve different degrees of centralisation and forced and voluntary relationships between citizens and the State. Whatever the intellectual rationale for indicative planning, it had little relevance for the Soviet experience. Central economic planning came to the Soviet Union as the servant of a specific strategy,[52] the objective of which was to bring about a revolutionary shift in factor allocations between the major sectors. This could be achieved only through a mechanism which would mobilise and concentrate resources on a small number of selected targets and prevent their dissipation to sectors of low importance. The task of the planner, therefore, was not that of coordinating plans within a consistent framework, but rather to impose on society the vision of the political leadership and to devise the mechanisms which would translate the political objectives into operational outcomes.[53] Soviet central planning was almost exclusively an instrument of mobilisation. The first objective set out in the first Five Year Plan was to so increase investment as to double the fixed capital stock in five years.[54] The Plan went through numerous drafts, as Stalin demanded more and more improbable targets for steel, cement, non-ferrous metals and machine tools. Consumer goods were inevitably sacrificed, and to avoid the consequences of the goods famine which had so concerned Preobrazhenski, centralised planning had to be accompanied by a comprehensive programme of agrarian collectivisation to force down the living standards of the peasants and enable the Party to expropriate the agricultural surplus to feed the industrial proletariat. In fact the Party's objectives were more than likely attainable without having to double the capital stock in one five year period,[55] but the *ad hoc* basis of Stalinist-planning precluded rational calculation of means and ends.

Industrialisation reduced *per capita* income and collectivisation brought about a prodigious increase in the industrial labour supply, on a scale unmatched in any other country. In 1929, 1 million households lived on collective farms; by 1930 this number had increased to 14 million. The social consequences of so great a dislocation left even many of the superindustrialists aghast.

The maelstrom has been explained as a psychological excess of revolutionary zeal by Bolshevik cadres, who, once the process started, believed it essential to complete the transformation as quickly as possible, and to destroy what many regarded as the counter-revolutionary influence of the Kulaks.[56] For Stalin, industrial and military goods had become ends in themselves. The goal of production became, not the maximisation of welfare, but the creation of more industrial goods, steel, cement, machinery, and of course weapons which was at least consistent with the quantitative objective of catching up and overtaking the capitalist countries. Consumption became little more than a means of production, the allocation to which was determined by the minimum necessary to provide an adequate supply of labour, and to avoid political unrest. In a state governed by terror, that minimum quantity was small indeed.

The one consistent objective was to guarantee to top priority branches the resources necessary to meet their goals. A powerful defence industry was an integral part of the industrialisation programme, and after the mid-1930s, possibly the single most important policy objective.[57] Military production provided a powerful rationale for, and justification of, the massive concentration of economic and political power in the Soviet system of central planning.[58] To the extent that military objectives were important, even decisive, influences on the practice of Soviet central planning so was defence responsible for the systemic and policy induced inefficiencies which have characterised the planning system since its inception.

Central economic planning is totally consistent with the Marxist view of the market as inefficient and unjust. Nevertheless, even within a centrally planned framework, politically determined objectives can be attained by more or less efficient methods. Even if planners reject the market as a satisfactory allocative device, there do exist capitalist procedures which, suitably modified to the socialist environment, could be used to assist the planners in their allocative tasks. The degree to which such devices are rejected depends upon the ideological perspective of the planners; on the economic distance which they seek to shift allocations away from that which would have prevailed in a free market. Given Stalin's preferences, central planning offered the only way they could be achieved, and was in terms of those preferences, by and large successful. The process was costly, however, for those whose lives were directly touched by the great transformation and those who have since had to accept the economic consequences of lower living standards.

The first Five Year Plan was initially drafted as an operational programme which, by laying out a description of the current state of the economy and a blueprint for the desired direction and pace of change, would give systematic assistance to the planners. The plan quickly lost contact with reality as Stalin insisted on more rapid expansion and greater distortions in sectoral allocations. Unattainable targets were laid down, and though the wild excesses of the first plan have not subsequently been repeated, the concept of planning as propaganda has been sustained into the modern period.[59] No plan has achieved all its stated civilian targets, even for high priority goods, the sixth Five Year Plan was discarded before even it was approved, and others have been severely modified before the conclusion of the plan period. Even the supposedly more operational one year plans have had to be amended during the course of the year as enterprises promised seriously to underfulfil or overfulfil norms and targets. Plans which respond to, rather than determine, outcomes are operationally limited but are valuable as exhortatory devices.

Although planning was sanctioned by Marxist theory and was not in itself irrational, its particular manifestation in the Soviet Union reflected the unique social circumstances of time and place.

The overriding objective was economic growth, the prerequisite for military–economic power and for catching up with and overtaking the capitalist countries. Other desirable criteria, such as microeconomic efficiency, high consumer living standards or equalising incomes were dismissed as either being irrelevant, or had to be postponed until the revolution had been secured domestically and the capitalist counter-revolutionary impulses checked. Realpolitik and Marxist theory combined to give a heightened emphasis to the quantitative parameters of planning, and from the outset, physical comparisons with the economic peformance of other countries became the touchstone of progress.[60]

The emphasis on easily understood and monitored physical quantities economised on one of the major factor constraints, efficient economic managers, who were also ideologically sound. In view of the limited theoretical understanding of the dynamics of central planning and lack of information on economic and technical linkages, it was impossible for planners to model more than a comparatively small number of branches. The tasks of planners and managers were simplified if targets were set, norms agreed and performance monitored in physical dimensions. As a matter of principle and of expediency, economic industrial and military success came to be measured in quantitative terms – more steel, more cement, more machine tools, more armaments.

Planners ignored efficiency criteria not only because they might influence economic outcomes, such as reducing growth rates but also because economic efficiency was a static capitalist concept, irrelevant to a socialist society which had determined upon a mode of production totally incompatible with that which preceeded it. The teleological view, which in the 1920s asserted that socialist expansion should not be governed by the 'facts' of the current state of the economy, still lingered into the 1930s.

Markets were anathema, and so by definition must be everything which made them work. Chief among these was price. There was little attempt to distinguish between operational functionalism and the social framework within which prices had historically functioned. Although prices in a Marxist society were to reflect socially necessary labour time incurred in production, it has not been possible to devise a price system independent of the prior evaluation of what is socially necessary. There can thus be no systematic evaluation of the social costs and benefits of the most desired outcomes, or the most efficient way of achieving objectives after they have been determined. Prices do not precede but follow the allocative decision and therefore cannot influence it. The rate of interest and rent were not only the price of capital and land, but also the unnecessary and exploitative portion of national income which accrued to a particular class, due to their possession of a particular array of property rights, rather than as a reward for their essential contribution to economic well-being. These also had to be abolished, especially since, as some argued, interest rates, by artificially raising the price of capital, would lower the organic composition of capital and therefore hold back investment and growth.[61] Thus the monetary basis for rational economic calculation was rejected as bourgeoisie formalism, of little relevance for socialist planners. The function of planners was to work out and improve the technical relations between the economic branches[62] much as if the Soviet Union was one giant factory. The objective was not consistent balance, so that when input and output plans failed to mesh, which was usual, the practical response would be the transfer of resources from the residual to the key branches. Although this solved the immediate problem, it was detrimental in the long run in that it forced Soviet planners into an empiric and eclectic mode of evaluation,[63] which was emphasised by Stalin's rigid prohibition of theoretical debate which might lead to conclusions about desirable economic means and ends other than those he had determined upon. The failure of economists to engage in theoretical debate to increase understanding of how planned economies work, and thereby to add to the disembodied parameters of growth, remained characteristic of Soviet planning long after it had been shown to be inimical to Soviet objectives.

The rejection of capitalist procedures increased the difficulty of trading with capitalist countries and strengthened autarchic tendencies which were in any case strongly entrenched. The creation of a powerful armaments industry was doubly influential in this respect, for an excessive reliance on key inputs from countries which were avowedly hostile would make the State unnecessarily vulnerable.[64] The Soviets for a few years pursued a policy of borrowing foreign civilian and military capital and technology from capitalist countries,[65] but in 1932 moved to isolate the country from the rest of the world, and by 1939 only 1 per cent of GNP was derived from foreign trade. Although international trade is normally a powerful expansionary economic force, it is difficult to calculate how costly was autarchy in the 1930s, in view of the higly protectionist policies then being followed by the depressed capitalist nations.

In terms of the leadership's own criteria, central planning was effective though inefficient. It enabled the planners to mobilise economic forces, many of which had traditionally lain dormant or which had been only partially exploited, and by so doing to simultaneously achieve their economic and military goals. The Soviet Union, in a remarkably short period, grew to assume the status of a major industrial and military power and, building upon the industrial expansion of the 1930s, became after the war one of the two military superpowers. It did produce more steel, more cement and more machine tools than any other country in the world, capitalist or otherwise. (This is not the place to consider whether these were valid objectives or whether they might have been achieved by other means, or even whether the sacrifice was worth it.) The mechanism which had been devised and put into operation in the 1930s served well the interests of the military, and the economic performance sustained those who urged that increasing investment would of itself create the required growth rate. The outcome was partly fortuitous, however, for though planning effectively mobilised resources, it gave little incentive to use them efficiently, and only so long as consumption could be squeezed and the dynamic economies of scale characteristic of newly industrialising economies remained available were the economic and military objectives not in serious competition.

Soviet planning did not emerge fully formed in the 1930s, but was modified as planners increased their understanding of the dynamics of socialist growth and responded to economic and social opportunities and problems. The processes of change did not stop with the Second World War, but the post-war planning system was essentially that which had been created in the 1930s. The defence sector continues to influence economic performance to a high degree and the system designed to bring about such an outcome remains an acute source of economic inefficiency.

The period of demobilisation after the Second World War and of comparatively low spending on armaments lasted only briefly, brought to an end by the Korean War, after which defence expenditures grew at a steady, though not excessive, rate. As economic growth declined from the very high rates achieved in the 1950s, the secular expansion of the armaments branches appropriated a growing proportion of the nation's resources. When, in response to international crises, the rate of military expansion increased above the long-term norm, the additional appropriations of economic resources by the military branches increased more than proportionately. Each time defence spending increased above the trend, it brought about a 'prompt and unambiguous' effect on the other macroeconomic components, especially on investment, which declined by nearly the full amount of the increase.[66]

Consumption was constantly squeezed to levels far below those prevailing in other countries at roughly similar levels of development, but once the broad sector allocations had been determined, the resource claimant most competitive with defence at the margin for the output of the capital goods branches was and remains civilian investment.[67] The basic pattern was established early in the 1950s, when increased military spending during the Korean War was accompanied by declining growth of investment which, however, increased again after the end of hostilities. In 1960–3, when defence spending was again pushed above trend, investment growth decreased, and the pattern remains to the present day.[68]

Technological improvements are usually embodied in new machinery and equipment,[69] equally important inputs for the production of civilian and military goods. The output of the machinery and equipment sector, the Machine Building and Metal Working branches (MBMW), is therefore of particular importance to economic growth. Although Soviet statistics do not distinguish between civilian and military end use, it is possible, by the method of residuals, to construct estimates of sectoral appropriations which reveal a clear and unambiguous trend for the growth in military allocations (Table 3.3) to exceed the overall rate of expansion of durable goods.

Table 3.3 Growth rate of machinery

	All engineering	Defence
1958–68	11%	19%
1970–82	7%	11%

Source: *Allocation of Resources in the Soviet Union and China, 1983*. Hearings before the subcommittee on International Trade, Finance and Security. Economics of the Joint Economic Committee, Congress of the United States (Washington, DC 1984) p. 1.

Such large differences in overall growth rates must inevitably increase the proportion of durable goods output apportioned for security purposes. The average military share grew from 19.0 per cent in 1965 to 30.1 per cent in 1980, and to 40 per cent in 1982 of the MBMW branch. The CIA has recently calculated the marginal share of new machinery for defence at a remarkable 60 per cent[70] though this has been challenged as being unrealistic[71] and is in any case inconsistent with separate data on the civilian share.

Since the average proportion of durable output allocated for civilian consumption is only 10 per cent the measurable decline has been small, and the brunt of the burden has fallen on civilian durable investment goods, the share of which has fallen from 70.2 per cent to 60 per cent of total output.[72]

Machinery and labour are complementary inputs, and the growing allocation of material resources to the defence branches has been accompanied by a parallel movement of labour. Between 1962 and 1980 employment in the civilian machinery branches increased by 35 per cent, but by 67 per cent in the military-related branches, which are estimated to employ up to 60 per cent of machine workers.[73]

Quantitative data cannot reveal the dimension of qualitative preference in end use allocations. The defence branches lay prior claim to the best quality materials, the most advanced machinery, and to the most clever scientists, engineers and economic managers which in a society where technological progress is otherwise poorly stimulated, may well be the most severe resource cost of all.

Soviet enterprises, squeezed between tight plans on the one hand, and capital and machinery shortage on the other, have pursued inefficient investment practices, in particular conservative capital retirement and replacement policies. Soviet retirement rates, averaging 1.6 per cent p.a., fall far short of the American figure of 3.6 per cent p.a., and whereas 50 per cent of American gross investment is for replacing capital taken out of service, the figure for the USSR, is only 23 per cent.[74] The productivity consequences of an ageing capital stock were amplified by inadequate investment in new machinery and equipment in civilian industries, the potent carriers of new technology. The combined effect was to increase incremental capital ratios (Table 3.4) in all sectors of the civilian economy.

Economists using more formal econometric techniques have sought to measure the effect of defence priority on the major macroeconomic variables and on overall economic growth. The usefulness of the results depend on the reliability of the data and on the appropriateness of the statistical relationships specified in the models. Since the models are based on avowedly capitalist concepts, they are unlikely to replicate Soviet circumstances exactly, but do indicate within broad magnitudes the dimensions of the civilian–military trade-off. The techniques are simple enough in principle. A statistical correlation based on historical data is calculated for military expenditures and the civilian macroeconomic end uses. Assuming that the model remains a valid statistical description of the economy, variations in economic growth, civilian investment and consumption can be estimated for different hypothetical growth rates of the indepen-

Table 3.4 Incremental capital output ratios

	1960	1970	1980
Economy	1.6	2.2	3.3
Industry	1.5	2.1	3.8
Agriculture	0.6	1.0	2.9

Source: R. Leggett, 'Soviet Investment Policy in the 11th Five Year Plan', in *Soviet Economy in the 1980s: Problems and Prospects*, Part One, JEC (Washington, DC, 1982) p. 133.

dent variable, defence spending. The technique thus allows a statistical comparison of the beneficial or adverse consequences to the civilian economy of changing the rate of growth of defence spending and, assuming that this is within the control of the political authorities, gives a broad assessment of the outcomes of different policy mixes.

The, perhaps surprising, conclusion, which obtains from most such calculations, is that quite large changes in the rate of increase of defence expenditures have only limited impact on the rate of growth of GDP, industry and of agriculture.[75] If the baseline assumption is that defence expenditures grow at around 4.5 per cent p.a., equal to the long-term trend from around 1960 to 1976 or so, the economy will grow at approximately 2 per cent p.a. If it is then assumed that the growth rate of defence spending declines to zero, and the output of the MBMW branches which would have been allocated for military production is instead redistributed to civilian investment, GDP will grow by only 0.17 per cent faster than the baseline projection. If, on the other hand, defence were assumed to grow by 9 per cent p.a., GDP could be expected to grow only negligibly slower. The effects of such severe changes in military spending on civilian end use is more marked, with growth ranging from 0.83 to 2.68 per cent for consumption, which could have a significant effect on improvements in living standards, and from 2.0 to 3.4 per cent for investment. Assumptions about different degrees of resource transfer can be incorporated into the models. If, in addition to MBMW outputs R&D resources are also transferred, and furthermore it is assumed that defence-based resources are more efficient on average than those in the civilian branches, only marginal improvement is obtained over the baseline case.[76] Different models yield slightly different outcomes, but in each case the general conclusion holds that large changes in the rate of defence growth yield only minor costs or benefits to the civilian economy, and therefore that the measurable defence burden is low. If correct, these models imply that Soviet leaders can anticipate little immediate economic benefit by reducing the rate of growth of defence spending in the light of a more difficult domestic economy or accommodating international environment.

The explanation for the comparatively small impact on civilian growth is twofold. In the first place, even though the Soviet defence sector is larger than that in most developed countries, it is still a comparatively small proportion of total GNP. Changes to a comparatively small component of a larger total inevitably have small consequences on the larger variable. In addition, the inefficiency of Soviet investment during the 1970s yields a low output elasticity of capital, so that quite large additions to the capital stock produce comparatively small increases in output.

The inference that defence expenditures have only a marginal effect on civilian output is misleading. Apart from the conceptual and statistical problems with the models themselves, a number of crucial qualifications must be made. Even if it were true that over a brief period of time the trade-off between the civilian and military sectors was small, foregone exponential civilian growth over a long period of time would be cumulatively large. The models measure the marginal adjustment of economic variables around an average level, whereas a consistently different allocation in past periods would have changed the average level, and by the current decade consumption and investment would be much larger than in fact they are. The models assume symmetry between expansion and contraction of defence spending, whereas there is a strong likelihood that outcomes may in fact be asymmetrical, i.e. that the detrimental impact of more rapid growth of defence spending will exceed the beneficial consequences of lower defence growth because of the effects on bottle-necks, which discernibly reduced growth rates in the Tenth and Eleventh Five Year Plans. They also indicate that the statistical cost to society of a given rate of military expansion has increased. Whereas in the 1970s the economy could simultaneously attain over 3 per cent p.a. growth in consumption and 4.5 per cent p.a. growth in defence expenditures, by the 1980s, due to more adverse economic performance, a 4.5 per cent rate of increase in defence would constrain consumption to 2.6 per cent p.a.[77]

Policy-makers who have to calculate the security and civilian benefits of alternative allocations at a point of time are less interested in the historical relationships between economic sectors than in the crucial policy question of how newly created resources are allocated between civilian and military outputs. One item of relevant information is the proportion of investment goods output that may be required for a given rate of expansion of military output. The marginal cost in terms of new resources foregone far exceeds the historical average. If military production continued growing at the long-run rate of 4.5 per cent, then given certain, not implausible assumptions, the defence branches would, by the year 2000, absorb upward of 25 per cent of new material resources created between 1985 and 2000. Figures for the crucial durable goods sectors show by the same basic calculations that by 1995 defence could absorb up to 90 per cent of all new durable goods output; that is, virtually no new capital goods of the type most conducive to technological progress would be available for civilian investment, an impossible state of affairs, especially given the thrust of the Gorbachev modernisation programme.

The statistical models are sensitive to fairly modest changes in some of the key assumptions. Variations in the assumed rate of increase in productivity have an especially potent effect on growth and hence on the trade-off between civilian and military outcomes. During the 1970s, total factor productivity increased at an annual average rate of 0.7 per cent, but the trend was downward. If average productivity growth is maintained to the 1990s, growth in defence spending of around 4.5 per cent p.a. is compatible with an increase in total real consumption of just under 3.0 per cent p.a., an acceptable, though far from spectacular increase in living standards.[78] Economic targets in the eleventh Five Year Plan are predicated on the assumption that total factor productivity grows at a high 0.9 per cent p.a., in which case civilian consumption and military growth can occur at around 4 per cent p.a. If, however, the downward productivity trend continues unabated, as some Western economists predict, to a worst case rate of −1.0 per cent, aggregate consumption can grow by only 0.52 per cent, which means a reduction in real *per capita* consumption, and must jeopardise many of the calculations on which long-term economic expansion is predicated. Higher or lower growth in defence spending will also have corresponding consequences on consumption for each assumed growth rate in total factor productivity.

The models allow reverse sequence analysis, i.e. for a given consumption target the effect on defence of assumed differences in productivity (Table 3.5) can be calculated. It must be emphasized

Table 3.5 Trade-off between consumption and military spending

	Factor productivity		
	−0.1 p.a.	0.1 p.a.	0.9% p.a.
Target consumption	1.5% p.a.	1.5% p.a.	1.5% p.a.
Defence growth	NIL	7.8% p.a.	10.5% p.a.

Source: M. Hopkin and M. Kennedy. *Comparisons and Implications of Alternative Views of the Soviet Economy* (Santa Monica: Rand, R-3075-NA, 1984).

that the models are no more than statistical artifacts, and the outcomes depend critically on the assumptions of structural relationships and on the data base which may in the event turn out to be untrue or incorrect. They do however indicate broad magnitude.

Despite the large numbers employed in total Soviet R&D, skilled scientists and engineers remain in short supply. In 1970, although over 3 million people worked in some capacity in R&D, the numbers of highly qualified personnel was little over 545 000.[79] Military R&D accounts for around 50 per cent or so of total expenditures, but 60 per cent of R&D personnel. And of those not working directly in scientific institutes, over 70 per cent are employed in the MBMW branches, a high proportion of whose output is destined for military end use.

Preoccupation with the military usefulness of new or existing technology has often overly determined the pattern of development in key industrial sectors. Soviet haste in developing computer hardware most useful for defence and basic science analysis, instead of that economically useful for planning and management, has been one explanation[80] for the ten year gap behind Western computer technology which the Soviet authorities are so anxious to close.

Military R&D is bounded with restrictions, which not only reduce the efficiency of information flows between different institutes within the defence sector, but also between it and the civilian branches. Spin-off effects do reduce the burden of resources foregone to the civilian economy, but the departmentalism endemic in the Soviet economy is especially virulent in military-related R&D, where security considerations give an added reason for and justification of secrecy. For instance, the sectoral distribution of patents shows there to be less linkages between defence and the civilian sectors than between different branches within the civilian economy.[81] Military spin-off effects have been limited, largely, to management techniques which have little security implications, and unlike capitalist economies, the lack of a profit-oriented sector seeking to exploit military development for private gain inhibits the flow of information, personnel, materials and technology. The economic incentive from both supply and demand to generate military civilian spin-offs is weak, and the administrative mechanisms are largely ineffectual.

Some Soviet economists have argued that Soviet economic planning, designed for the unique circumstances of the 1930s, is less relevant to the intensive growth model which lies at the core of the Gorbachev modernisation programme.[82] The constituency for reform is weak, for in a bureaucratically administered economy the new is necessarily under-represented compared with the conservative forces ranged on the side of the *status quo*, amongst which are the defence chiefs and the military industrial producers. Despite the increasing inefficiency of the current planning system of which the military are aware, economic centralisation has over the years served the armed forces well. Defence has been possibly the major beneficiary of central planning, and military chiefs and Defence Industry ministers must be reluctant to throw over the system for another whose outcomes are more uncertain, the economic benefits of which may not be attainable for a number of years in any case. Defence chiefs have in the past successfully opposed reform which might undermine their prior claims to economic resources,[83] and on balance are still likely to oppose a root and branch reform of the system unless a serious economic crisis ensues. Military doctrine is, however, predicated on the fact that in the final analysis military power depends on an effective and efficient economy.[84] So far the military have gone along with the Gorbachev modernisation programme, because it offers them the possibility of modern weapons and systems in the future, and since the capital base necessary to produce the next generation of weapons is largely in place, the current economic squeeze may have only a small immediate impact.[85] It is only when, in due course, new capital investment has to be undertaken for the next round of weapons modernisation that the implication of the programme will become politically sensitive. At that time the support of the army to proposals and projects which may erode its traditional status in Soviet society may be critical.

The real burden of defence spending depends as much on the

performance and requirements of the civilian economy as on the military sector. If long-term growth rates remain low and competing demands intense as at present, the allocation between civilian and military production will remain one of the crucial policy choices facing Soviet leaders.[86]

4 Economic Growth

In his analysis of capitalist growth, Marx distinguished between what he termed simple reproduction, whereby the material product used up in production was exactly replaced and the far more important extended reproduction, which resulted in a continual increase in society's material product. Extended reproduction, according to Marx, could only occur by allocating an increasing proportion of the nation's resources for investment. Capital was identified as the primary source of growth. Lenin extended the Marxian analysis, arguing that in industrialised societies almost the sole limit to economic growth was the proportion of the economy's resources which was allocated to investment, especially to the capital goods sectors. Marx certainly, and Lenin possibly, were concerned to explain the dynamics of capitalist growth, but since by the 1920s the economic theory of socialist societies was virtually non-existent, the role which both men gave to capital and their status within the Party led to their views on investment being accepted by Soviet economists and politicians as being also valid to socialist economies, even though the institutional framework and incentive systems were quite different. Thus when, towards the conclusion of the turbulent 1920s, Stalin and the Party determined upon the optimal economic system and developmental strategy, Marxism–Leninism provided both a guideline to and an ideological justification of the preferred policy.

Industrial capital had to be supported by complementary supply of labour, otherwise diminishing returns would rapidly set in. Since the Soviet Union in 1928 was still largely agrarian, farmers had to be forced, against their will if necessary, to move in large numbers from the land to the towns, by collectivising agricultural production. Hence the intellectual rationalisation for the two revolutionary institutional changes which so transformed Soviet society in the 1930s, and which have since characterised it.[1] Central economic planning gave the Party the power to determine the distribution of the nation's resources between consumption and investment in accordance with Marxist–Leninist theory, while collectivisation enabled planners to control the level of real wages in the countryside and to force the required migration to the more productive, expanding industrial sectors.

Although Marxian theory, especially as developed by Soviet economists after 1922, provides a very sophisticated analysis of the appropriate distribution between Department I goods, the means of production, and Department II goods, the means of consumption, the actual Soviet strategy for growth in the 1930s was determined by much cruder considerations,[2] being little more than the identification of a small number of key investment sectors such as steel, energy, machine tools and, of course, armaments, as being particularly crucial for early and rapid expansion. Problems of Marxian value could be postponed for future consideration.

The preferred strategy was what later came to be called extensive growth, based primarily on identifying resources which were un- or underexploited, and mobilising as many in as short a period of time as possible to produce the investment goods necessary for extended reproduction. Considerations of allocative efficiency which were central to capitalist economic calculation were largely ignored. Indeed, not only were considerations of microeconomic efficiency and, therefore, of economy, unimportant, but the Bolsheviks viewed them as devices to undermine the socialist strategy. An economy constrained by market price, especially a charge on capital, would reduce the organic composition of capital by forcing investment below that considered necessary for socialist expansion.[3] Rent, interest and profit were appropriate only for an exploitative property-owning society which, since the USSR was not, had no relevance for, and should have no consequence on, the allocation and growth of economic resources. Since the economy was conceived as one large firm, managed by the Party on behalf of society at large, the task of the planners was to identify the technical coefficients between the different branches, and to achieve as quickly as possible the objectives which had been politically and previously determined. Therefore, even where prices were used to expedite the planning process, they had an accounting function only and had no consequence on outcomes. Those commodities for which rent or interest payments would have been substantial were by definition underpriced, encouraging excessive usage and waste. The cost of capital was low, for enterprise managers did not have to pay interest payments, the cost of raw materials was low because rent was excluded and the cost of labour was held down by collectivisation and inflation, which reduced the urban wage and squeezed consumption opportunities to a minimum. For an economy experiencing large-scale structural changes in a predetermined direction, market prices are often only partially useful,[4] but even so strategic objectives, after they have been identified on political criteria, can be achieved more or less efficiently, and relative prices can play a useful role in encouraging thrift and economy. The rejection of objective market constraints on expansion reflected an earlier teleological view according to which socialist development should not be constrained by capitalist rates of technological or economic transformation. Once the political objectives had been decided, the sole function of the Soviet planner was to identify the engineering coefficients which would most quickly turn the theoretical plans into material reality.

The economy was richly endowed, possessing enormous reserves of petroleum, coal, iron ore, copper and timber. In 1929, 82 per cent of the population worked in what was, in general, labour intensive and low-productivity agriculture. The opportunities for quick and cheap economic expansion were abundantly available, and given the leadership's objective, the extensive growth model was not inherently irrational. It is always dangerous to encapsulate overall economic performance in a single statistic, and the index number problem is particularly acute for an economy which experienced such great structural changes as did the Soviet Union in the 1930s. Recalculation of the raw Soviet data into a more familiar Western accounting framework reduces the growth rate below the official figures, often quite substantially.[5] Nevertheless, even after due allowance has been made for the various conceptual and statistical problems of interpreting the Soviet data, output other than agriculture grew in real terms at rates rarely bettered in world experience (Table 4.1).

Table 4.1 Annual rates of Soviet growth 1929–38

	1929	1930	1931	1932	1933	1934	1935	1936	1937	1938
Net material product		16.0	21.0	16.8	11.3	6.5	15.2	19.2	29.3	12.0	8.9
Industrial gross output		19.7	22.2	20.7	14.6	5.2	19.2	22.7	28.7	11.2	11.7
Agricultural gross output		−2.4	−3.3	−2.6	−6.1	−5.6	5.0	12.3	−8.4	22.9	−10.5

Source: D. Dyker, *The Future of the Soviet Economic Planning System* (London: Croom Helm, 1985) pp. 15, 30.

The producer goods branches grew at an annual average rate of over 20 per cent p.a.[6] Whereas in 1928–9 investment accounted for 19.5 per cent of GNP, by 1929–30 fully 36 per cent of the nation's resources were allocated for expanding the capital stock, and though such an extraordinary ratio could not be maintained indefinitely, at no time did it fall below 25 per cent. The growth rate of individual investment industries reflected this hectic pace of economic expansion; machine tools grew at an annual average rate of 16 per cent p.a. and steel at 22 per cent p.a. Diminishing returns to capital were postponed by virtue of the enormous complementary transfer of labour to the towns. Between 1929 and 1939 the urban population increased by 32 million people, and by the end of the decade 32 per cent of the population lived in urban areas.[7]

Even on its own terms, the frenetic unbalanced growth created strains on the allocative mechanism, which reduced average growth below expectations and quite probably below potential. Gross industrial output varied between rates of 28 per cent in 1936 and 5 per cent in 1933, and even key industrial inputs failed to meet planned targets. Between 1929 and 1933 steel production which was planned to increase by 3.4 million tons, actually grew by only 0.1 million tons.

The growth performance was certainly impressive, but not unique, especially in view of the primitive base from which expansion took off. Growth and transformation are little understood phenomena, in particular why it is that some countries take off to sustained growth while others fail to take advantage of apparently favourable circumstances. Once sustained expansion does occur, growth in the initial period tends to be high. In purely statistical terms, a given absolute expansion in production results in higher growth rates when related to a small initial base. There are, however, economic reasons why growth should normally be high in the early years. In newly industrialising countries a high proportion of the capital stock is necessarily new and of low average age. Thus only a small portion of capital is likely to be economically or technically obsolescent, and a high proportion of gross investment represents a net addition to the capital stock to create a high rate of capital accumulation.[8] Growth, especially from a comparatively primitive base, is normally accompanied by structural change, in particular an increase in the absolute and relative size of manufacturing at the expense of agriculture, and historically the rate of economic growth is significantly correlated with the relative rate of expansion of the manufacturing sector, which normally generates higher levels of growth and productivity[9] because, more than in other branches of the economy, manufacturing exploits dynamic economies of scale and embodied technological progress. In the USSR this developmental tendency was pushed to its limits and in the short period the economy benefited from the economic and technical returns to unbalanced growth.

Capital productivity in developing countries may be increased by the low cost of embodied technological change. Follower countries can benefit from technical progress elsewhere in the international economy without themselves having to incur the R&D costs, though certain preconditions must exist if they are to maximise the opportunities provided by the technological leader. There must exist a substantial gap between the follower and the leader, plus a sufficiently well developed economic, social, scientific and technological infrastructure to allow it to maximise the potential borrowing opportunities.[10] In 1928 the Soviet Union could be so categorised and the first Five Year Plan contained a specific commitment to seek out and apply the benefits of foreign technology to Soviet industry. Agreements were signed with firms from most developed countries to buy licences or to encourage inward investment in both the civilian and the military sectors. Autarchy after 1933 reflected a clear change in international perspective. Although the bulk of Soviet technologies in use have historically been of foreign origin,[11] the structure of central planning inhibited the efficient exploitation of trade and investment opportunities. Stalin laid down a policy of large expenditures on R&D, highly oriented towards Sovietising foreign technology, which, however efficient, relegated the Soviet Union to the status of chronic technological follower.

The Great Patriotic War only briefly interrupted the pace of expansion and the pre-war level of industrial output was regained in only three years.[12] Economic expansion after the war, though less frenetic, was more sustained (Table 4.2), and induced an increasingly confident leadership to predict that within a matter of years the USSR would attain and then surpass capitalist economic achievement (an assertion which Western leaders were not at that time disposed to reject out of hand).

Stalin's death was followed by a distinct shift in emphasis, even though the basic strategy remained. Stalin's model had worked in part because agriculture in particular and consumer goods in general were forced into the status of residual claimants for economic resources, 'a bothersome appendage'.[13] In 1938, over 60 per cent of the population lived and worked on the land, yet the agricultural sector

Table 4.2 Soviet economic growth, 1951–61

	1951–8	1958–61
National income produced (Soviet data)	11.4	9.1
GNP (Greenslade/CIA)	6.0	5.8
Industrial output (Soviet data)	13.1	10.4
Industrial Output (Greenslade/CIA)	12.0	11.3

Source: P. Hanson, 'Economic Constraints on Soviet Policies in the 1980s', *International Affairs*, Winter 1980–1, p. 22.

which was generally primitive and undercapitalised, received only 10 per cent of gross capital investment that year. Because so much agricultural capital was destroyed during and as a consequence of collectivisation, actual investment in the rural economy far exceeded that which the strategy had projected. Even so, real living standards declined, and in 1938 the index of consumer goods production stood at 346, compared with 734 for producer goods (1928 = 100). Labour discipline had been imposed by terror. As Khrushchev and later leaders dismantled much of Stalin's coercive apparatus discipline had to be induced rather than forced, effective only through the provision of material incentives and higher living standards for industrial workers and, later, peasants. The supply of food and industrial consumer goods was increased, but the overall growth of material output was sufficiently high for the increased provision of consumer goods not to impose a fundamental change in priority between the investment and the consumption branches.[14]

Economic growth is the cumulative consequence of two basic forces in the economy, the rate at which new resource and factor inputs are mobilised and the efficiency with which they are used, and in all economic systems both mechanisms exist to a greater or lesser degree. The social benefits of economic growth depend in part on the relative contribution of quantity and quality. Other things being equal, growth which is largely based on increased efficiency is less costly and more sustainable in the long run than that obtained mainly by increasing the quantities of factors of production and natural resources. Despite the sophisticated econometric techniques available to economists, it has proved extraordinarily difficult to account for growth in modern societies, and many aspects of the Soviet ex-

Table 4.3 Rates of expansion 1950–62

	USSR	Japan	USA	N.W. Europe
1. National income	6.1	10.1	3.3	4.8
2. Total factor input	3.9	4.2	1.7	1.6
a. labour	2.1	1.9	1.4	1.0
b. capital	8.9	10.5	3.5	4.5
c. land	1.7			
3. Output per unit of input	1.7	5.5	1.3	3.4

Source: A.S. Cohn, 'The Soviet Path to Economic Growth: A Comparative Analysis', *Review of Income and Wealth*, 1976, p. 53.

perience are still unclear. Growth accounting techniques used in the West are based on models designed to explain expansion in capitalist countries and many, though not all, of the assumptions upon which they are based may be less appropriate to a planned economy. Thus, though it may be argued that basic economic forces prevail irrespective of the system of allocation, the conclusions from the models should be understood as only indicating broad tendencies.

A comparison of the Soviet experience with those of a group of advanced countries (Tables 4.3 and 4.4) may serve to highlight some of the most characteristic features of Soviet growth in the post-war period, the most notable of which during the immediate post-Stalinist period being the tremendous rate of increase of the capital stock.

As Table 4.3 shows, the Soviet Union was not unique, for Japan achieved an even higher rate of growth of the capital stock. What distinguishes the USSR from the capitalist countries is the relatively small contribution to the achieved growth rate made by increased efficiency measured by productivity.

Table 4.4 Contributions to economic growth

	USSR	Japan	USA	N.W. Europe
Total factor input	70.0	39.9	58.7	35.7
labour	25.2	13.0	33.7	17.4
capital	44.6	26.9	25.9	18.1
Output per unit of input	30.2	60.1	41.3	64.5

Source: A.S. Cohn, 'The Soviet Path to Economic Growth: A Comparative Analysis', *Revue of Income and Wealth*, 1976, p. 53.

Table 4.5 Soviet economic growth 1960–80

	1961–5	1966–70	1971–5	1976–80	1980–2
National income (Soviet figures)	6.5	7.7	5.7	4.2	
GNP (Greenslade/CIA)	5.0	5.5	3.7	3.0	1.2
Industrial output (Soviet figures)	8.6	8.5	7.4	4.7	
Industrial output (Greenslade/CIA)	7.0	6.8	6.0	3.5	3.0

Source: P. Hanson, 'Economic Constraints on Soviet Policies', *International Affairs*, vol. 57, no. 1, 1980–1, p. 22.

Although in Aggregate Production Function models upon which the tables are based productivity is measured as a residual, i.e. a catch-all to capture everything which cannot be explicitly explained, it does broadly indicate the comparative inefficiency of the Soviet growth process. The simultaneous large increase in capital and low productivity suggests that only modest success was achieved in using the expanding capital stock to improve the efficiency with which the nation's resources were being used. This is unexpected, for a comparatively less efficient economy as was the Soviet Union might be expected to benefit from the advantages of late development. The experience of Japan demonstrates clearly that a very high rate of capital formation was not incompatible with equally rapid improvements in economic efficiency, and in living standards.

By the 1960s, the high point of Soviet expansion had been reached, and though growth rates remained high by world standards, the trend rate was secularly downward (Table 4.5). The achieved rate of growth for national income and industrial production was lower in each decade than the preceeding one, and, with just one exception, was lower in each succeeding Five Year Plan period.[15]

In view of the particular importance of factor inputs to Soviet expansion, it is necessary to understand how they grew in the postwar period, and how that growth effected the eventual economic outcome.

The Soviet Union was unique of the developed industrial countries in being able to increase the supply of land sufficiently to make a discernible impact on growth. Despite its enormous land mass, only a comparatively small percentage is available for secure arable farming, much land being marginal, located in areas of low or uncertain precipitation and of poor soil. Along with reforms to increase the efficiency of agriculture, Khrushchev between 1954 and 1957, brought 36 million hectares of marginal land, mainly in Siberia and Kazakhstan, into production, which in a few years increased the cultivated area by around 25 per cent. The Virgin Lands were chiefly sown with grain and, helped by good weather, initially achieved a comparatively high level of output and of productivity, which could not be sustained however. The very marginal nature of the land made it especially vulnerable to adverse weather since Soviet planners failed to invest against declining yields by providing the complementary inputs of machinery, fertilisers. Indeed, they often made the outcome worse than it need have been by planting inappropriate crops, influenced partly by Khrushchev's mania for maize. Nevertheless, average agricultural output in 1954–8 exceeded that for the previous five years by 40 per cent, much of which was due to the Virgin Lands programme.[16] The land's non-agricultural output could also be easily expanded for supplies of coal, oil, timber and ferrous and non-ferrous metals were economically accessible. The underpricing of land and basic raw material inputs in the absence of rent gave an additional fillip to the extensive but ultimately inefficient use of the nation's primary resources. Coal was abundantly available in the Donbas, close to large centres of population, and although the oil areas were found further afield in the Urals the cost of lifting and transporting was easily sustainable.

Labour supply is only partly under planners' control, being influenced by demographic, and also social and cultural factors, but for much of the period labour trends were favourable. Between 1950 and 1960, the population increased by 11 per cent, due in large part to beneficial demographic expansion. In the fifth and sixth Five Year Plan periods the country enjoyed a natural rate of increase of 1.7 per cent p.a.,[17] but by the ninth Five Year Plan the beneficial demographic trends were largely spent. Declining birth rates and, latterly, accelerating death rates combined to reduce the natural rate of increase. In 1950–5, the population increased by 16 million people, in 1965–70 by 11.9 million. Though the average annual growth rate in the 1960s, at 1.3 per cent p.a., was less than the previous decade, it was still enough to provide a large potential addition to the labour supply.

The portion of the population which is potentially available for work, the labour supply, is influenced by non-demographic factors which for much of the period reversed the population trends. That is, the labour supply increased more in the second half of the 1960s. In 1961–5, it grew by 4.7 million people, in 1966–70 by 10.5 million. The apparent paradox is explained by the fact that, because of the Second World War, fewer young people reached working age in 1960–5, while at the same time education reforms increased the number of students in the labour supply age group staying in full-time education. By the second half of the decade these temporary factors had worked themselves out, and whereas between 1960 and 1965, 8.7 million full-time students were enrolled, only 3.0 million enrolled between 1966 and 1976.

The labour force, i.e. that portion of the labour pool which actually offers itself for employment, showed a more modest but more regular pattern of expansion. The civilian labour force grew by 1.3 per cent in the first half of the decade, an increase of 6.9 million people, and by 8.9 million in the second half of the decade.[18] The industrial labour force grew by 3.9 per cent p.a. Higher participation rates particularly of females, which in the age group 20–29 years of age reached 86 per cent, added significantly to the labour pool.

The high participation rates were achieved by a combination of coercion and inducement. On the one hand, a series of anti-parasite laws passed at the end of the 1950s gave considerable powers to state and city officials to force (especially young) people who were considered eligible but were not working, to look for employment, sometimes at menial levels. Since unemployment did not officially exist in the socialist state, there need be no provision for able-bodied people who were without work and hence no unemployment pay. On the other hand, new nursery facilities increased female participation in the child-bearing age groups who were often tempted towards employment by the prospect of growing consumption opportunities. Furthermore, a modest policy of building factories in small towns with high male but low female job opportunities, brought women who would otherwise be unemployed, and who could not migrate, into employment.[19]

By the eighth Five Year Plan, participation rates had been boosted to levels beyond which it would be difficult to increase. Indeed, improved welfare provision for people at the age of retirement might even reduce them. In 1965, collective farmers and their families were brought into the State Social Insurance Scheme, which made it easier for this group of workers, who numbered between 25 and 30 million people, to retire at an earlier age than had previously been the case.

Although the most dramatic migration from agriculture to industry, where productivity was three times as high, had already occurred, it was for much of the 1960s far from insubstantial, and about 1 million people left the land each year. In 1950, 61 per cent of the population lived in rural areas. By 1960 this had decreased to 51 per cent, and in 1970 to 43 per cent.

The quality of the labour input was quite as important for economic expansion. Although private consumption opportunities had been severely circumscribed, education and health provision had increased during the 1930s adding to the stock of human capital which is a potent explanator of economic progress. During the 1930s the numbers of young people receiving a general and a specialist education increased dramatically. In 1928, 12 million students received a general education (primary and full secondary school), by 1939 this had increased to almost 33 million. In the same period, the number of graduates from specialised higher education institutes increased from 28 000 to 98 000, and the trend continued after the war. By 1960, the number receiving a general education had increased to 36 million, and a specialised higher education to 343 000.[20]

For socialist planners, labour was an enabling factor which allowed the capital stock to expand without inducing diminishing returns. The key to economic growth was a high rate of investment, which ideally should increase faster than GNP. During the 1950s investment increased rapidly, by an average of 13 per cent p.a., and some years as high as 20 per cent p.a. Such a pace could not be maintained, and in the 1960s the long-term average growth of capital formation fell to the more modest but, by world standards, still rapid rate of 7.5 per cent p.a. Industrial investment grew even more furiously; during the 1950s at an annual average rate of 22 per cent, and in the 1960s at 13 per cent (in constant prices).[21] Even when, after Stalin's death, consumer demand increasingly constrained planners' choices, the priority of investment was not seriously challenged. The share of investment in end use allocations doubled between 1950 and 1968 and the consumption proportion of industrial output fell.[22]

The rapid expansion of the capital stock was associated for a while with a high rate of labour productivity, due largely to the benefits of youth, a low-replacement ratio and a still rapid structural transformation. In 1951–60, labour productivity increased at an annual average rate of 7.5 per cent p.a.,[23] in excess of most industrialised capitalist economies. Since the capital stock grew faster than national output, capital productivity was negative for most sectors of the economy, indicating a falling rate of return on investment. During the

Table 4.6 The slowdown in Soviet growth

	1951–5	1955–60	1961–5	1966–70	1971–5	1976–80
Net material product (Soviet figs.)	11.4	9.2	6.6	7.7	5.7	4.2
GNP (CIA estimates)	5.5	5.9	5.0	5.2	3.7	2.7

Source: D. Dyker, *The Future of the Soviet Economic Planning System* (London: Croom Helm, 1985) p. 40.

mid-1960s the benefits of youth ceased to compensate for systemic inefficiency and as the growth of labour productivity declined the growth in total factor productivity fell to only 1.8 per cent p.a.[24]

Virtually all the macroeconomic growth indices showed a steady secular decline. Capital formation fell in successive decades from an average rate of 13 to 7 to 4 per cent, while total factor productivity fell from 1.8 per cent p.a. in the 1960s to 0.1 per cent in 1970–5.[25] Incremental capital/output ratios worsened. In 1950, a 10 per cent increase in the capital stock increased output by 9 per cent. By 1970 the same 10 per cent increase in capital produced only a 4 per cent increase in output.[26] The growth indices which had long moved steadily but slowly downward, in the middle years of the decade fell precipitously.

Discontinuous growth of the sort experienced by the Soviet Union in the mid 1970s may be explained by exogenous shocks. Agricultural output, which in 1976 still accounted for over 25 per cent of net material product, suffered a series of below average harvests, down to 140 million metric tons in 1975–6. Economic recession in the capitalist countries had some, probably marginal, effect on growth, while the particularly severe winter of 1981–2 froze railway lines, machinery and plant, and had a very discernible impact on economic output. Exogenous shocks, though real enough, did not explain the root cause of the economic decline, as Gorbachev himself later admitted.[27] The real explanation was endogenous to the growth process itself. Soviet planning had been designed to deal with a specific set of circumstances which had existed in the 1930s. The dominant ideology, the economic and social goals and the objective economic circumstances, all conjoined to determine what was then perceived by Soviet planners to be the optimal strategy and organisational structure, and there can be no gainsaying Soviet success. The Soviet Union does produce more coal, steel and petroleum than any other country. However, the criteria for economic success seldom are as crude as physical targets alone imply, and in more advanced societies progress is measured in qualitative terms less amenable to raw quantification.[28] Though the Soviet system was reasonably designed for extensive growth, the model, based as it was on mobilising large quantities of resource inputs, was less appropriate for the requirements of complex modern economies.[29] Physical resources are ultimately limited, and hence costly, and the extensive growth model always contained within itself the seeds of economic slowdown, which had been postponed for a time by the compensating benefits of late industrialisation. As the economy aged, these inevitably declined in potency and were gradually but inexorably overwhelmed by the endogenous inefficiencies of the planned system.

By the same token, economic performance might have been anticipated to improve. Though Western economists have on the whole been largely dismissive of the beneficial impact of what has been described as the 'treadmill of economic reform',[30] there is every reason to believe that, from a learning-by-doing perspective, planners' understanding of the methodology and practical issues of managing the economy should have increased.[31] Soviet planners are aware of, and have made some limited use of, economising concepts such as rent and interest, have put most enterprises on an economic accounting basis, have an understanding of mathematical optimising techniques,[32] and seek targets other than crude output. Improvements in economic organisation, however marginal, should further increase the efficiency of planning. Such improvements, real though they may be at local level, have not however gone to the root cause of the economic problem.

High investment is normally correlated with rapid economic or technological obsolescence, which reduces the average age of the capital stock, and since newer vintage machines tend to be more efficient, especially if they embody new technology they increase the average level of productivity. New capital also increases industrial flexibility reducing the cost of structural transformation which is part of the process of economic change in dynamic societies. If investment grows faster than the other factors of production, especially labour, which is usually the case, the capital labour ratio will necessarily increase, which, other things being equal, will also increase the productivity of labour. If, however the growth of capital exceeds output, the productivity of capital will decline. The effectiveness of investment in increasing output thus depends on how efficiently enterprises substitute capital for labour, and the degree to which machines incorporate new technology. The summary index usually used to measure these forces is factor productivity.

Econometric investigation shows that the gradual and then severe decline in Soviet post-war growth was due to both forces, though it is difficult to isolate and give a precise weighting to the two trends.[33] It is also likely that the relative importance of the two explanations differed over the entire period as a consequence of the changing economic structure.[34] The early post-war period witnessed a particularly rapid expansion of capital relative to labour which resulted in a low output elasticity of substitution.[35] That is though the average contribution of capital to growth was high because of the advantages of youth, the additional benefits from new capital formation were rapidly declining. However, as the growth of the capital stock declined and the difference between it and labour were reduced, especially if measured in efficiency rather than physical units,[36] output elasticity became a less potent explanator of economic performance.

For the period as a whole the single most powerful explanator of declining growth is likely to have been total factor productivity,[37] which was low at the beginning of the period, and declined steadily in almost every branch of the economy. It was, moreover, especially significant in explaining the steep decline during the tenth Five Year Plan.[38]

For a given social and cultural environment, the reasons for economic decline are much the same as those for economic progress, that is, the rate at which factors of production are increased and the efficiency with which they are used.

For the eighth and ninth Five Year Plan periods the demographic trend was marginally less favourable than had been the case in the previous quarter century. The labour force increased at an annual average rate of 1.9 per cent p.a. in 1970–5, and by 1.5 per cent in 1976–80, which added 24 million more people to the labour force over the decade.[39] The aggregate data conceals what has emerged as a major problem for the planners and managers, that of a severe global and regional imbalance between supply and demand. So great was the anticipated problem that in 1976 the Union Republic State Committee on Labour and Social Questions was created to deal with labour issues. Migration from the farms, which had traditionally provided an economically cheap mechanism for increasing growth, had largely ceased, for agriculture, like the industrial sector itself, had and has problems of labour shortage. Declining birth rates and, almost unique to the Soviet Union, rising death rates,[40] plus a retired population which is growing both absolutely and proportionately resulted in quite modest manpower targets being underfulfilled, in some cases by as much as 25 per cent. The rates of labour participation are already so high that there is little likelihood of relief from that direction, though old age pensions have been adjusted to make it worthwhile for people in the retired age group which total 15% of the population to take on jobs after they have finished full-time work. Nursery facilities are being increased to induce married women to take on part-time work.

The overall problem is bedevilled by regional unevenness, for labour shortage in some economic regions is offset by surplus in others. There is little migration from labour surplus to deficit regions and small prospect of it increasing to ease the economic problems of both. Soviet industrial expansion has been heavily and deliberately concentrated in a comparatively small geographical area of the Soviet land mass in the Western provinces of the RSFSR, the Ukraine and the Baltic States. More than 80 per cent of the nation's industrial plant is located in this economic region, which is also necessarily the major area of employment. The population growth in RSFSR is particularly low, due partly to the very success of the official drive to increase female participation which has reduced the number of children which women of child-bearing age bear. The population in the RSFSR is barely replacing itself, and the region is experiencing a net loss of the labour force. The other major area of labour shortage is Siberia, which has come to assume such importance to the rhythm of Soviet economic activity. The indigenous population is small and unskilled in the industrial arts. The weather and lack of social, educational and cultural facilities conspire to make it an unattractive place to live, so that despite higher than average wages and better terms of employment, inward permanent migration is small. Planners are therefore obliged to meet the acute shortage in many sectors through a policy of brigade contracting, which means the expensive transportation of groups of workers to their place of work for given periods of time, rather than permanent settlement.

In contrast to the RSFSR and Siberia, the largely Muslim Republics of Central Asia are labour abundant, and population has been increasing at 3 per cent p.a. There is a high proportion of women of child-bearing age, and each woman in that age group on average bears more children than in the Russian Republic. The Republics are still largely agrarian, but despite an inferior economic status the Muslim farmers have been and still are reluctant to move to higher paid industrial jobs in Siberia or the RSFSR.[41]

Paradoxically, the shortage is aggravated by economic and social institutions which encourage inefficient and wasteful utilisation in enterprises and farms. Bonuses are still highly geared to gross output targets,[42] failure to meet which imposes greater penalties on enterprises than low productivity due to excess labour. Labour hoarding so ties up inefficient labour that, according to one Soviet source, if it could be released to productive employment, production might increase by between 10 and 12 per cent.[43] Furthermore, the State virtually guarantees employment to anyone seeking work. Even though living conditions were low, Soviet workers did at least have the compensation of knowing that they could always expect to be continuously employed. Pressure was brought on managers not to sack workers who were lazy or ineffective, and those whose jobs were replaced by more efficient machines or better organisation were found work elsewhere within the enterprise. This, though socially acceptable, did reduce the incentive to innovate and employ labour efficiently. In one well known experiment where enterprise managers could keep and distribute between themselves and the workers the financial reward of higher productivity 15 per cent of the workers left the enterprise in a four year period. Productivity increased by 10 per cent, and average wages by 9 per cent.[44] The outcome provoked such a political outcry by the unions however that, despite its effectiveness, the experiment was scaled down and its major objective abandoned. The protection given to labour has reduced enterprise flexibility and therefore the ease with which obsolete or redundant branches are phased out and new ones brought in.[45] In periods of excess labour demand, restrictive working practices which have been in place over a long period of time are more growth inhibiting than in periods of excess supply. Since labour is not coerced, it must be induced to move to areas of shortage by economic inducement, usually by letting wage differentials reflect relative surplus and shortage and to bring about a shift in the desirable direction. For Soviet leaders this economic solution may have the undesirable consequence of increasing income differentials in a manner inconsistent with the social objectives of the State. In the 1930s, rapid growth was accompanied by a gross widening of wage and salary differentials and in the 1950s the policy was reversed, and relative wage differentials,

Table 4.7 Growth of fixed investment and capital stock

	Economy		Industry	
	Fixed I.	K. Stock	Fixed I.	K. Stock
1960–5	6.3	8.5	6.8	9.1
1965–70	7.6	7.5	6.8	8.7
1970–5	7.0	7.9	6.8	8.6
1975–80	3.5	7.0	3.9	7.5

Source: S. Cohn, *Declining Soviet Capital Productivity and the Soviet Military Industrial Complex*. US Arms Control and Disarmament Agency, *World Military Expenditures and Arms Transfers* (Washington, DC, 1984).

especially those between the industrial and rural workers, gradually declined. One of the objectives of Gorbachev's labour policy is to increase market flexibility and to this purpose he has urged that people be paid a reward equivalent to their economic contribution, even to the degree that there should be no upper limit to earnings,[46] which will undoubtedly widen differentials again.

Economic models show the capital stock to be a highly significant explanator of Soviet growth, and although trends in investment precede those for capital, which incorporates previous investment, the two variables eventually converge. Therefore expansion in investment (Table 4.7) has a powerful effect on long-term potential growth.

Table 4.7 highlights the sharp decrease in the growth of investment since 1975. The cause was initially a policy decision to reduce the rate of growth of new capital formation for at most a few years, to enable planners to regain control of the investment process, which had become increasingly inefficient and wasteful, after which it would be allowed to increase again on a more effective basis.[47] Long-term trends imposed their own momentum upon the planners, however, and whatever the expectations may have been at the beginning of the Five Year Plan, the growth in investment continued to decline, to reach what was, by Soviet standards, a crisis rate of only 2.5 per cent in the final year of the tenth Five Year Plan. After a modest improvement, investment again grew rapidly in the eleventh Five Year Plan to exceed planned targets, though a disputed degree of inflation in the machinery branches[48] may have reduced the rate of real growth in new capital below the nominal figures.

Investment adds to the nation's growth potential, but it is equally the case that the rate of growth of output has an impact on how much

Table 4.8 Incremental capital output ratios

	1960	1970	1980
Economy	1.6	2.2	3.3
Industry	1.5	2.1	3.8
Agriculture	0.6	1.0	2.9

Source: R. Legget, 'Soviet Investment Policy in the 11th Five Year Plan' in *Soviet Economy in the 1980s: Problems and Prospects*, Part 1, JEC (Washington, DC, 1982) p. 133.

Table 4.9 Capital productivity

	1959–60	1966–70	1970–5	1976–9
Industry	–4.2	–2.2	–2.8	–3.3
Agriculture	–4.9	–4.3	–8.0	–5.2
Economy	–3.4	–1.9	–3.8	–2.9

Source: S. Cohn, 'Sources of Low Productivity in Soviet Capital Investment', in *Soviet Economy in the 1980s: Problem and Prospects*, Part 1. JEC (Washington, DC, 1982) p. 172.

resources are available for investment in subsequent periods.[49] The precise inter-relationships depend upon an admixture of technological, economic, social and poltical factors. Over the long run, however, low growth of national output will make it more difficult to sustain given additions to the capital stock, especially if demands on the social product by other claimants are high, and once started the cumulative downward spiral may be difficult to reverse.

Incremental Capital Output Ratios (Table 4.8) measure the effectiveness of new capital in increasing output. During the post-war period they show a secular increase extending to all sectors of the economy. Whereas in 1970 each additional ruble of output required an input of three rubles of capital, by 1980 the same increase in output required six rubles of capital.[50]

Higher growth of capital over gross material product led necessarily to negative capital productivity figures (Table 4.9), and indicate so low a rate of return on capital that in capitalist societies market pressure would have forced a reassessment of the appropriateness of the existing strategy long before it was eventually undertaken by the Soviet planners in 1976.[51]

Table 4.10 Labour productivity

	1960–70	1970–5	1975–80	1980–2
All sectors	3.5	2.1	1.4	
Industry	3.5	4.3	1.9	1.4

Source: D. Bond and H. Levine. 'The eleventh Five Year Plan, 1981–5', in S. Bialer and T. Gustafson, *Russia at the Crossroads* (London: Allen & Unwin, 1982) pp. 88–9.

Table 4.11 Total factor productivity

	1960–70	1970–5	1975–80	1980–2
All sectors	1.5	0.1	−0.4	−2.0
Industry	0.2	1.0	−0.7	−1.0

Source: D. Bond and H. Levine, 'The eleventh Five Year Plan, 1981–5', pp. 88–9.

The poor capital performance necessarily reduced labour and total factor productivity (Tables 4.10 and 4.11).

The Japanese experience shows that high investment ratios need not necessarily result in low-factor productivity, for Japanese firms managed to offset diminishing returns to a rapidly increasing capital stock by embodying new technology in machinery and equipment. (It is, of course, the case that the Japanese economic performance far surpassed that of most other capitalist economies as well.) On the other hand, probably the single most important long term explanation of the downward trend in Soviet growth was poor technological performance.[52] Part of the explanation lay outside the control of the planners and would have occurred irrespective of policy or system. The exogenous factors were, however, made more virulent by the systemic inefficiencies of central planning and by the nation's economic and industrial policies.

Progressive ageing of the industrial economy led to diminishing returns to investment in the resource base. Fuels and raw materials which still account for a disproportionately high ratio of national output, had for many years been cheaply exploited by virtue of favourable geography and geology. Oil in the Urals region, coal in the Donbas, and wood and timber products from the ubiquitous forests, meant that output could be increased at comparatively low investment costs. Eventually, and inevitably, as the easy deposits were exhausted, drillers, miners and loggers had to work in harsher climatic and geographic environments, further from the centres of consumption, with more primitive infrastructure facilities. Energy and metallurgy are capital intensive activities with long pay back periods five to ten years in a major oil field, and ten to fifteen years in a large metallurgical complex.[53] Soviet industrial strategies to expand output as rapidly as possible required little consideration of the most efficient means of exploiting the natural resources, and accelerated the ageing process. In the 1930s, and even in the 1960s, the nation's resource potential appeared limitless, creating what has been described as a gusher mentality. Oil trusts lifted the oil by water injection techniques which maximised current output but at the cost of a high incidence of flooding. The failure to charge rent induced mining and timber trusts to work the most accessible oil, coal or trees, and when the marginal cost of working existing mines or timber stands exceeded the cost of starting anew, to move on to new mines or stands. So inefficient were the resource extracting techniques that up to 50 per cent of oil and 30 per cent of usable timber was left in or on the ground.[54] Inefficient pricing policies give little user incentive to economise on scarce resources with the result that the Soviet Union is an inefficient user of energy, metal and other material inputs.

For many decades Soviet economists rejected the notion of economic obsolescence as being irrelevant to the dynamics of socialist expansion. Since the objective was to create as large a capital base as possible, it was clearly inadmissible to sacrifice plant and machinery which were technically still viable. Moreover, given tight planning constraints, there was little incentive for firms to scrap machinery and equipment which could be used to meet particularly tight deadlines or brought back to production, irrespective of cost, in the event of breakdown or shortage. In the early years, economic obsolescence was not a severe problem by virtue of the young average age of the capital stock, but after reaching economic maturity, it did as in all industrial societies, become an issue, and eventually the concept was introduced into the managerial lexicon. The formal change had only a minor effect on the retirement policy of enterprise managers, however, who still kept working capital as long as possible, and retirement rates fell below official amortisation rules.[55] They also fall short of those in many other industrialised societies. On average, 1.6 per cent of the capital stock is retired each year, compared with 3.6 per cent for the USA. For the industrial sector, the respective ratios are

2 per cent and 4.2 per cent.[56] Older capital stock is less productive, embodies more primitive technologies and holds back the nation's growth potential.

Corresponding to low retirement ratios are similar rates of capital replacement, which also fall well below those which prevail in market oriented economies. In the Soviet Union, 23 per cent of industrial investment is allocated for replacement of capital worn out in the production process, compared with around 50 per cent for the USA[57] and in consequence, service lives for Soviet plant exceed those for the USA by substantial margins (Table 4.12).

Table 4.12 Comparative service lives of industrial assets (years)

	USA	USSR
Electric power	18.2	39
Ferrous metals	1.8	29
Machinery	8–12	26

Source: S. Cohn, *Deficiencies in Soviet Investment Policies and the Technological Imperative*. Soviet Economy in a New Perspective: A Compendium of Papers submitted to the Joint Economic Committee (Washington, DC, 1976) p. 455.

Although the stock of capital is increased, this is achieved only at the expense of economic efficiency, for a high proportion of gross investment each year is diverted to keep in working order old machinery which, naturally enough, tends to break down more frequently than newer equipment. In 1976, for instance, 29 billion rubles were allocated for repair, equivalent to 25 per cent of capital invested that year. Forty per cent of the machine tool park is being set aside for repair instead of being used for the more productive work of building new machinery and equipment.[58]

The ageing capital stock coincided with an inefficient distribution of the labour force, where up to 49 per cent work at low paid, low productivity auxilliary jobs such as packaging, transportation and warehousing.[59] An effective programme of labour saving investment could not only increase productivity, but also release labour to the deficit regions.

Since by design capital is cheap, enterprises and Ministries have little incentive to economise, but instead compete for more capital funds than they can effectively use. Consequently, they are often unable to complete construction projects in a reasonable period of time, due to a combination of poor management control and inadequate supplies of complementary inputs. Gestation for construction projects is lengthy, and the pay-back period inevitably postponed, during which resources already committed yield no return. The time between initiating a construction project and its full-scale production, is on average more than double that for the USA. Unfinished construction in 1980 amounted to 80 per cent of total fixed investment, equivalent to 6 per cent of the entire capital stock, and more than doubled over the decade.[60]

The end use allocation of investment funds also reduced economic efficiency. Consistent with the extensive growth model, a disproportionately small (by capitalist norms) ratio of total investment is allocated to machinery and equipment. It is easier to plan new construction, and green field sites minimise the disruption to existing work practices. Given the primitive capital base, such a policy was initially rational, indeed necessary, but with maturity it is less appropriate. Factories are longer lived than machinery, which are the more potent carriers of new technology,[61] and failure to invest sufficiently in equipment holds back the rate of technological progress.

The cumulative impact of inefficient investment provoked during the tenth Five Year Plan a reappraisal of its proper role in the growth model, which encompassed both its overall dimension and sectoral distribution.

On the one hand, given the resource constraints and the manifest difficulty of absorbing newly installed plant and machinery into the existing capital stock, investment, it was argued, had been excessive. Gosplan studies had revealed a trade-off between the rate of investment spending and the average length of gestation periods.[62] If investment grew too rapidly compared with other factor inputs, in particular labour, in the industrial heartland, new projects would take longer to assimilated complete, older equipment kept in production and retirement rates reduced. Capital wastage, implied by the high and increasing ICOR, could only be reduced by adjusting investment to levels commensurate with other factor and management resources.

Investment remains, however, the most potent source of productivity gains, and to cut back on growth of the capital stock might well worsen the productivity performance. The Soviet leadership had already identified productivity as the major source of economic expansion in future Five Year Plans, which was to be significantly influenced by embodying new technology in machines and equipment.

Many industrial branches were already working below capacity because of bottle-necks and delays, and enterprise capital stock was only partially exploited. If investment were reduced, the long-run obsolescence and retirement rates would remain unchanged and modernisation delayed yet again. According to this argument, what was required was not so much a reduction in the rate of growth of investment as a substantial reallocation between end uses. Improved labour productivity, based on modernisation and new machinery and equipment, was an absolute precondition for intensive growth, which by the middle years of the decade had been identified as the appropriate response to declining economic performance.

The immediate outcome was twofold. The rate of growth of investment decreased in two stages, first in 1975, and then again in 1979,[63] and for the first time in the State's history, investment was planned to grow at a lower rate than national income. The implication quite clearly was that a higher proportion of the achieved growth rate would have to be obtained from better utilisation of the factors of production. In addition to improving the economic mechanism, higher productivity was to be achieved by allocating a higher proportion, up to 50 per cent, of the slower growing investment to machinery and equipment; and the renovation of existing equipment, rather than constructing new, was given particular emphasis.[64] Although renovation might prove to be more disruptive of normal work patterns to the enterprise, and hence not attractive to managers, the savings to the economy were considerable. Capital investment channelled into reconstruction can yield twice as high a return as new construction[65] because of cheaper construction, speedier withdrawal of obsolete machines and shorter construction time.

The strategy was however risky, with a high probability of failure, based as it was on the assumption that declining efficiency of the investment mechanism was capable of solution by better management, a technocratic solution consistent with Soviet response to economic problems. To attain growth rates faster than the minimum politically acceptable, lower rates of increase of capital and labour had to be compensated by improvements in productivity, and ICOR reduced from those currently prevailing, a reversal of long-term trends.

The success of the strategy depended on the intensification of production which, if it was to be more than merely cosmetic, required long-term changes in economic management. In the short term, the criteria by which intensification may be measured, indicate at best modest success and at worst failure.⁶⁶ Uncompleted construction was marginally reduced, but retirement rates remain largely unchanged. Indeed, it is most unlikely that the investment branches would have been able to meet both extra civilian as well as military demands had the investment strategy brought about the planned increase in retirement and scrapping.

The modest level of achievement is underlined by economic performance in the eleventh Five Year Plan. Despite the theoretical rationale for a new growth strategy, traditional planning norms were soon re-established and investment again grew rapidly relative to the other macroeconomic variables. Although the consumption goods sector has, and is, planned to increase faster than the investment goods sector, the difference of only a few percentage points clearly indicates the problems which planners face in meeting the prerequisites for intensive growth. Expansion has been modest, at around 2.6 per cent p.a. Industrial growth has been higher, however, at 4.2 per cent p.a., growth being dragged down by a succession of poor agricultural outputs. Although up to 90 per cent of increased output has been caused by higher productivity,⁶⁷ it is clear that forecasts of the higher growth which would accommodate the competition between the civilian and military claimants for new resources have not been entirely fulfilled, and explain the urgency of Gorbachev's proposals to stimulate the economy.

Western and Soviet growth forecasts about growth of productivity and technological change differ fundamentally. Those offered by Western economists assume that the most recent trends will by and large be maintained, consistent with the belief that low growth is partly systemic in origin and that the basic form of economic organisation and management will be little changed into the foreseeable future. Improvements in the economic mechanism already in place, or apparently being contemplated by the leadership, will yield only marginal long run improvements. Many of the exogenous factors which have adversely influenced capital productivity during the past decade or so will remain, and may even increase in virulence. The resource base will continue to deteriorate requiring large injections of capital, in increasingly distant and geologically difficult areas, the full return on which may not occur until the next decade. Investment in infrastructure, in consumer durable goods which have high capital output ratios, and in the increasingly urgent area of environmental control, will sustain the demand for capital. The Soviet economy, it is argued, is simply not well organised to maximise efficiency and technological progress.

The Soviet leaders have a more optimistic, though far from blinkered, assessment of how intensified production might be brought about. On the one hand, improvements in the economic mechanism should reduce some of the waste associated with departmental planning. The superministries in energy, machine tools and agriculture, it is argued, will destroy some of the departmental barriers endemic to ministerial planning. Labour discipline has been increased by a variety of means, ranging from Andropov-style sweeps of streets and shops to wage reforms which make workers more immediately responsible for their own rewards and investment in machinery will reduce the average age of the capital stock. Transcending all is the unknown and unforecastable impact of political will. Economic outcomes in the Soviet Union have always been responsive to the political dimension which Western-style econometrics cannot model. In reality, of course other things do not remain equal. Mr Gorbachev's Soviet Union is different from Mr Brezhnev's. The key question is how different. Mr Gorbachev clearly believes it to be great.

5 Competing Claims

From the first economic plan, steel became the quintessential symbol of Soviet modernisation and progress.[1] Not only was it a basic requirement for economic and military power, it was also the measuring rod by which Soviet leaders assessed the comparative performance of the economy, and in a short period of time the Soviet Union became the largest steel producer in the world. By 1980, output of crude steel was 149 m. tons p.a., and of rolled steel 103m. tons p.a. It was, one imagines, with some indignation that in 1986 Gorbachev publicly acknowledged that, despite the scale of output, the nation was in the grip of a steel shortage.[2] Production in 1980 was below target by around 12 per cent, and despite reducing targets to modest levels, was in 1984, at 154m. tons and 107m. tons respectively, also below plan. So severe was the shortfall that it was perhaps the single most important explanation for the comparatively poor performance in the transportation and the machinery branches in the tenth Five Year Plan,[3] and may even have held back production of military goods. Investment in plant and equipment was inadequate to the degree that additions to steel-making capacity in 1980 fell below that for 1975 by fully one-third.

One reason for the unsatisfactory performance was the poorly compensated consequences of ageing in the two basic inputs, iron ore and coal. Although the Soviet Union is richly endowed with extensive reserves of both, the more accessible supplies have been exhausted, and Soviet planners, apparently caught unawares by the speed of decline, have failed to invest in modernisation, in transportation facilities and in preparing new areas for commercial exploitation.

In 1980, 245m. tons of iron ore was mined, some 30m. tons below target. By 1984 output had increased to 247m. tons, an annual rate of increase of only 0.8 per cent, due partly to exhaustion in the established mining areas. Between 1950 and 1970 the average ferrous content of working deposits declined from 50 to 40 per cent, and to 35 per cent in the next decade a process which inevitably required a compensating programme of ore enrichment. In 1950, only 37 per cent of ore required enrichment. By 1980 this had increased to 87 per cent, and a higher proportion of new output had to be used to make up for depletions. In 1966–70, 3m. tons of capacity was withdrawn from production compared with 8m. tons of new capacity. By 1976–80 the same quantity of gross additions were offset by withdrawal of 6m. tons. Exhaustion forced the mining trusts to work at lower depths, which increased the time and hence the cost required to bring a new mine to the production stage. The overall result of ageing was such a deterioration in the technical and economic parameters that, whereas in the 1960s investment costs per ton of usable ore totalled 61 rubles, by the late 1970s this had increased to 102 rubles.[4]

Coking coal, the other major input, faced a similar range of problems. Peak output of 186m. tons occurred in 1977, followed by a collapse in production to 175m. tons in 1981, and a subsequent slow recovery to 1985. Declining investment, and productivity in the key Donetzk and Kuznetsk basins were the consequence of long-term policies to concentrate investment on the cheaper and more versatile hydrocarbons. The mining conditions in the Donbas coal areas have been described as amongst the most adverse in the world, and failure to modernise mining and production techniques to compensate for the poor and worsening conditions has been the major cause of the poor output and productivity. Currently up to 80 per cent of gross annual commissionings of new mine capacity is required to offset depletion and exhaustion.[5]

The absence of a much more extensive enrichment programme than the Soviets have been prepared to finance must inevitably result in a concentration on low quality output, and it was the lack of high quality speciality steels, rather than of overall production, which held back production of machines, consumer durable goods and military equipment in the tenth Five Year Plan. Current shortages derive from earlier planning failures to increase capacity in sheet and speciality steels, but despite shortages of high quality products, as late as 1980 90 per cent of investment in finishing capacity was concentrated on increasing production of crude steel. Consequently, the yield of rolled steel has fallen below that of most other major steel producers. The 1984 yield of 69 per cent, no higher than that obtained in 1950, fell below that obtained in the USA by 5 per cent, and in Japan by 8 per cent. An improvement in yield offers substantial benefit to the steel-makers; a 1 per cent improvement saving the equivalent of 2.2m. tons of crude steel. Modern production techniques are not widely disseminated throughout the branch and Incremental Capital Output Ratios are higher than technically they need be. Planners have launched a large-scale investment programme to renovate the fixed assets in the ferrous metallurgy industry, among them new investment in the reconstruction of the Magnitogorsk and Kuznetsk Metallurgical Combines, and in extending ore enrichment and sintering plants and finishing mills to produce rolled and pipe steel.[6] As well as increasing output of rolled steel to over 116m. tons, the Draft Guidelines for 1990 incorporate plans to modernise production by increasing the smelting of oxygen-converter and electric steel by 30 to 40 per cent, and continuous casting of steel by 100 per cent, which will however yield a return only in the long term. In the short period, the failure to expand capacity at a sufficiently rapid pace, especially at the high quality end,[7] has had a detrimental impact on the machinery branches which are crucial to the Gorbachev modernisation programme.

The Soviet machine park is the largest in the world, and the machine branches are efficient producers of high volume, general purpose standardised machines and tools. Despite the importance of machinery and equipment as carriers of new technology, the quantitative and qualitative indices have until recently, when Gorbachev pushed the branch to centre stage, been quite modest. Between 1971 and 1980 machine building grew at an annual average rate of 0.47 p.a.[8] Addition to capacity in 1982 was only 82 per cent of that achieved in 1974, and for some key sectors such as metal-cutting lathes only 74 per cent. Production of machinery and equipment for the energy branches fell 20 per cent below target, and for some individual items for the strategic energy sectors such as pipe borers and coal cutters, actually declined.[9] The unexceptional quantity indices were matched by an equally modest performance in meeting quality targets. Industrial pricing policies and reward criteria give producers and users little incentive to economise, and Soviet machines, though sturdy and effective, are heavy and resource intensive, often of the metal-cutting rather than the more efficient metal-stamping types, so that compared with American norms the Soviet economy uses 50 per cent more metal per unit of GNP.[10] The new investment strategy in 1976 was designed in part to improve such qualitative indices, but has achieved only modest success to date. A special conference of industrialists and planners, called under the chairmanship of the influential Abel Abenbegyan in 1985, concluded that the Soviet machine tool branch lags behind international best practice in the degree to which high quality products are diffused throughout the economy by up to ten to fifteen years.[11] Furthermore, the lag appears to be positively correlated with the degree of technological sophistication and is greatest for the most advanced tools. Forge and press machines account for 20 per cent of Soviet output, compared with 31 per cent for the USA, finishing machines 59 per cent and 30 per cent, and grinding tools 29 per cent and 49 per cent respectively. For the most advanced, numerically controlled machine centres capable of working simultaneously in three axes, the degree of American superiority is overwhelming. These account for less than 3 per cent of the Soviet inventory, compared with 40 per cent for the USA.[12]

A high proportion of tools are made in large batches, with a standardised range of performance parameters, and the average quality level of the equipment which can be produced is often below potential. More metal is wasted and more man-hours are required per unit of output. The report estimated that between 30 per cent and 50 per cent of the productive potential in equipment design may be dissipated because of the shortage of high quality cutting tools.[13] Fully 30 per cent of current machine types incorporate obsolescent technical parameters so that despite the scale of production, the domestic stock has had to be regularly supplemented by imports from more advanced specialist capitalist producers which, in 1967 amounted to $75m. By 1980 the figure had increased to $700m.[14]

Many of the industry problems are common to the economy in general. Organisation and planning is often shared between a number of ministries, and the pervasive departmentalism reduces quantity and quality below potential. Ministries tend to monopolise the most profitable work of their enterprises and refuse to hand over their best equipment to other ministries. High quality tools need specialised skills and equipment, most effectively produced in small plants responsive to customised demands. In the American industry 89 per cent of total output is produced in small shops making custom-made tools in small batches for individual customers. In the Soviet Union, the pervasive belief in large-scale production means that only 33 per cent of the total output is produced in specialised small plants.[15] Ministries and enterprises, knowledgeable of the delays and shortfalls that attend the supply plan, compensate by building 'in house' production facilities, and over 16 per cent of tool-makers are employed in 'user' and therefore non-specialist plants. While this common practice reduces the likelihood of an enterprise failing to meet its target, it does reduce the degree of specialisation, and *inter alia* the skills to produce high quality tools.

The quality of the output cannot be divorced from that of other major inputs. In addition to a shortage of quality steels a high proportion of the Soviet labour force is insufficiently skilled to manufacture and operate sophisticated tools, to the extent that the number being installed exceed the number of operators by a ratio of 50 per cent.[16] There is often little incentive for employees to incur training costs for, in accordance with the social policy of reducing wage differentials, the rewards of higher grading may not be commensurate with the costs involved. Between 1945 and 1982 the ratio of engineers' pay to that of industrial operatives fell from 2.3:1 to 1.1:1,[17] though Gorbachev's support for a reversal of that trend should eventually improve recruitment.

Gorbachev identified the low quality of the machine stock as a major explanation for poor economic performance, and insisted that 'paramount attention' be paid to the branch,[18] especially for high quality tools. In 1984–5, metal-cutting machine tools grew at 9 per cent p.a., but growth of the most advanced programmed control centres grew by fully 28 per cent,[19] much in excess of industrial production as a whole, and the branch was one of the few to substantially exceed targets. The draft guidelines for the twelfth Five Year Plan project expansion of machine tool building as a 'top priority',[20] especially for computer equipment, instrument-making electric and electronic equipment. In a major reorganisation of branch management, the Council of Ministers in 1985 created a superministry, the Coordinating Bureau for Machine Tools, which has the ultimate authority to allocate economic resources throughout the industry and which may even include military users. Qualitatively, however, problems remain. A recent Soviet report made it clear that no fundamental improvement had occurred,[21] for which the industry itself had to bear major responsibility. The transition to the production of highly automated tools and machines is slow and customer complaints about output quality are widespread.

Even though the Soviet Union is a major industrial power, the atrophied pattern of industrial and geographical development, with the primary sector still accounting for around 40 per cent of GNP make considerable demands on the transportation sector, which Soviet spokesmen admit is operating under great strain. Large volumes of often low-value goods must be transported, sometimes over long distances. Railroads move all the economy's output of coal, timber and metallurgical ores, and a high percentage of metal and machine products. The sector absorbs over 12 per cent of total investment, and moves an average 24 tons per person, over twice the average freight carriage in the USA. Transportation bottle-necks were especially severe in the winters of 1980–1 and 1982,[22] creating such a critical constraint that one of Andropov's first decisions when he became General Secretary was to sack the Minister for Railways and a number of senior officials, giving a member of the Politburo special responsibility for improving the overall performance. Andropov-style discipline campaigns have been highly effective in increasing turnover and productivity,[23] and the decline in freight turnover which occurred up to 1982 has since been reversed, increasing in 1984 at almost 3 per cent p.a. Over the long period, freight shipments have increased *pari passu* with economic growth and given the planned eastward expansion of oil, gas, coal, timber and metallurgical industries to areas even more distant from the centres of consumption the ratio is unlikely to be reduced in the near future. When the major strategic decision to shift production decisively to the Siberian economic region is made, which many economists believe to be inevitable, the demands for further major capital investment in transportation will be irresistible. The capital constraint in transportation has been one of the reasons why planners have not yet fully committed resources on the scale required to exploit the Siberian economic potential effectively. Part of the investment cost has already been incurred, the Baikal Amur Mainline railway and the Orenburg pipeline system for instance, but will only pay back if the complementary infrastructure is also built, and already the average length of railway freight journeys has increased from 861 kilometres in 1970 to 923 kilometres in 1980.[24] The bare statistics conceal many of the qualitative problems, however. The existing track has been inadequately maintained and freight cars are often unsuited for the specific loads which they carry. Grain and fertilisers are shipped in open-topped trucks, which create large spillage and wind-blown waste of up to 4bn rubles p.a.

The Soviet rail network, probably the largest in the world, is matched by a road system which is primitive outside the major cities and is especially irksome for the agricultural sector. Hard surfaced roads from State and Collective Farms are limited, and many lack year round transportation connection with the outside world. Food is wasted, and valuable time spent by farmers, who sometimes spend three or four days taking one or a few animals to be sold or slaughtered due to the poor quality of the roads. Quick transportation is especially important for high quality perishable goods such as vegetables, fruit and some dairy products, for which the income elasticity of demand is high. Although targets for car ownership are still modest, the demand for roads and associated services by private motorists and the Agro-industrial complex must increase with living standards and the Draft Guidelines target construction of 167 000km of hard surface motor roads by 1990, of which 92 000km will be intra-farm roads in rural areas.

By far the most dynamic branch of the transportation network is the system of gas and oil pipelines, the dimensions of which have increased prodigiously in the past few plan periods. Rail, which until recently carried most of the petroleum, has been almost entirely superseded and currently carries only 5 per cent or so of domestic shipments. All the natural gas is moved by pipeline. Growth in energy, especially in natural gas extraction, has exceeded that of any other industrial sector, with the recent exception of a narrow range of advanced machine tools. The economy is highly resource intensive, and apart from one brief period from 1965 to 1975, growth in energy consumption has exceeded that of the national economy. The output elasticity of demand is greater than one, and in contrast to the capitalist nations, the Soviet Union has failed to economise on energy untilisation following the increase in petroleum prices after 1974.[25] For Soviet planners energy is the driving force of the economy, so that failure to match supply to demand not only at the macro level, but for each major energy source, will directly impact on economic prosperity. The sector is doubly important for economic well-being because together oil and gas account for over 50 per cent of hard currency earnings.

In 1950, 65 per cent of domestic energy consumption was derived from solid fuel, mainly coal, which was, however, expensive to mine and to transport. Petroleum, on the other hand, was so cheap, that, as with most other industrialised countries, Soviet planners converted the energy balance away from coal towards the more efficient, versatile and profitable hydrocarbons, initially oil, and then natural gas. The resource saving was enormous. The investment required to produce an additional unit of energy from petroleum was far below that for coal, and the export potential further increased the net return on investment. Reserves were enormous and available in areas which were geologically not too difficult to work. Petroleum had been lifted from Baku and elsewhere before the war, but in the post-war period the most rapid additions to capacity were in the giant fields in the Urals–Volga region, where the oil lay in relatively shallow deposits which did not require deep drilling, and water injection techniques gave rapid recovery rates. Although the fields were located some distance from the major centres of consumption, petroleum has the great advantage over coal in being relatively cheap to transport, and since it was used largely as an industrial input, was only lightly refined. Thus, although the capital requirements for such a major transformation were not insubstantial, the state of the art technology was not especially advanced and was well within the capacity of indigenous producers.

Expansion was rapid. By 1980, only 34 per cent of Soviet consumption of primary energy was obtained from coal. The proportion of oil burnt in electrical stations increased from 7.5 to 22.5 per cent, while coal fell from 70.9 to 6.1 per cent.[26] So productive was the Urals–Volga region that the enormous expansion and structural transformation made very modest demands on investment resources.[27] Planners were lulled by the quick and easy returns into what later Soviet critics described as 'gusher mentality', and neglected to modernise drilling and lifting equipment and also, crucially, it later transpired, to prospect and map new geological areas in preparation for the period when output in existing mature fields peaked or declined.[28]

So long as domestic oil was cheap and abundant, and world prices low, Soviet energy policy, though inefficient, was on its own terms rational. Changes in the domestic and the international energy markets in the 1970s destroyed the assumptions on which that policy had been predicated. In 1974, petroleum prices increased tenfold and increased again in 1979, and as a major exporter, the Soviet Union benefited by up to $2bn, over the next decade. Domestic structural constraints and international obligations reduced the extent of the benefit well below potential, however, as coincidentally the total domestic energy balance turned adverse. Reserves of coal, oil and gas remained abundant, and the problems for energy planners were of declining productivity and of adverse geographical and sectoral balance. Although all energy sources are ultimately substitutable, specific capital investments in each of the major branches severely limit the degree of flexibility in the short period. Since the economy is not naturally sensitive to economic stimulus, supply and demand has to be planned and directed not only for the energy sector as a whole, but for each major energy source. Even if aggregate supply equalled

Table 5.1 Average annual growth of output, inputs and productivity in the fuel industries 1961–82

	1961–5	1966–71	1970–5	1976–80	1981–2
Outputs	6.3	5.0	5.0	3.1	1.6
Inputs	3.6	3.8	3.5	4.3	5.3
Productivity	2.6	1.2	1.4	−1.1	−3.6

Source: G. Schroeder, 'The Slowdown in Soviet Industry 1976–1982', Soviet Economy, 1985, p. 43.

demand, excess capacity in one branch might be only partially effective in making up a shortfall elsewhere, and specific geographical or industrial shortage could still ensue.

For the first half of the 1970s output grew at a rate of 5.0 per cent p.a., not far short of the average rate of 5.6 per cent attained in the previous decade. In the second half of the decade the rate of increase fell to 3.1 per cent p.a. (Table 5.1). Although this might partially be explained by declining growth of GNP, and hence of demand, or by improved energy utilisation, it is unlikely that planners would willingly sanction so large a decrease in growth rates, given its high export potential. Since 1976 neither coal nor oil output reached planned targets, even though they had been reduced to modest levels. For both branches the normal processes of ageing was brought on by inefficient planning and management.

In the tenth Five Year Plan period, output in the once productive Ob oilfields begun to decline, and in the most accessible West Siberian fields peaked, so that a larger share of new output was required to replace that lost through ageing. In 1970, 45 per cent of new capacity was required to compensate for declining production in the Ob fields; by 1976–80 this had increased to 74 per cent. A similar process occurred in the coal industry, in particular in the Donbas coalfields. Soviet pricing policies were especially perverse in the resource sector, where the lack of proper rental and interest charges induced a wasteful pattern of production. Drilling teams had little incentive to maximise the return from mature oil wells, for as depth, and therefore cost, increased, it became more profitable to drill new wells. Water injection methods maximised production in the short period, but at the inevitable expense of flooding the well and also potential oil or condensate bearing deposits in the vicinity. Up to 50 per cent of potential reserves may be left in the ground after the oil combines move on.

Planners and politicians, who for varying reasons have short time horizons, neglected the warnings given by the technical experts that declining output of oil and and coal from the traditional areas had to be compensated by investment in new fields. Furthermore, a series of inefficient strategic decisions led to a concentration of investment in upstream facilities, which though rational in its own terms, neglected to survey and map new structures, so that when production and productivity in existing fields began to decline so dramatically, reserves were not readily available to fill the gap and the ratio of reserves to current output declined. The oil and coal-bearing strata which were discovered were often in geologically difficult areas and in lower quantities than in the traditional fields. Drilling depths increased from 2000 to 3000 metres to more aggressive geological environments. No new giant fields of Samotlar proportions have been discovered, and in 1983, for the first time, oil production declined, and has done so, by small quantities, each year since.[29] Industry targets have been adjusted downwards to the degree that those determined for 1985 were much the same as were originally set for 1980 in the tenth Five Year Plan.

The changing energy balance could not have been attained without heavy investment in building new oil-fired and converting existing coal into oil-fired power stations. By the mid 1970s almost 50 per cent of the nation's power stations burnt oil or gas beneath their boilers. The increase in oil prices after 1974 rendered this policy uneconomic, for the relative benefit to the economy of oil over coal as a source of steam was exceeded by a considerable margin by its more profitable utilisation elsewhere, either as an input in the petro-chemical industry, or as an earner of hard currency. The opportunity cost of using oil as a source of power when coal was a technically adequate substitute, created enormous opportunity costs for society. Energy planners responded in the proper manner by instituting a policy of reconverting back to coal, where technically feasible, and of ensuring that all new power stations would be coal-fired. Reserves of deep and strip mine coal and of lignite were abundant enough to last over 200 years, and offered an effective long-term solution to the rising real costs in petroleum extraction.

At almost precisely the moment when the new policy was articulated, the planners' assumptions were destroyed by an apparently unanticipated worsening of the economic and technical parameters in the coal industry. Output growth declined from an average rate of around 5 per cent p.a. in the ninth Five Year Plan period, to just over 3 per cent p.a. in the period 1976–80, and was associated with, and partly caused by, a concomitant decline in productivity growth, which fell from an average annual rate of 1.47 per cent p.a. in 1971–5 to −1.1 per cent in 1976–80.[30] As a consequence output fell below target, in some years by considerable margins. In 1980, for instance, production, at 716m. tons, was 74m. tons short of plan. Production targets were adjusted downward and those set for 1985, in the eleventh Five Year Plan, at 770 to 800m. tons, were originally established in the previous plan guidelines for 1980.

The old established coal-mining fields in the Donbas suffered a decline in both the quantity and the quality of the coal produced. Peak production of 220m. tons p.a. has fallen to an annual rate of around 200m. tons p.a.[31] and easily worked seams have long been exhausted. Despite adverse mining conditions the Donbas is well located, being close to the major industrial centres, which reduced the very substantial transportation costs, so that planners continued to invest in the Donbas despite declining productivity, consistent inability to meet targets, and better long-term prospects elsewhere.

The alternatives were the enormous coal and lignite deposits in Siberia. Although mining costs are relatively low, especially if strip mining techniques can be utilised, the Siberian fields suffered in comparison with the Donbas by being distant from the major centres of consumption and in having so little of the social and technical infrastructure in place. Coal transportation is expensive, and accounts for a high proportion of total costs, and in light of the constraints on the railway network, a major expansion of one or other of the giant Siberian fields would have imposed impossible short-term strains on existing resources. The most extensive deposits lie in the Kansk–Achinsk basin, but the coal and lignite, though cheap to strip mine, is of low calorific value, and transportation of the unrefined raw material to the industrial centres is prohibitively expensive. Although there do exist outline long-term plans to increase output from the current level of 58m. tons p.a. to over 1bn tons p.a.,[32] the means to attain such a large expansion have not been determined. Various possibilities exist: to burn the coal at mine mouth and transport it westward in the form of electricity along the long-distance high voltage power line; to process it into a more malleable form, easily transportable by pipeline; or to use it as the basis for a mine mouth metallurgical industry, where the high value added to the metal end product reduces the real cost of transportation.

A second investment strategy would be to concentrate on expanding production in the Ekibastuz region. This coal is also of low quality, with a high rock and ash content. Plans exist to build four mine mouth power stations, with a combined capacity of 16m. kw,[33] and construction has started on the 15 000kw d.c. and the 1150v. a.c. Ekibastuz-Centre transmission line.

The third possible long-term coal strategy is to expand coking coal mining in the Kuzbas region. Unlike the other two regions Kuzbas coal is of high quality, productivity is almost three times as high as in the Donbas, and industry engineers estimate that at full production, output might exceed 300m. tons p.a. Despite its high quality, however, transportation costs make Kuzbas coal prohibitive at the moment.[34]

A coal-based energy policy has the further disadvantage of yielding a return only in the long run. The sharp deterioration in the oil and coal sectors and the absolute need to meet short-term energy targets forced economic planners, after 1979, to switch resources to a crash programme of expansion in natural gas, the only energy source which offered the potential for a rapid enough expansion to close the imbalance.

Gas reserves are estimated to be around 30 per cent of world total, and output growth has been extremely rapid, increasing at an average annual rate of around 8 per cent since 1975. It is, moreover, the only fuel source which has consistently exceeded targets and which, unlike the other fuels, have been revised upwards as output has expanded. Plans for natural gas production project an annual average increase of around 40bn cubic metres to 835 to 850bn cubic metres by 1990. In the current Plan period 75 per cent of the projected increase in energy for the economy overall, and 90 per cent of that for the European part of the economy, is to be obtained from natural gas.

The rapid expansion in output was achieved almost entirely by concentrating investment in the West Siberian gas fields, in particular in the enormously productive Tuymen oblast. By 1985, Siberia supplied 60 per cent of the planned output of 630bn cubic metres. The 1985 Siberian target of 330–370bn cu. m. represented an increase of 90 per cent over the 1980 output, and the single Urengoi field, with a target output of 250bn cu. m., was to account for all the increase in output in the eleventh Five Year Plan.[35]

The physical dimensions of the investment programme are daunting. The gas is located in geologically difficult and climatically severe areas, and drilling occurs at deep levels, where the gas is often mixed with condensate, which make conventional injection methods inappropriate. Infrastructure, in what is often virgin territory, is virtually non-existent and the economic and social capital has to be created alongside the wells and the immediately productive gas equipment. Because it contributes little to current output, social capital tends to be neglected, so that even when the wells may be ready to produce overhead capital is incomplete, sometimes 75 per cent short of target; a classic Soviet response of meeting short-term targets at the expense of the long term. The tundra makes road laying difficult and expensive, and labour has been reluctant to move to such harsh conditions with so few social facilities, even though the economic rewards are great. The gas ministry response of flying in teams of contract workers to work fixed term periods, although relatively successful, is expensive and draws skilled technicians away from their current employment in other sectors which is disruptive and inimical to high productivity.

The major cost in the industry is, however, transportation and distribution, which can exceed that for petroleum by up to a factor of five. Estimates of construction costs for the Urengoi fields vary from an average low of 1bn rubles per 1000 km to 1.5bn rubles per 1000 km, with the figure rising to 1.7bn rubles per 1000 km in some particularly severe stretches of terrain.[36] The pipeline system consists of six lines of 56-inch diameter pipes transporting the natural gas some 2000 km to the central industrial region, and one even longer pipeline to Czechoslovakia, and eventually to Westen Europe,in fulfilment of the long-term contracts for gas sales which the country has agreed with West Germany and other capitalist countries. The total budget for the pipeline was 45bn rubles, which in the eleventh Five Year Plan absorbed 7 per cent of total capital investment. The Urengoi pipelines required 30m. tons of rolled steel, 25 per cent of total domestic output.[37] Construction teams had to build 102bn cu. m. of new cooling and processing plants in addition to the usual complement of compressor stations, boosters, drilling and lifting equipment, etc. Despite this huge investment, output in the Tuymen oblast has consistently fallen short of target. Although the Urengoi pipeline is now largely in place, planned expansion into the even more northerly and remote Yamburg and Yakutia regions of Western Siberia, where construction costs can be up to four times more expensive, will sustain capital investment in the gas industry at a high level.

Despite the poor performance in coal mining, the peaking of oil production and the high cost of expanding natural gas in Siberia, pessimistic assumptions that by the middle of the current decade the Soviet Union would become a net energy importer have not and are unlikely to materialise. The problem for Soviet planners is the more sophisticated one of matching potential imbalance between demand and supply in the three major fuel sources. The huge gas investment programme has inevitably drawn resources away from coal and oil. The share of gas in energy investment increased to 32 per cent in 1980, and given the demands by other high priority, non-energy claimants, it is unlikely that the energy sector as a whole will be able to claim more than a proportionate increase of the nation's resources. There exists, therefore, a real possibility that in the light of insufficient investment, demand for oil and coal may at some particular time or place exceed supply, while gas supply may exceed demand. For despite the very large price changes which have occurred in the domestic and international energy markets since 1974, the real adjustment between the different energy sources has been minimal. The entirely rational policy of converting oil-fired power stations to coal has been ineffective in practice. No oil-fired stations have been converted to coal and few new coal-burning stations have been commissioned. In view of the failure to meet coal targets, that is not entirely unwelcome. The gas-based policy, also a rational response to short-term crisis, may nonetheless lead to the sort of long-term neglect which was the proximate cause of the current crisis.

Neither producers nor consumers are induced to economise in response to higher prices, as is the case in market economies. Poor techniques result in upward of 8 per cent of the natural gas being wasted after it has been brought up from the wells. In the USA the utilisation of casinghead gas exceeds 95 per cent of potential, compared with only 35 per cent for the Tuymen region, and Soviet calculations show that 22m. tons of standard fuel, equivalent to 15m. tons of petroleum, could be saved each year if Soviet practices were brought up to best American levels.[38]

Soviet industrial enterprises use more energy per unit of output than their American counterparts, and the USSR has a considerably higher output elasticity of demand, 1.26 per cent, compared with 0.6 per cent for the USA. More significantly, perhaps, is that after a brief

Table 5.2 Westward movement of fuel from Soviet Asia

	1970	1975	1980
Oil (m.t.)	15	133	242
Gas (bn.m^3)	44	104	224
Coal (net)	65	96	1200

Source: L. Dienes, *The Soviet Energy Policy: Soviet Economy in a Time of Change*. A Compendium of Papers submitted by the Joint Economic Committee. Congress of the United States (Washington, 1979) p. 208.

period between 1965 and 1975, when the output elasticity fell below one, it has again risen above unity despite Soviet policy to economise. Soviet plans identify energy saving as a major source of balancing supply and demand.

The energy sector more than in any other country is characterised by geographical imbalance between supply and demand. Eighty per cent of deposits lie east of the Urals, whereas 80 per cent of demand is located to the west (Table 5.2). Current production in the industrial central region fell short of demand by fully 50 per cent, and every European economic region has become a net energy importer. The marginal imbalance is even more critical, however, for in the plans little more than 10 per cent of additional supplies of oil and coal, and none of additional gas, are to be obtained from the western regions. Transportation accounts for a high proportion of the final price of energy to the consumer, and the eastward shift in production imposes a real resource cost on the economy.

Nuclear energy differs from the other major fuels in that it is largely unaffected by problems of space. Its peculiar and increasing difficulties are related to capital and technology. Even though the Soviet Union commissioned the first nuclear reactor to produce electricity for peaceful purposes, the 100 MWe (LGR) reactor at Troitsk in Siberia, in 1958, growth in the following fifteen years or so was modest. Given the Soviet Union's cheap and abundant hydrocarbon resources, the enormous capital costs and uncertain outcome associated with the new technology and military related priorities, this was a perfectly rational response to the objective economic circumstances. After the tenfold oil-price increase in 1974, the nuclear construction programme was put on a new footing. Capacity increased at an annual average rate of 35 per cent p.a., and by 1980, twenty-nine reactors were in operation, producing 70.5 billion Kwh of electricity and with a nuclear capacity of 13.5 million Kw.[39] Nuclear energy was considered particularly efficient for the fuel deficit western part of the economy.

The eleventh Five Year Plan called for additional investment to bring total generating capacity to over 37 000 MWe by 1985, which, if achieved, would mean that up to 15 per cent of total Soviet electrical power, and 25 per cent in European Soviet Union, would be obtained from nuclear stations. Indeed, plans call for all the increase in electrical power in the European USSR to be nuclear in origin. However, plan shortfall which has dogged the industry, (as those for all countries) has held growth below target. Between 1976 and 1980, capacity fell 5000 MWe short of planned expansion to 18 400 MWe, and the 1985 output has also fallen short of the target.[40] Nevertheless, industry engineers were pressing ahead in building not only more, but also bigger reactors. By 1980, seven high capacity reactors, capable of generating 1000 MWe each, were under construction, and planners were forecasting that within a few years the Leningrad will and the Chernobyl stations would have a generating capacity of 4000 MWe. In addition, Soviet engineers are pushing ahead with development and construction of fast breeders. By 1980, they had commissioned a BN 600 (600 MWe) reactor, and although work is proceeding on the logical next stage, the BN 800, so confident are they of being able to overcome the technical, operational and problem disposal associated with the breeder cycle, that they are already working on the construction of a larger and technologically sophisticated BN 1600 (1600 MWe).[41] Although branch targets have been consistently underfulfilled, the commissioning of the giant Atomic Power Machinery Complex (ATOMASH) in Volgodonsk in 1981, is planned to put the industry on a more secure basis. ATOMASH is designed as a conveyor for the serial production of large capacity atomic power stations using electricity generated from nearby nuclear reactors. When fully operational, this one facility will be capable of producing component parts for 3 million KWe reactor sets p.a.

Nuclear power stations are highly capital intensive, the most important component in their lifetime costs being amortisation. They do, on the other hand, offer large savings on fuel costs which amount to only 15–20 per cent of total, compared with 60 per cent for fossil fuel-burning stations. For every 1 million KWe generated by a nuclear power station using 30 tons of enriched uranium, there is an estimated annual savings of 2.5 million tons of coal. The total commissioned during the Five Year Plan should save 45 million tons of fuel per year and hundreds of thousands of railroad cars equivalent.[42]

Although some scientists had periodically expressed concern about the appropriateness of siting policies, these were usually brushed aside by official insistence that Soviet engineers had solved the technical problems of the fuel cycle. The generally low importance accorded to environmental factors and the need to increase output quickly, more than compensated for the doubts about the advisability of the ambitious nuclear programme.[43] The accident to the Chernobyl reactor in April 1986 has thrown into considerable disarray previous calculations about nuclear expansion. At the time of writing, Soviet officials have publicly insisted that the nuclear programme will continue. Even so, the pace of expansion will be held back, and the additional safety measures which are virtually bound to be incorporated must increase construction costs. Given the tight constraints which exist in the other energy sectors, a major withdrawal from the nuclear commitment seems unlikely, although the planned expansion of 400 to 600 per cent by the year 2000 must be unlikely.

The broad outlines of the energy programme clearly bring into focus the short-term horizons of planners. Investment in coal, the long-run option, has been postponed, to allow the rapid expansion of natural gas, the short-term option. Soviet energy absorbs fully 30 per cent of all industrial investment, and if that in complementary activities is included, the ratio increases to 50 per cent. The sheer scale of the sector is such that once planning decisions have been made operational, they are difficult and expensive to reverse.

Soviet planning is usually effective in attaining clearly articulated, high priority, extensive goals. Though current reports indicate that Tuymen targets are underfulfilled, there is every likelihood that in view of the political importance which the Party has accorded the Siberian targets, they will, in the main, be achieved. The coordination of energy policy has been hindered by organisational duplication for each fuel branch has its own array of overlapping research, procurement, transportation and supply bodies. Not until the magnitude of the crisis was revealed in the last few years of the 1970s did Brezhnev himself appear to take personal control. Although there is no evidence that Gorbachev has personally involved himself in the details of the energy sector, the lines of authority have been more clearly delineated, and currently Victor Dolgikh, who is a member of the Politburo, appears to have assumed political control over the execution of energy policy, which should bring together to a degree the centrifugal pull of departmentalism and interbranch rivalry. Numerous high level ministers have been sacked to improve performance, and interdepartmental programme-oriented commissions have been created in Tuymen, along with a special section in GOSPLAN, to improve planning and coordination.

Soviet economists and political leaders recognise that the extensive growth model, devised for the particular circumstances of the 1930s, is no longer appropriate for an economy at the stage of development attained by the USSR.[44] The twelfth Five Year Plan, for instance, requires 90 per cent of the projected increase in industrial production to be obtained from higher productivity. Although Gorbachev and his fellow Politburo members are strongly committed to improving labour efficiency through more rigorous prosecution of the discipline campaigns,[45] they also recognise that a permanent improvement requires more organic changes in labour and in consumer markets.

Soviet plans to intensify material production encompass wide-ranging improvements in the economic mechanism, not all of which are resource demanding. Even so, higher productivity cannot be obtained without increasing material living standards, for even in a socialist society better performance is acknowledged to be responsive, probably in large part, to economic incentives. Stalin had reduced the importance of material rewards by creating a system of terror, and he could afford to reduce consumption in general, and agriculture in particular, to the status of residual resource claimant. When his coercive apparatus was dismantled, better work habits had to be induced through economic reward and the greater the planned contribution of productivity to the wealth-creating process the greater will be the demands for personal and collective consumption. The Draft Guidelines to 1990 project a faster rate of expansion of sector B consumption goods than sector A investment goods, though recent performance has been disappointing.[46]

Despite the policy of forcible transfer of resources from agriculture to industry, net investment in Soviet agriculture in the 1930s was in the event quite substantial.[47] Nevertheless, agriculture was for Soviet planners an irrelevant appendage, and at Stalin's death in 1953 the sector was absolutely and relatively more backward than in 1928.[48] The industry was undercapitalised and inefficient, labour productivity being less than 25 per cent of that in the USA. Post-Stalinist planners sought a more balanced growth, to improve living standards which was formalised in the Party Plenum of 1965. The consequence on

Table 5.3 Production of basic types of agricultural output (annual average in mill. tons)

	1951–65	1976–80	Growth in %
Grain	130.3	205.0	157
Sugar beet	59.3	88.7	150
Vegetables	16.9	26.3	156
Fruit and grapes	6.5	15.2	234
Meat (slaughter weight)	9.3	14.8	159
Milk	64.7	92.7	143
Eggs (bn)	28.7	63.1	220

Source: Pravda, 25 May 1982.

agricultural output and food production was dramatic. Since 1965, gross output increased from an average annual total of 82.6 bn rubles to 124 bn rubles in 1980, and to 131 bn rubles in 1984, a rate of advance in excess of that achieved on balance by capitalist countries. A detailed breakdown of the achieved growth illustrates the broad basis of the improvement (Table 5.3).

Since the growth of food production outstripped that of the population, *per capita* consumption of all basic foodstuffs increased (Table 5.4).

Table 5.4 Per capita increase in food consumption 1965–80

All agricultural products	28%
Meat and meat products	42%
Milk and milk products	25%
Eggs	100%
Vegetables	33%
Sugar	30%

Source: Pravda, 25 May 1982.

The calorific value of the average Soviet diet, at 3443 calories per day, exceeds that of most European countries, and is not far short of the American level. Moreover, a change in diet has reduced the percentage of the calorie intake obtained from starches and increased that obtained from higher quality foods. Surveys by international organisations, using Soviet data, put the USSR towards the top of the food league in some respects,[49] and there can be little doubt that, over the long period, agricultural performance has been quite noteworthy.[50]

The generally favourable picture painted by these and other similar statistics conflict with reports of shortage, often seasonal, low quality, poor choice and of queues. They also do not connect with other statistics, which show the sector in a much less favourable light, nor, perhaps most crucially, with the manifest evidence of official concern shown by Soviet leaders.

Although there is no reason to believe that Soviet food statistics are falsified, they are often incomplete. Thus, although the Soviets are towards the top of the table with regard to beef consumption, they are towards the bottom in terms of overall meat consumption. Many of the food statistics include elements which, under strict definition, might be considered waste products, not appropriate for human consumption.[51] The figures also conceal the irregularity of supply, which is a major source of irritation and a real cost to the consumer.

Geographical and climatic conditions make agricultural output highly vulnerable to adverse weather conditions, though better organisation and equipment could offset these factors to some degree, as happens in other countries with a not too dissimilar range of climatic conditions, such as Canada. Not only is output seasonal, but it is also liable to far wider annual variations than for most countries. The grain harvest varied in one seven year period from 140m. metric tons in 1975–6, to 237m. metric tons in 1978–9, and back to 160m. metric tons in 1981–2. Although consumption does not vary by such wide margins due to stock adjustments and recourse to imports, availability and hence welfare are adversely affected by such wide dispersion around the average.

Despite the noteworthy long-term performance, recent trends in growth of output and productivity have been downward (Table 5.5).

Table 5.5 Average annual rates of growth of agricultural inputs and outputs

	1951–60	1961–70	1971–80
Output	4.8	3.0	1.8
Input	2.7	2.1	1.6
Factor productivity	2.1	1.0	0.2

Source: D. Diamond et al., 'Agricultural Production', *The Soviet Economy: Towards the Year 2000* (London: Allen & Unwin, 1983) p. 146.

Soviet consumers have a high income elasticity of demand for food especially high quality meat, dairy produce and fresh vegetables, and failure to meet rising expectations are politically damaging. Food riots in Gorky, Togliatti, and elsewhere, and special distribution of food outside the normal retail network at the place of work to placate particularly important industrial groups, attest the sensitivity of the food balance.[52]

Since the mid 1960s, consumption has been sustained, especially in years of poor harvests, partly through imports from capitalist economies. Not only was this expensive, in 1981, for instance, imports of grain and meat cost the equivalent of $9 bn,[53] but it was also politically and strategically damaging to be dependant on imports from countries, many of which were ideologically opposed to the very existence of the regime, and ever ready to threaten and on occasion to prosecute embargo.[54] The Soviet dependence on imported food and feed increased from 8 per cent of total imports in 1971–5 to 27 per cent in 1975–80, equivalent to 102 million tons of grain which, according to one calculation, accounted for almost all of the *per capita* increase in food consumption during the period.[55] Food imports are not of themselves evidence of economic inefficiency and many countries sensibly pursue policies of food importation, but given the proportion of the nation's resources devoted to food production, the currency constraint on imports of manufactured goods forgone, and the political sensitivity of excessive dependence on capitalist sources, its characterisation as the Achilles heel of the economy is well made.

Excess demand for food, as reflected in queues and empty shelves, is only partly a function of inefficient production for prices have remained essentially static for many decades. The last major revision of food prices occurred in the mid 1960s, although prices of individual foodstuffs have increased since that time. Income elasticity of demand is high, but the leadership has, for good or bad, refused to sanction the price increase which alone would choke off excess demand. Procurement prices, to stimulate production, have been increased consistently, so that the cost to the State of buying food from the State and Collective Farms far exceeds the price charged to the consumers in the shops. In 1981, for instance, the price of meat was only 50 per cent of its cost, and similar gaps exist for other foodstuffs. The difference between cost and price is met by official subsidy, which in 1980 alone cost the State over 31 bn rubles.[56]

Labour trends throughout the post-war period have been adverse, for though migration has not attained the scale of the 1930s, farmers, usually young, migrate to the towns each year to take advantage of higher wages and the greater range of social amenities which cities normally provide, so that much of the investment to increase rural skills is wasted. In 1979, for instance, the various agricultural schools, institutes and colleges graduated 1.14 million trained students, of which only 32 000 joined the agrarian labour force,[57] the others, presumably, having moved to use their acquired skills in higher paying industrial enterprises. A high proportion of those who remain are elderly and female. Almost 65 per cent of the rural population are women who are likely to be untrained, have low skill attainments, and are less likely to seek full-time work.[58] Periods of peak demand are often characterised by labour shortages, and regular farm labour must be supplemented by casual labour from the armed forces, industrial workers, and even school children, whose education, so it is argued, suffers accordingly.[59]

The Soviet response to agricultural crisis was the familiar one of throwing money at the problem. From the mid 1950s investment increased at an annual average rate of over 9 per cent, until by 1981–2 up to 27 per cent of the nation's new capital resources, amounting to 172 bn rubles, was allocated to agriculture. Increased capitalisation, however, failed to provoke a commensurate and presumably anticipated increase in productivity, which has on average remained at around 25 per cent of best practice elsewhere. Not only was the average productivity low, but by the tenth Five Year Plan it appeared to be decreasing (though the figures are heavily influenced by a succession of poor harvests). To obtain 100 rubles of agricultural output in 1966–70 required inputs of 70 rubles, by 1971–5 this had increased to 89 rubles, and by 1976–80 to 107 rubles.[60]

Poor performance in agriculture was made more acute by failure to invest in complementary industrial branches, which have consistently failed to meet targets for new agricultural machinery and equipment. State and Collective farmers work with 65 per cent of the estimated required number of combine harvesters, 65 per cent of beet harvesters, and only 43 per cent of commercial fertiliser spreaders.[61] In 1980, 84k of fertiliser per acre was applied, compared with 117k per acre for the USA, and 480k per acre for West Germany. Failure to build enough all-weather roads, grain silos, cold storage facilities, specialised trucks, and even such mundane products as sacks, have caused enormous wastage of agriculture goods. Crops lie unharvested or unpicked in the fields, rotting on roadsides and in warehouses, spilling out of open railway trucks, and animals are kept beyond optimum slaughter weight. It has been estimated that up to 20 per cent of the grain, fruit and vegetable crops, and 50 per cent of the potato crop fail to reach their ultimate destinations each year because of shortcomings in the service sector.[62]

So serious did the Party view these that the 1982 Plenary Session of the Communist Party identified the provision of reliable food supplies to the population as the 'central problem of the current decade', and implemented a Food Programme which was to delineate the framework of agricultural policy till 1990.[63]

Low food prices deliberately held in check for over two decades, had become part of people's expectations and by 1980 were politically impossible to increase to equate supply and demand, so that apart from a handful of luxury goods, the Programme did not sanction a general increase in food prices. Although the Party must eventually face up to the incompatibility of low prices and an efficient agrarian sector, at its inception at least, the Programme concentrated exclusively on supply.

Low growth in a constrained economy, meant that even for agriculture, investment could not grow at the high rates which had obtained in previous plan periods. After 1982, agricultural investment was projected to grow *pari passu* with national income, which still implied a total sum of 189 bn rubles in the eleventh Five Year Plan, equal to 27 per cent of total investment. In addition, a further 44 bn rubles was allocated for investment in the auxilliary industrial branches, bringing the total in the agro-industrial complex to an enormous 33 per cent. The Programme identifies key sectors such as road building to facilitate transportation of farm produce to local markets, processing plants, warehouses, etc. to reduce wastage, and housing, schools, cultural and social amenities to improve the economic living standards of the State and Collective farmers. Detailed components include 160 billion rubles for housing, cultural and consumer-service facilities and roads, 3.7 million tractors, 1.1 million grain harvesting combines, increasing the supply of electricity to agriculture to between 210 and 235 bn Kw; to guarantee delivery of 30–37 million tons of universal fertiliser, to increase the acreage of irrigated land to 25 million hectares, in addition to an increase in quality; to produce 3 million railway trucks, 76 000 refrigerated trucks and to increase packaged food to 60–70 per cent of total sales volume.[64] This far from exhaustive list indicates the extent of the resource commitment in the Food Programme.

The preamble to the Programme and statements made by political leaders and planners elsewhere reiterate the view that in agriculture, as elsewhere, extensive production has lost much of its capacity to meet demand for more and better quality food, so that capital investment is only one strand in a comprehensive programme of administrative and economic improvements designed to shift production to a more intensive mode based on higher efficiency and productivity. However, the analysis of the change in organisation, the economic mechanism and the role of private farming, which do not in themselves have strong resource implications, will take us too far afield.

Although quality food has a high elasticity of demand, rising incomes and more sophisticated tastes have also created growing demands for more and better quality non-food consumption goods. With the exception of those goods and services which increase the economic potential of the workers, consumption had low priority for Stalin. Living standards were brutally suppressed, those of 1928 were not again achieved till 1950. Investment in health and education however was substantial, presumably for narrowly economic reasons.[65] Health standards, literacy and technical training levels approached and in some cases exceeded those achieved in many capitalist countries. Collective consumption goods such as public transport and communications also achieved a respectable standing in the planners' preference, but at the neglect of private consumption.

After Stalin's death private consumption attained greater prominence, and increased at an annual average rate of 3.4 per cent. Clothing increased fourfold, and consumer durable goods 14 per cent p.a. The overall quality of consumption goods also improved as successive plans gave priority to different types of consumption goods. In the 1950s, housing was in first place, then retail outlets, and in the 1970s food production. Overall there can be little doubt that consumption opportunities have increased very substantially.[66] Eighty per cent of the population own a television set and 70 per cent a washing machine. Yet from many perspectives non-food consumption remains unsatisfactory. Despite improvements for the mass of consumers, living standards remain relatively low, below many of the East European countries, and also in some cases below the norms established by Soviet scientists. The allocation of household budgets show on average a profile typical of countries at a comparatively low standard of living. Food and clothing account for 65 per cent of the household budget, and housing only 9 per cent, whereas in most developed countries, food and clothing account for between 27 per cent and 40 per cent, and housing 21–25 per cent,[67] although part of the explanation is likely to be due to price effects such as highly subsidised housing. The array of goods and services distorted by poorly structured norms and incentives fail to match higher incomes and tastes. Unsold goods sometimes amount to over 4 bn rubles, and the consumer is not helped by the underdeveloped state of retail and distribution in which 12 per cent of the working population are employed compared with 33 per cent in the USA.[68]

Housing is a particular source of welfare dissatisfaction.[69] In 1928, a minimum housing norm of 9.0c.m. per person was established, but throughout the Stalinist period low investment led to a decline in the stock of available housing, compared with the rapidly increasing urban population. After Stalin's death, investment increased to the extent that 22 per cent was allocated to a crash house building programme, and in 1959 a record number of 2.7 million dwellings was built. Even though *per capita* living space has increased from 8.8 to 13.6 square metres, marriages exceed new dwellings and demand exceeds supply. By 1983, investment in housing construction had fallen again to 14 per cent, and the housing target was underfulfilled by 4 per cent. In 1980, over 30 per cent of urban dwellers lived communally, sharing facilities with non-family members.[70]

The organisation of consumer goods production reflected its lowly status, for it would have been inconsistent to give consumer representatives a powerful voice in the decision-making process if their claims were politically deemed to be secondary. Thus no single ministry was or is designated as being solely responsible for coordinating and planning the production and distribution of consumer goods. Up to 34 per cent of consumer production is carried out in plants nominally in the heavy and defence branches, for which it is a secondary activity, and therefore most liable to interruption and delay. Because there is no single coordinating ministry; in furniture for instance there exist up to thirty-five branches and ministries, quality control is often low, with a poor degree of standardisation. Plants in the branches which do exclusively produce consumer goods are generally of lower quality, using old technology and inferior inputs.

The adverse consequences of poor organisation and low investment are made worse by policies to hold down prices of food, housing and many, though not all, consumer goods. Excess demand is reflected in queues, hidden inflation and the so-called coloured markets, which add to the frustration of consumers.[71] The intensification of production is predicated on there being an appropriate supply of consumer goods, and the Draft Guidelines plan a more rapid growth of consumer over investment goods. Nevertheless, the share of consumption in GNP has fallen from 62 per cent in 1950 to 53 per cent in 1980,[72] and Soviet leaders have sought to reduce expectations by warning the people that significant improvements in living standards will have to be postponed to the 1990s and beyond.

Production and consumption are everywhere necessarily spatial, but the unique geographical characteristics of the Soviet land mass give an additional boost to the resource cost, because of the maldistribution between the centres of production and the supply of factors and resources.

Production is highly concentrated, 80 per cent of the industrial capital being located west of the Ural mountains. In this economic region the rate of growth of the labour force has declined, and in the RSFSR its absolute size has fallen and will continue to do so in the future. In the Central Asian Republics, on the other hand, demographic growth is high which offers the possibility of some relief from the labour constraint. Migration from the Asian Republics is low and, despite the attractions of higher wages and better material living conditions elsewhere to an increasingly educated and sophisticated labour force, is projected to remain so.

Soviet industrial development, planned from Moscow, has deliberately benefited the Centre, and has imposed upon the Asian Republics an atrophied pattern of economic expansion. Investment in the labour surplus areas was largely concentrated in exploiting natural resources, which were then transported to the industrial centres for processing. Even though Uzbekistan, Khazakstan and Khirghiztan produce 90 per cent of the total output of cotton fibres, production of made up textiles accounts for only 5 per cent, and sewn garments 4 per cent, of total production.[73] All indices of economic development are lower than for the USSR on average. The infrastructure is less well developed, the percentage of workers with technical and managerial skills and their efficiency is low. Construction costs are higher, productivity lower, and capital output ratios higher. A major strategy of investment in Central Asia to take advantage of the underemployed labour resources would have to accept the consequences of lower returns, which would increase ICOR. It would also imply reducing the proportion of investment resources available to other economic regions which probably have higher priority for Russian central planners. Despite labour shortage elsewhere and the possible political costs of continued neglect, Soviet plans for the medium term do not indicate a massive redirection of investment to Central Asia.

Soviet planners are unlikely to be so complaisant about the economic potential of Siberia, however, for the effectiveness with which its enormous resource wealth is exploited has a crucial impact on the rhythm of Soviet economic expansion. The vast land mass contains over 90 per cent of the reserves of petroleum gas and alum, as well as gold, timber, ferrous and non-ferrous deposits, which still account for more than 40 per cent of GNP equivalent. Soviet rhetoric has long underscored the importance of the Siberian economic region, but developmental strategies have been more conservative. In 1965, the percentage of industrial output from Siberia was 8.2 per cent, while it received 15.7 per cent of total industrial investment. Ten years later, at the threshold of the big gas investment programme, investment had increased to 16.2 per cent and production as a proportion of aggregate had increased to only 8.8 per cent.[74]

The reason for the reluctance to commit resources on a scale commensurate with its potential are not hard to find. Harsh weather, difficult geology, poor infrastructure, long distances from centres of consumption and labour shortages have combined to reduce most indices of economic efficiency below the USSR average. The investment necessary to exploit the region's resources potential will be great, with a long pay back period. Meanwhile current policy to renovate and re-equip capital will necessarily focus investment on the existing stock in the mature industrial centres. Planners have an acute dilemma over the appropriate regional balance. They may, however, be unable to postpone for much longer the strategic commitment to the massive transfer of investment resources necessary for the effective exploitation of the Siberian economy. Some decisions have already been made, for instance natural gas and the BAM railway, but the resource demands remain. Major expansion programmes have been published for some of the giant metallurgical, timber-processing and petrochemical complexes, but the key strategic planning decisions have yet to be made.

The far from complete account of expansion in key economic sectors shows clearly that demands for material resources will remain high. Military producers must anticipate intensified competition for the more slowly growing resources likely to be available to the end of the century.

6 External Relations

Alliance theory shows that though the collective provision of security may impose some unwanted costs on members, it does increase the overall level of deterrence against threat and protection in the event of war.[1] As a member of the Warsaw Pact, the Soviet Union must be presumed to benefit from the joint provision of military activities in the Socialist Commonwealth, and also to incur costs which it otherwise might avoid, many of which are unconventional in nature[2] and which confound the analysis of the economic dimension of Warsaw Pact alliance.

As the largest country in the Warsaw Pact, the Soviet Union's expenditure in absolute terms exceeds that of any other member country. In addition, however, as the largest country it also pays a disproportionate share of the burden of the public good. (The theory normally applies to countries which voluntarily join alliances.) Its unique position allows it also to appropriate a correspondingly disproportionate share of the conventional economic and technological benefits which obtain from the international division of labour.

The non-Soviet East European countries make a significant material contribution to Collective security. (Henceforth, Eastern Europe will include the non-Soviet European members of the Warsaw Pact.) They have 1 million men under arms, produce 33 per cent of Pact tanks and armoured vehicles, provide 60 per cent of its divisional tactical aircraft and 50 per cent of fighter aircraft in the Central Region, which in the event of war would be immediately transferred to Soviet command.[3] Overall, however, the Soviet Union dominates, supplying more than 66 per cent of conventional and nuclear capability and virtually all the Pact's advanced weapons systems.[4] Converting the known East European military strength into its economic analogue is difficult for, like the Soviet Union itself, official East European budget data are generally unreliable.[5]

The East European countries do not make known the different components of overall defence expenditures, but offer only aggregate and partial data, and Western estimates must overcome similar obstacles to those for the Soviet Union itself. The research input is less elaborate, and the estimating techniques are correspondingly less secure. The failure to provide a consistent set of data based on systematic estimation techniques persuade some that extant information precludes a broad-based analysis of the economic dimension of East European military expenditures.[6] Though the data are admittedly incomplete, broad magnitudes are sufficiently known to support a proximate analysis of trends and contributions.[7]

The first problem, as always, is definition. The most careful analysis of East European defence expenditures concludes that published budget data include the direct cost of maintaining military personnel, procurement and the maintenance of military equipment and supplies. The figures exclude, moreover, defence-related R&D and military investment.[8] Even though a high degree of uncertainty pertains to all R&D estimates, the exclusion of this category from the East European data is probably less critical, for it is almost certainly the case that R&D outlays are not a significant proportion of total expenditures, for the Soviet Union has appropriated to itself the major R&D activity in the Warsaw Pact.[9] As in the Soviet Union, there is almost certainly a substantial though inexactly quantifiable degree of subsidisation of the military by the civilian branches, so that official data in local currency is likely to underestimate the real cost of military production. For comparison purposes it is useful to recost data from local into a common currency, the dollar. The conversion and index number procedures create the same problems for East European currencies as for the ruble. Thus the dollar estimates of the narrowly defined defence burden exceed those calculated in the local currencies, usually by substantial margins, sometimes by a factor of more than two, with a general tendency for the gap to be largest for the less developed economies. In 1981, the East European members of the Warsaw Pact spent the equivalent of $32 bn on military related activities,[10] a far from inconsiderable economic contribution to block collective security. The strictures which were emphasised in Chapter 1 about the usefulness of dollar estimates of Soviet military spending apply equally to dollar estimates of East European defence spending. Estimates in dollars and local currencies show expenditure totals as follows (Table 6.1):

Measured in local currencies or in dollars (Table 6.2), the East European defence burden falls far short of that incurred by the USSR. This is partly due to the public good aspect of collective defence spending. It also reflects the different resource capability of the various countries and, because of their only partial identification with Soviet objectives, their differing assessment of threat and ben-

Table 6.1 East European defence expenditures in local currencies and dollars

	1970	1975	1980	1983	Growth % 1970–1983	1983 in dollars (bn)
			in local currency			
Bulgaria (m. leva)	324					4
Czechoslovakia (bn crowas)	14.9	19.7	22.9	23.8	3.7	6
GDR (bn marks)	6.7	9.6	13.1	15.9	6.9	5
Hungary (bn forints)	9.8	11.8	16.4	21.0	6.0	3
Poland (bn zlotys)	35.7	50.2	65.3	89.1	7.3	9
Rumania (bn lei)	7.1	9.7	11.8	11.7	3.9	5

Source: T. Clements, 'The Cost of Defense in the Non-Soviet Warsaw Pact: A Historical Perspective' in J.E.C., *East European Economies: Slow Growth in the 1980s*, 1985, pp. 453 and 470.

Table 6.2 Defence as percentage of GNP 1982

	Domestic	Dollar
Bulgaria	3.2	10.1
Czechoslovakia	3.5	5.2
GDR	4.2	5.8
Hungary	2.2	4.5
Poland	4.0	7.0
Rumania	1.4	4.6

Source: T. Alton *et al*, 'East European Defense Expenditures' in J.E.C. *East European Economies: Slow Growth in the 1980s*, 1985, pp. 477–8.

efit, and hence of the appropriate level of defence spending.[11] On average, therefore, the East Europeans spend around 3.5 per cent of GNP measured in domestic currency, considerably less than the 15 to 17 per cent which the Soviet Union currently allocates. The country which is least prepared to incur costs for collective benefit is Rumania, which has on many occasions distanced itself from Soviet foreign policy. Conversion problems between the dollar and local currencies make it difficult to show unambiguously which country is most supportive of Warsaw Pact military objectives, as measured by the defence quotient. Measured in dollars, Poland has the highest defence quotient; in local currency it is the GDR.

Soviet military economic objectives in the Warsaw Pact are diverse, and sometimes conflicting. On the one hand, it has sought to ease the burden of its own spending by periodically exhorting the other members of the alliance to shoulder a larger share of the collective burden. The European response has been at best mixed. In 1965, when the overall economic environment was favourable, most of the allies responded enthusiastically. In 1978, the Soviet Union, again conscious of its increasing burden, called upon each East European country to increase its contribution by an additional 5 per cent.[12] This time, however, the Soviet request coincided with a worsening economic performance in Eastern Europe, and apart from the GDR, which by many criteria has become the Soviet Union's most dependable ally (and for which it has been duly rewarded), the response was unenthusiastic. In contrast to the first half of the 1970s, when defence spending increased faster on average than in the USSR, between 1976 and 1981 it increased at an annual average rate of only 1.9 per cent p.a. Since 1982, in spite of a continued adverse economic environment, the nominal rate of defence growth has increased again, to an average rate of 4.7 per cent,[13] partly due to higher inflation and partly to continued Soviet subsidisation of their economies. The Soviet Union is probably reluctant to be too insistent because in Eastern Europe, as in its own economy, defence spending reduces overall economic efficiency,[14] and, given the delicate economic and social balance, too large or too rapid a diversion of resources away from the civilian economy might so provoke economic and political dislocation and disturbance as to require subsequent rescue by the Soviet Union. It is also the case that since the interests of individual East European countries do not exactly coincide with the Soviet Union or with any other single country, excessive spending by one country might disentangle the complex web of military, economic and political ties which bind together the often disparate strands of the alliance.

The alliance creates a guaranteed international market for Soviet weapons, which allows longer production runs for Soviet military enterprises, increases economies of scale, and makes it easier to justify production and expenditures which might otherwise be considered excessively expensive if incurred solely for domestic forces. Up to 25 per cent of the new generation of fighter aircraft currently under research and production are to be allocated to Pact forces,[15] which could significantly ameliorate the heavy R&D costs incurred in the development of new aircraft. The USSR reaps further economic reward by insisting upon a high degree of product standardisation in the division of Socialist labour.

Many of the Pact members were substantial armaments producers in their own right before the Second World War, Czech and German arms, especially, having a high reputation in Europe. They possessed a stock of human, and in some cases, material capital upon which post-war production could be organised. Military integration is made more effective if troops use standardised weapons and equipment which have common elements and which are interchangeable as circumstances warrant. There is also considerable economic reward if production can be coordinated to produce common weapons or components. In NATO, for instance, failure to pursue an effective policy of standardised production and utilisation has been estimated to cost between $10 bn and $15 bn p.a.[16] Although no simple extrapolation is possible to the quite different circumstances of the Warsaw Pact, and the inefficiencies and secrecy of Soviet practices reduce the actual benefit below potential, the figure does indicate the broad order of magnitude of the economies which may be earned from a coordinated programme of production and deployment. East European production designed in effect to meet Soviet requirements, inhibits the expansion of indigenous manufacture in more preferred directions, and the failure to reconcile the sometimes conflicting objectives of the Soviet Union and its allies has created a degree of intra-block tension.

Since Stalin's death, the block's military economy has been characterised by a high and increasing degree of formal weapons coordination as the Soviet Union has brought indigenous East European producers within the ambit of its own plans, through a series of bilateral and multilateral agreements. In 1965, military–economic coordination was formalised via a Political Consultative Commission.[17] A further reorganisation in 1970 created a Joint Technical Committee, which has the stated objective of giving the East Europeans a greater role in the development and production of new weapons, to coordinate R&D and to increase military industrial specialisation.[18] Although the Soviet Union has made heavy demands on, for instance, Hungarian electronic technology, it has kept to itself the major R&D effort. Soviet leaders have refused to provide advanced military scientific and technological information to the East Europeans, which has effectively prevented them from pursuing an indigenous research effort. They have been barred from participation in modernisation programmes, which makes them totally dependent on the USSR. Not only are they militarily dependent for advanced weapons, but the Soviet quest for security has reduced the indigenous armaments industries in Eastern Europe to little more than integrated satellites of its own military economic sector. The main block weapons are almost exclusively of Soviet origin, either of design or production, and no non-Soviet developed armaments have been introduced into the armies of all the Warsaw Pact countries.[19] East European armaments producers can buy production licences to manufacture Soviet designed weapons, or can modify Soviet designs to make them compatible with their own technological capabilities, but they are not, and under the circumstances cannot be, innovative producers.

The degree of modernisation in the different forces varies, reflecting in all probability the extent to which the USSR can politically push its allies in particular directions. It has sought to decrease the proportion of indigenous production gradually and to impose upon its allies a uniform standardisation, based almost exclusively upon its own designs. As the Soviet Union tools up to produce new or more advanced weapons systems, it sells the design of existing models to the most appropriate East European producers. Despite some resistance to Soviet pressures, the East Europeans have in the final analysis only limited choice over the type and quantity of weapons they produce. Although the formal institutions of the Warsaw Pact allow for the possibility of a common exchange of research documents or joint production of technologically advanced systems, the flow is essentially unidirectional. Advanced research is almost exclusively a Soviet activity which, though it reduces the cost of modernisation for East Europeans, leaves them in the category of second- or third-class technological powers. The degree of standardisation which has been attained, though much greater than in NATO, is still far from uniform as countries cling where possible to indigenous design and production to give them some limited measure of independence, and there are instances of individual weapons or components produced in one country being incompatible with the stock available to the alliance as a whole.[20]

The Soviet aim of increasing the Socialist division of labour is not limited to the defence sector, for the group of countries which in 1955 formed the Warsaw Pact were by and large the very same group of countries which had in 1949 created the Council for Mutual Economic Assistance. During the 1930s the USSR pursued the policy of autarchy to such effect that at the outset of the Second World War overseas trade accounted for less than 1 per cent of its GNP,[21] and in the official textbooks international trade was deemed quite unimportant to the wealth-creating process. Given the size and the resource diversity of the economy autarchy, though not economically rational, did not create unmanageable economic costs. The economic circumstances of the other CMEA members were quite different, being smaller, with a narrower range of indigenous natural resources. Traditionally, international trade had been a more potent generator of economic wealth, and most of them had in the pre-war period extensive trading contacts throughout Europe, in particular with Germany. The collapse of the German economy after the war created an economic vacuum into which the Soviets quickly moved, at the same time forcing the East Europeans to a trade pattern and policy which was quite at variance with their tradition and economic potential. Statistical calculation suggests that membership of the CMEA was costly for both the USSR and the East Europeans,[22] and from the outset it clearly had a non-economic *raison d'être* (though for the East Europeans, of course, membership was not a matter of choice).

During the Stalin period the CMEA had little impact on economic outcomes, for though Socialist trade increased such that by 1950 it accounted on average for 70 per cent of East European exports, this was due more to the normal process of economic recovery and bilateral agreements than to trade creation or diversion along customs union lines.

The CMEA was also irrelevant to Stalin's policy of extracting economic revenge from Eastern Europe for the human and material losses sustained by the Soviet Union during the Great Patriotic War. This took two basic forms; war reparations and the creation of exploitative joint stock companies. Although the Soviet Union might claim to be entitled to some repayment for the damage to its economy, the scale and the nature of reparations extracted from economies totally or largely disabled by war created costs which Soviet policy itself subsequently indicates to have been excessive. Most of the reparation cost was in the form of dismantled European plant and equipment shipped to the Soviet Union, cheap raw material exports and payment for Soviet troops stationed on indigenous territory. In addition, the Soviet Union formed joint stock companies with host nations, financed in equal part by the two countries. Since the Soviet share usually comprised captured local investment material, the whole costs were effectively borne by the host nation, largely for Soviet benefit. Net East European transfers in the period 1945–55 are estimated to have amounted to the equivalent of $23 bn, of which the GDR alone paid $19 bn. Because of inefficient planning and the problems of organising the exchange in dislocated economies, the net Soviet receipt was in the region of $19 bn.[23] Former allies, Czechoslovakia, Poland and Yugoslavia, were also forcibly brought into the Soviet economic sphere on disadvantageous terms as Stalin sought to transform the whole of Easter Europe into a Soviet economic satellite.

Riots and revolution in the GDR, Poland and Hungary, which were partly economic in origin, forced upon the post-Stalin leadership a reappraisal of the utility of a policy of savage exploitation, and after 1955 it reversed the net financial flow, paying back around $2.6 bn to the East Europeans. In addition, the Soviets cancelled what they asserted was their legitimate right to further payments of $9.4 bn, which enabled them to claim that the Soviet real contribution to East European economic recovery after 1955 was of the order of $12 bn.

In the first ten years or so Soviet economic relations with its partners were very much in accord with the predictions of a simple theory of economic warfare.[24] A country's power to extract unequal economic concessions from another depends on the degree of mutual economic interdependence between the two countries. Although questions of political will, etc. are never entirely absent, the economic dimensions of dependence are influenced by such criteria as the absolute and relative contribution of international trade to GNP in each country, the relative importance of each partner in the total trade of the other, the pattern of trade and the degree to which alternative suppliers or markets may be found in the event of threatened or actual embargo. According to all these criteria, the Soviet Union was well placed to extract economic tribute from the other East European countries. To the Soviet Union, international trade was unimportant, whereas for the smaller economies, trade before the war had been a powerful generator of economic wealth and still was comparatively more so than for the USSR. Because such a high proportion of East European exports were, forcibly, shipped to the USSR, which effectively cut them off from the mainstream of capitalist development, they had few alternative markets, and lack of effective competition reduced their overall quality and diminished their long-term competitiveness in world markets. East European imports from the Soviet Union, on the other hand, were mainly in the form of strategically important non-food raw materials, interruptions to the supply of which would have adverse and immediate impact on production and on living standards, and for which alternative markets were readily available. Eastern Europe exported soft goods to the Soviet Union and imported hard goods. Economic dependence was of course matched by a powerful military and political dominance. The Soviet Union had an overwhelming bargaining position, but after 1960 or so, and in contrast to the predictions of simple theory and to previous experience, it appears to have been unwilling or unable to exploit its power, for intra-CMEA trade and payments moved to a much more equitable pattern for the East Europeans.

The irrational price systems which prevailed in each COMECON country made the systematic calculation of costs and benefits of international exchange and the settling of net deficits and surpluses almost impossible. Efficient trade and settlement required an acceptable common unit of account which, in the absence of a Socialist alternative, was agreed would be the appropriate world price for each good or commodity. The Bucharest pricing procedure established intra-CMEA settlements on the basis of the world price for each good in the prior five year period. Since international trade was dominated by capitalist firms and nations, world prices were effectively those prevailing in capitalist markets, which was itself an ironic judgement on the economic rationality of socialist exchange. The actual settlement prices usually diverged from those prevailing in world markets to a greater or smaller extent by, for instance, purging such capitalist elements as monopoly profit, as being inappropriate for Socialist countries. In many cases it was difficult to identify what was the world price, due to different qualities, discounts, premiums, and so on.

In societies constrained by absolute shortage, the price of a single commodity only incompletely captures the net transfer of resources between trading partners, for prices reflected relative bargaining power at each stage of the negotiations and high price for one commodity might be compensated by low price elsewhere, or a low price might be compensated by countries having to buy commodities they did not really wish to buy as part of an agreement. Thus, despite being nominally based on world prices, CMEA procedures allowed for considerable departures, depending on the relative strengths and objectives of the bargainers.

Even so, up till the mid 1970s relative price movements show a deep and consistent worsening of the Soviet terms of trade with its COMECON partners. On average, during the period, the price of East European manufacturing exports exceeded world prices by 20–40 per cent, while Soviet exports of energy and raw materials exceeded world prices by only 0–20 per cent[25] and the Soviet terms of trade are estimated to have deteriorated by around 20 per cent. The Soviet loss was greater than a straightforward price calculation might indicate. Soviet exports of petroleum and raw material were of a quality which could be sold for hard currency in competitive world markets, and which could be used to buy imports from capitalist countries. The protected and hence low quality East European manufactures could only be sold amongst themselves or, more typically, to the USSR. That is, high quality and low-priced Soviet hard currency exports were exchanged for low quality and high priced East European soft currency imports.

The Soviet Union was also unable or unwilling to exploit its apparent bargaining power to impose on its allies its vision of the optimal degree and pace of socialist integration.[26] In 1962, Khrushchev proposed an ambitious programme of supranational management through a series of coordination agreements to integrate economic planning in each member country, and in 1966 further measures for deeper economic integration were proposed by the Soviet Union. These were successfully resisted by the East Europeans, with Rumania usually in the vanguard, as by and large were all Soviet initiatives for formal integration.

The CMEA was not without economic benefit for the Soviet Union, however. Eastern Europe was forced into a complementary trading pattern, which guaranteed secure markets and sources of supply which served Soviet quantity planning, and were not liable to interruption by unpredictable markets and aggressive capitalist opponents ever ready to threaten embargo. Although they resisted formal integration, the East Europeans were prepared to participate in joint investment schemes on Soviet soil, in particular those which promised them eventual pay-back in the form of energy and power. The giant 'Peace' electricity grid to link national electricity systems and the 'Friendship' oil pipeline from the Urals were tangible results of intra-CMEA investment in this period.

It is clear that Soviet behaviour in subsidising its partners and failing to obtain the degree of economic integration it apparently desired was inconsistent with the view of the Soviet Union as a dominant bargainer. Although prices derived from a mutually agreed formula, and were therefore partially predetermined, that formula was not inviolable and was itself presumably changeable had the Soviet Union so wished, and actual prices depended to a large extent on bilateral negotiation. The apparent paradox of a dominant bargainer resisting the opportunity to maximise the net return from its power was magnified by the circumstances of the 1970s.

Solid and hydrocarbon energy reserves are very unevenly distributed in the CMEA countries. The Soviet Union has abundant reserves of all energy resources, the GDR and Poland are, or have been, exporters of coal and lignite, but apart from Rumania, which has been largely self-sufficient during the post-war period, oil reserves are limited to the Soviet Union. Over a period of years the energy deficient countries increased their dependence on Soviet imports, as they and even the two major coal producers diversified their energy balance to a greater dependence on oil. Oil was also a basic input into the chemical industry, which was a major growth sector for many of the more industrially advanced countries. The East Europeans, as was the Soviet Union itself, were inefficient users of oil for the price system gave little incentive to economise. One of the early fruits of economic union between the USSR and its partners had been the construction of the Druzba (Friendship) pipeline, in 1958, to transport Soviet oil to Poland, the GDR, Czechoslovakia and Hungary. That was followed by long-term bilateral arrangements to sell agreed quantities of Soviet oil at fixed price in return for East European investment in Soviet oilfields and the international pipeline system. Throughout the 1960s, Soviet oil exports increased at an annual average rate of 12 per cent, and by 1970 totalled 38m. tons p.a. So long as the oil was cheap and abundant, East European dependence, though increasing their strategic vulnerability, was economically rational. Alternative supplies were cheaply available, so that when in 1972, in response to the growing opportunity cost of selling to soft currency markets, the USSR urged its allies to seek supplies elsewhere, they quickly agreed alternative arrangements with OPEC producers. Poland doubled its storage capacity, while Hungary and Czechoslovakia joined with Yugoslavia to plan an Adriatic pipeline to transport Kuwaiti oil to their industrial consumers.

The tenfold increase in oil prices in 1974, and later in 1979, effectively destroyed East European and Soviet plans for energy diversification. The cost to the East Europeans of alternative supplies at world prices would have been prohibitive, and the Soviet Union had to accept its role as the almost exclusive non-indigenous supplier of energy to Eastern Europe. From 1970 to 1979 Soviet exports accounted for 90 per cent of the increase in energy consumption in Bulgaria, the GDR and Hungary, and for 85 per cent in Czechoslovakia. They increased at an annual average rate of 9.5 per cent p.a. in 1971–5, and by 6.0 per cent in 1976–80.[27] By the end of the decade exports of energy had increased to around 80m. tons p.a.

However, the Bucharest principle, which tied prices to those prevailing in 1966–70, imposed intolerable burdens on the USSR. In 1971–4, for instance, the Soviets forewent a possible improvement in its terms of trade of around 35 per cent,[28] and in 1976, a year ahead of schedule, it not only increased the price of energy exports, but induced the CMEA to accept a new pricing formula. Under the new 'Moscow' principle, intra-CMEA prices were to be based on a rolling five year average of world prices, so they would change annually, but with a time-lag. This also was an instance of the Soviet Union failing to press an apparent advantage, for it originally proposed the elimination of any time-lag, and then one of only three years.

Nevertheless, Soviet benefit was instantaneous and large. In 1975 its terms of trade improved by 11 per cent, imposing an additional burden of $3.3 bn on the East European importers, and by 1980, by fully 40 per cent, yielding a gain of over $2000 m. in four years.[29]

The increase in oil prices was the source of not only the greatest windfall profit for the Soviet Union, but also, paradoxically, of its greatest opportunity cost. Even though the terms of trade moved so adversely against the East Europeans, they none the less benefited greatly from the highly accommodating stance which the USSR took in its economic relations with them. The Moscow principle postponed debilitating price increases, giving the East Europeans some time to adjust to new economic circumstances, and the terms of trade increased far slower than if intra-CMEA trade had been based upon prices charged in world markets. Slower adjustment meant for the USSR price increases foregone. Estimates of the implicit subsidy given by lower prices vary, but by 1980 may have been of the order of $34 bn. Though the Soviet terms of trade improved by 30 per cent, it forewent another 30 per cent,[30] and in 1981 Soviet oil was 70 per cent below the world price level.[31]

The Soviet opportunity cost exceeded even this large sum, however, for by selling oil to the East Europeans in exchange for soft goods or claims against future goods, it forewent sales to hard currency markets. Not only did it get less for its exports, but with the lower sum it bought inferior quality manufactured goods. Meanwhile, in 1976–80 the Soviet economic performance overall, and the oil industry in particular, worsened. Between 1960 and 1980 the cost of raising and shipping an extra 1 million barrels of oil increased 3.75 times. At the same time, hard currency imports also increased, from $8.6 bn in 1974 to $27.7 bn in 1981. Although hard currency exports matched higher imports, this was due very largely to higher earnings from fuel, which accounted for 68 per cent of total hard currency earnings, and the net hard currency debt to the West increased from $1.6 bn in 1974 to $12.4 bn in 1981.[32]

Soviet generosity to its allies was even so not finished. Socialist exchange was traditionally based on bilateral clearing, and credit between any pair of countries was kept strictly limited. During the 1970s many of the more developed East European countries pursued an import-led growth policy predicated on the assumption that imports of high quality Western machinery would accelerate the transformation to intensive production. Western government and bank credit was readily available and short period debts were to be paid off by increasing industrial exports in the future.

In the event, however, exports failed to grow as projected, for various reasons, and the balance of payments and international debt position of many East European countries became critically adverse. Social upheaval is not an exclusively economic phenomenon, but it has in Eastern Europe been affected by economic performance and expectations which induced a cautious Soviet policy to the East European deficits. Instead of insisting on the transfer of real resources by eliminating the deficits in accordance with traditional Socialist practice, the Soviet Union agreed to credit its allies by accepting a large build-up of balance of payments surpluses. From a relatively modest figure of $105 m. rubles in 1974, the Soviet surplus increased in three years almost twentyfold, to $1.9 bn rubles. By 1983 the total East European debt in transferable rubles amounted to almost $30 bn,[33] in addition to which the Soviet Union granted a series of long-term loans to assist readjustment to the new set of economic circumstances.

Estimation of the total subsidy to the East Europeans is controversial, depending on a number of sometimes questionable assumptions about counterfactual alternatives. One careful estimate suggests that between 1973 and 1980 alone the subsidy totalled $60 bn; $26 bn being attributable to buying manufactured goods from Eastern Europe at higher than world prices, and $34 bn to selling energy at less than world prices.[34] Estimates based on a different set of assumptions push the total figure to $110 bn.[35] Whatever the 'correct' figure, the scale of the opportunity cost is quite at variance with the Soviet position as a powerful, exploitative bargainer.

The Soviet Union, like all other countries, was caught unawares by the magnitude of the OPEC price increase in 1974 and later in 1979; and the benefit forgone must partly have been simply accidental, a reflection of the Moscow pricing formula, and a stroke of good fortune.[36] However, the Soviet Union probably could, if it so wished, have altered the price mechanism, as it had done in 1975, and the balance of payments surpluses certainly reflect policy judgements rather than luck.

The subsidy may have been implicit acknowledgement of the value to the USSR of other economic benefits made available to it by the East Europeans. Though energy and raw materials accounted for over 50 per cent of total exports revenue, these are non-renewable and increasingly costly assets. It was anxious to diversify its export patterns, but autarchic policies had eliminated effective market pressure to sustain quality, and exports of machinery and equipment were generally uncompetitive in world markets. Although the USSR produced 12 per cent of world industrial production, it accounted for only 2 per cent of world industrial exports. Soft East European markets offered easy outlets for its industrial products,[37] unlikely to be interrupted by capitalist embargo. Some of the more developed nations also sold to the USSR manufactured goods of a higher quality than it produced domestically.

Soviet planners had consistently sought a tighter degree of international Socialist planning than the other nations had been prepared to countenance. With the exception of a few large integrated investment programmes, it had failed either to threaten the East Europeans with sufficient dire consequences or to offer sufficient inducement to bring about the level of integration it desired. Changing economic circumstances increased the weight of both threat and inducement, as the Soviet Union sought to persuade its allies of the virtues of its vision. In 1971, the Comprehensive Programme appeared to offer a possible framework for greater cooperation, and in 1976 the CMEA agreed to strengthen Socialist cooperation through an Agreed Plan for Multilateral Measures (APMIM) to coordinate a series of long-term special purpose programmes. The most visible outcome of the APMIM was the joint investment in the Soviet Orenberg pipeline and the Ust Ilim pulp mill, which received about $12 bn of block investment, about 50 per cent of which was paid for by the non-Soviet countries. The two schemes in addition required the East European partner to provide a block of high technology Western goods, and in the case of the pipeline, skilled specialist labour. Although the APMIM had identified ten economic areas for possible joint investment, only the Orenberg pipeline and the Ust Ilim cellulose plant were completed.

A second APMIM agreement identified five major areas for coordinated investment: energy and raw materials, machine building, food, industrial consumer goods and nuclear energy. A number of agreements in principle were signed, but in the light of European opposition the range of projects was gradually whittled away until only those associated with fuel transportation remained intact. The reduction in the number of schemes coincided with agreement for a looser integrated framework for joint investment. Instead of investing in each other's economy, calculation of respective costs and benefits often being difficult, the members agreed to a much weaker coordination of domestic investment within the CMEA framework. East European investment in the Soviet Union remains at a modest 3 per cent of total. Once more it appears that the East Europeans have collectively been able to thwart Soviet policy for a tighter degree of economic integration.

In sum, the economic benefits which the Soviet Union has obtained from Eastern Europe does not match the great opportunity cost it has incurred or the predictions of the economic model, given its powerful negotiating position. If we assume purposive behaviour by Soviet leaders, it must be the case that Eastern Europe offers non-economic, in addition to economic, benefits and the subsidy is the price which the Soviet Union pays. Although not amenable to precise calculation, Eastern Europe provides the USSR with unconventional tangible political, diplomatic, ideological and, significantly, military gains from trade,[38] and it is argued that Soviet subsidy broadly reflects the contribution each of its allies makes to Soviet security and political objectives.[39]

Russia's lack of natural boundaries and its history of invasion from East and West have traditionally led its leaders to give high and enduring priority to the defence of the homeland, and current policy is no departure from the norm. The Czars and their advisers sought to enhance their defensive capabilities through a series of more or less formal alliances, and the Warsaw Pact is a formalisation of Russian policy to create a buffer zone to protect the homeland from direct contact with potential enemies lying westwards.[40] This can be achieved only within an organisation which accepts Soviet hegemony. Given what Soviet leaders would view as reactionary resistance to socialist ideology and practice, old-style voluntary alliances were insufficiently secure. The economic burden may therefore be the price which the Soviet Union incurs to cement a less cohesive union to avoid paying even higher direct costs in Eastern Europe.[41] Economic specialisation is matched by a division of mission responsibility in the Warsaw Pact, whereby troops of different countries undertake specialist functions within the block control system.[42] The different histories and uncertain loyalties of the non-Soviet armies allow for only incomplete specialisation in this respect. The East Europeans offer training facilities, forward bases and, in the event of invasion, a clear corridor to the West European heartland, and they support, with varying degrees of enthusiasm, Soviet foreign policies. The alliance is weakened by the vulnerability of some countries to internal and external fissiparous pressures. Poland and the GDR are especially critical in this respect, and it is perhaps no accident that they receive the highest subsidy, both as a reward and as an inducement to continued loyalty and support. The GDR received credit equivalent to over 7 per cent of that country's trade turnover, reflecting both its relative bargaining strengths and weakness. As the most consistently supportive of Soviet military ambitions and a regular exporter of high quality manufactured products, the large surplus was partly in the way of a reward. It was also an insurance given the GDR's geographical, and hence political, vulnerability.[43] Soviet assistance to Poland, which in 1981 alone amounted to $5.5 m.[44] may also be seen as a means to secure its military and political investments in that country.

The proximity of the East European countries and their crucial role as buffer states means that they receive the largest portion of the

Soviet subsidy. They do not, however, exhaust spending for this purpose, for the Soviet Union also incurs expenditures elsewhere which complement to a greater or smaller measure its foreign policy objectives. For instance, imports of Cuban sugar embargoed by the USA, may have cost the equivalent of $2 bn p.a. in 1980.[45] The total cost of empire in 1980, much though not all of which was sustained for military-related objectives, was estimated to be between $32 and $43 bn, growing at over 8 per cent p.a. Over 60 per cent of the total costs are accounted for by trade subsidies, equivalent in value to between 2 and 3 per cent of GNP, and to 16 to 21 per cent of domestic military spending. The hard currency component of subsidy amounted to 85 per cent or so of total hard currency earnings that year, and it is clear that the indirect external economic costs of sustaining the military effort have a not insubstantial impact on civilian economic outcomes. The precise trade-off depends as always on the assumptions which are made concerning the growth and the efficiency of the civilian and military variables. If, as is widely assumed by Western economists, Soviet GNP growth will not exceed 3 per cent on average to 1990 and total factor productivity will not increase much beyond current levels, then growth of empire costs at the long-run rate of 8 per cent p.a. will hold back domestic consumption and investment to 2.5 per cent p.a. or so.[46]

The values of the unconventional gains from trade are critically dependent on the price of energy in CMEA and world markets. Falling oil prices have adversely effected Soviet earning potential, especially in view of the real costs which have to be incurred in transporting the oil to external markets. It has consistently refused to sign long-term agreements with capitalist nations for agreed sales at fixed prices, unlike natural gas, and therefore it must compete on spot or short-term markets with exporters, many of whose production costs are lower. Falling energy prices and lower long-term demand forecasts may also reduce the enthusiasm of West European importers to sign long- term sales agreements of natural gas.

Paradoxically, however, the opportunity cost of sustaining the East European economies will decline. East European countries which pay less for energy imports will, other things being equal, have lower deficits for the Soviets to finance. If economic circumstances in general and the balance of payments in particular improve, the Soviets may feel less constrained in seeking payment for their surpluses in Eastern Europe. East Europeans may have better opportunities of obtaining non-Soviet supplies, and the final irony may be that since CMEA prices lag behind falling world prices, the Soviet Union may even divert exports towards Eastern Europe, though demands for hard currency make a significant diversion unlikely. Unless the Soviet Union replaces indirect subsidy by more direct economic aid, Soviet military benefits in Eastern Europe will be more economically available.

Some of the more industrially advanced East European countries assist the Soviet Union by supporting its programme of arms sales to Third World countries, and Czechoslovakia has become a medium-sized armaments exporters in its own right. Czechoslovakia also played an important early role as a surrogate for a Soviet Union reluctant to pursue aggressive policies in the Third World, which might have brought it into conflict with the then dominant arms supplier, the USA. In 1955–6 the Czechs, in lieu of the USSR, arranged a $200 m. loan of military assistance to Egypt.[47]

Soviet autarchy under Stalin was non-discriminating, excluding less developed agrarian as well as the more developed industrialised economies. Russia, as an agrarian economy, had only weak trading links with other agricultural or raw material producers. They were also, for Stalin, quite unimportant in the climactic struggle between capitalism and socialism. Decolonisation, and Khrushchev's more expansive outlook on world affairs, in the late 1950s, led to a reassessment of the role of the less-developed countries in Soviet objectives, and to a more active Third World policy. Many leaders of newly independent countries welcomed the involvement, believing that Soviet-type planning offered a more controlled strategy of economic expansion than capitalist type growth. The USSR was also perceived as a likely alternative source of economic assistance. Though Stalin had devalued the international dimension of Marxist theory, the Soviet Union was ideologically supportive of the anti-imperialist philosophies of the newly independent countries. Marxism–Leninism explained imperialism as a necessary stage in capitalist expansion, and if this source of external sustenance could be weakened, capitalism as a dynamic system might itself be compromised.

Despite their almost unique experience in planning economic development, Soviet leaders soon lost their initial enthusiasm for economic aid as a foreign policy instrument. Programmes of economic assistance relevant to local Third World conditions were often difficult to devise and to execute, and the return was usually long term. Military assistance, however, the export of armaments, equipment technicians, military advisers, and the provision of training facilities for officers in the Soviet Union itself, offered a more immediate political return, and quickly replaced economic aid as the major foreign policy instrument in the Third World countries, which were the main importers of Soviet armaments outside the Warsaw Pact.

From the outset, arms sales were mainly instruments to facilitate the political objective of providing an entré for Soviet personnel and ideas into the Third World, to decouple the newly independent countries from their erstwhile colonial masters.[48] After the Sino-Soviet break in 1960, they were also a useful bulwark against Chinese initiatives in the Third World. Initial levels were modest, and by the end of 1957 only $400 million had been transferred to the Third World, mainly to Afghanistan, Syria and Egypt. Within less than a decade, however, both numbers of agreements and their monetary value had risen to substantial levels.

Detailed information on the numbers and types of weapons are regularly available and widely published. Their economic or financial equivalent are more difficult to obtain, however, for the Soviet Union, as with its domestic expenditures, offers no information on its armaments agreements, which must be estimated using a variety of techniques. One such is to obtain residuals from the divergence between aggregate and itemised trade statistics. Sums of money which cannot be matched with civilian physical outputs or services are assumed to represent arms sales. The sums, in rubles or local currencies, are usually converted to dollars to provide a common base for international comparison which, as always, creates problems about the appropriate dollar–ruble conversion ratio. A second method, using parametric estimating techniques, is analogous to that used by the CIA in estimating Soviet domestic procurement. Performance characteristics of the most closely identified major weapons which account for between 50 and 70 per cent of the total, are costed in dollars, from which figures for total value estimates are obtained.[49]

Detailed investigation of specific agreements with a small number of Arab states, using locally published information, shows that the estimating techniques both understate and distort the true value of Soviet armaments. They may understate the total sum by a factor of two, and conventional arms tend to be overpriced, and high technology weapons underpriced.[50] This type of detailed information, valuable though it is, limited, and analysis of the trade must proceed on the basis of generally available data. Calculation of the true value of the agreements is made more difficult by incomplete information on what proportion of each agreement is paid in hard currency, what is available as grant aid, and whether the agreement includes spare parts and maintenance costs, etc., which can often increase the value of an agreement by a factor of two.[51]

Data show a gradual increase during the 1960s, followed by a quickening in the pace of expansion during in the 1970s.

From the Soviet point of view, arms sales offered a cheap and effective way of increasing its presence in the Third World. On the demand side, insecurity and conflict within and between the less developed countries provided an apparently continuous increase in demand for military goods. When occasionally the conflict erupted into war, between India and Pakistan in 1965, Israel and the Arab countries in 1967, replacement sales increased as the combatants rebuilt their weapon stocks to make up for those destroyed in battle. Furthermore, many of the radical leaders who rejected the capitalist mode of production also rejected its most powerful exponent, the USA, and consciously sought alternative sources of arms. Since the USSR was the second largest military power with extensive stock and production facilities, it was the natural alternative to which they turned.

Armament exports were relatively cheap to supply, initially consisting in large part of fairly antiquated, second-line equipment, obtained from the large stocks habitually kept, and which had been swollen by the strategic reorientation of the defence forces in the mid-1950s. When agreements stipulated the sale of more modern weapons in current production, Soviet practice of keeping reserve capacity in defence plants, conjoined with large production runs, to keep down the marginal cost of exports. In short, arms agreements were easy to plan and to implement.

From the outset, the Soviets showed a high and surprising degree of commercial flair in marketing arms in the Third World, which imported over 75 per cent of total sales. The Chief Engineering Directorate, which had overall responsibility for coordinating arms sales between the different domestic and overseas agencies, showed itself to be sensitive to local conditions, offering a diversity of terms to accommodate Third World buyers.[52] As the technological follower in the superpower conflict, it produced weapons more suitable to local conditions than the sometimes too sophisticated American equivalent. Soviet design principles emphasised standardisation, commonality and evolutionary progress, and its enterprises built weapons which were robust, effective and, moreover, cheap. Cheap-

Table 6.3 Military and economic aid, 1955–60 (million $)

	Military aid	Economic aid
Middle East	1437	1217
South Asia	1695	180
Africa	735	33
East Asia	404	1136
Latin America	30	
TOTAL:	4291	2566

Source: Gu Guan-Fu, 'Soviet Aid to the Third World', *Soviet Studies*, vol. XXXV, no. 1, 1983, p. 74.

ness partly reflected lower quality, but also a deliberate policy of subsidy and generous financial terms. Credit was generally available at 2 per cent interest, the principal to be repaid over ten years, but with a grace period of one to three years.[53] When recipient countries, many of which were poor, were unable to meet the terms of the agreements, the Soviet Union was usually prepared to accept payment in soft currencies or in local raw materials, which could be resold on international markets. The combination of low prices, generous credit, quick and effective supply after signing agreements, increased demand for Soviet arms and quickly pushed it to rough equality with the USA. Pre-war the Soviet Union had accounted for 6 per cent of world armament sales. By 1970 this had increased to 30 per cent.

Despite its official ideological support for movements of national liberation and for established Socialist governments, the worldwide distribution of its sales shows a clearly opportunist response to local political circumstances. The Soviet Union was quite prepared to abandon its Marxist–Leninist principles if this was politically or strategically advantageous. It sold arms to conservative states which were ideologically opposed to the Socialist principles which it espoused, some of which even waged war on local communist insurgency parties, for instance, Pakistan, Iran, Egypt and Guinea.[54] From the beginning the distribution of sales (Table 6.3) shows a pronounced regional basis, with more than 70 per cent being concentrated in the Middle East and South Asia.

Economic and military aid roughly balanced for a period, but by 1960, the relative importance of the economic component had declined. Between 1954 and 1972 the Soviet Union signed economic aid agreements worth $18.2 bn, of which $8.2 bn was drawn, a take-up rate of 45 per cent. Over the same period, arms agreements worth $47.4 bn were signed with Third World countries, of which $35.3 bn was drawn, a take-up rate of 75 per cent.[55]

Even though the economic cost of producing weapons for sale was comparatively low, and economic motivation secondary, it was not entirely absent, and the Soviet Union did seek an economic return where possible, often of a non-monetary nature for example, landing rights in Mali and the Congo, and naval facilities in Guinea, Somalia and Egypt.[56]

During the 1970s, the world market changed dramatically. International tension remained high in most parts of the world which occasionally in the Middle East and South Asia erupted into local but fierce wars. The real catalyst of expansion in arms sales however, was higher oil prices, which increased the budgets of many of the most active belligerents. As the producer of the largest array and quantity of arms, the Soviet Union was well placed to meet the increased demand (Table 6.4).

Eighty per cent of exports were sent to the Middle East and North Africa, mainly to Iraq, Syria, Libya and Algeria, although India and Vietnam were also substantial recipients of Soviet military aid.[57]

For the recipient countries, the Soviet comparative advantage remained much as it had been before the oil price shock. It had large stocks, a built-in buffer capacity which could be taken up if necessary, and in the final analysis could switch from consumer to military production, since defence plants were often tooled for both markets. The time between agreement of sales and delivery of armaments was routinely around half that taken by American suppliers, and production lines of modified front line weapons were sometimes kept open specifically for exports to the Third World.[58] Prices were lower, with often substantial discounts from list prices, and standard weapons, though no longer obsolete, retained their basic characteristics of robustness, commonality and comparative ease of use and maintainance.

The nature as well as the dimension of the international arms trade changed, as did, for the Soviet Union, its motivation. The oil rich countries could and were prepared to pay for modern armaments of the highest quality, a demand which the Soviets had to meet or lose the market, and the quality of Soviet exports increased, reflecting the higher percentage of new equipment in the total package. In some cases, Arab countries were sold armaments from current production,

Table 6.4 Value of Soviet arms transfers to non-Communist developing countries (Mil $)

	Agreements	Deliveries
Cumulative		
1955–69	5875	5060
1970	1150	995
1971	1590	865
1972	1690	1215
1973	2890	3135
1974	5735	2225
1975	3325	2040
1976	5550	3085
1977	8715	4705
1978	2465	5400
1979	8335	6615
1980		6538
1981		4741
1982		4184
1983		4174
1984		2532

Source: 1955–79, R. Pajak, 'Soviet Arms Transfer', p. 161.
1980–4, SIPRI Yearbook, 1985, p. 346.

for instance the MIG 29, before even they were deployed to Warsaw Pact forces,[59] which may even account for otherwise unexplained delays in the modernisation of the Warsaw Pact inventory.[60]

The rich Middle Eastern states and those which they subsidized paid for the advanced weapons in hard currency, or its equivalent, and Soviet price and credit terms hardened. In 1980, 43 per cent of total agreements were invoiced in hard currency or equivalent, such as oil from Libya. Some, though not all, non-oil countries had to meet equally stringent terms. In the 1977 agreement with Zambia, for instance, the repayment period was only seven years, at commercial rates, but other countries such as India, which had long been a favoured customer, could still buy on soft terms,[61] for the Soviet Union still sought political or diplomatic returns from armaments sales. By the middle years of the decade, hard currency payments were running at around $1.5 bn p.a. In 1980, the sum had increased to $2.5 bn, and in 1983 to $3 bn.[62]

The hardening Soviet terms reflected also a relative change in the motivation for Soviet arms exports. Although political and strategic motives were never less than important, a deteriorating economic environment at home in conjunction with profitable opportunities abroad strengthened the economic rationale for arms exports.[63] The dimensions of Soviet trade did not make an East European type import-led growth plausible for the USSR. None the less, imports did increase throughout the decade. Those of food, though variable, depending on the domestic harvest, occasionally increased to $9 bn, and those of industrial goods to $14 bn of which around $1.7 bn or so might be classified as high technology imports. The balance of payments deficit increased, as did the debt to Western banks and governments, which by 1981 reached $12 bn,[64] though the debt–service ratio always remained within the bounds of commercial prudence. The worsening figures nevertheless reflected Soviet failure to increase exports of machinery and equipment to supplement the traditional oil and raw materials, and official concern about the worsening balance of payments position was reflected in the decision to hold oil exports to the Eastern Europe to the 1982 level, despite the burden which this would impose on its allies.

The *modus operandi* of central planning gives little commercial incentive to seek exports, for the export multiplier, in a fully employed, centrally planned economy, is small.[65] Armaments provide one of the very few categories of manufactures at which the USSR can compete on equal terms with capitalist nations. They offer means of obtaining hard currency, and are the most dynamic and largest element in trade with less-developed countries. The Soviet Union accounts for 12 per cent of world industrial production, but only 2 per cent of world trade in industrial products. It has accounted for 37 per cent of world trade in armaments, which can total 10 per cent of exports, and apart from energy and gold, are the nation's most important earner of hard currency. Although direct comparison with a specific component of imports is necessarily arbitrary, armaments exports are equivalent to almost all imports of machinery and equipment in certain years.

Given that overheads have in any case to be incurred to meet domestic production, exports at economic prices show a very real return to military investment, and the export ratio for many categories of weapons are very substantial (Table 6.5), though some others, such as strategic nuclear missiles, are not traded at all.

Although it is not our purpose to assess the foreign policy returns, it appears that though they may have been effective in first establishing, and then consolidating, a Soviet presence in the recipient countries, armaments have not of themselves been instrumental in bringing

Table 6.5 Estimates of the share of exports in Soviet arms production, 1972–83

	Average 1972–6	Average 1977–81	1982	1983
Armoured vehicles				
Heavy and medium tanks	27	17	16	11
Infantry combat vehicles[1]	3	6	18	12
Armoured personnel carriers[1]	43	18	20	
Armoured reconnaissance Vehicles	16	25	16	13
SP field artillery[2]	5	10	5	5
Towed field artillery[2]	33	20	4	7
Warships				
Major surface combatants	14	17	25	10
Minor surface combatants	17	37	36	22
Aircraft				
Fighters/fighter-bombers	33	36	36	26
Trainers	43	41	50	29
Helicopters[3]	9	27	25	22
Transports[3]	10	16	17	17

Source: SIPRI, 1985, p. 352.

[1] The figure for production includes imports.
[2] Artillery over 100-mm. calibre.
[3] Both civilian and military.

about major political gains. Egypt and Somalia have both, for various reasons, ejected the Soviet Union, and in less dramatic vein, India has maintained its diplomatic distance from the USSR, despite its favoured treatments and along with Syria buys armaments from other sources.

Sales are often part of a total package which requires the Soviet Union to incur maintenance and training costs for officers and men in recipient countries, and as the technological level of armaments increases, this component becomes increasingly important to recipients. Up to 19 500 foreign officers were being trained in the Soviet Union in 1981, while over 11 000 Soviet advisers and technicians were working in Third World countries.

The military aid burden is shared by the East European allies. The GDR has offered military aid mainly in the form of military training and advising, and has supported Soviet activities in a number of countries. The major arms exporters are Czechoslovakia and, to a lesser extent, Poland, both of which, like the Soviet Union itself, have sought armaments exports as profitable alternatives to waning civilian industrial exports, and are actively pursuing more commercially oriented policies. In Czechoslovakia, armaments currently account for 5 per cent of all exports, more than 40 per cent of which are sold to non-Warsaw Pact countries.

The East Europeans also assist with training and advising duties. In 1983, 2655 Europeans military personnel were working in the less developed countries, compared with 17 525 Russians, and after 1971 they agreed to coordinate the training of Third World officers. Artillery and tank training is largely carried out in Czechoslovakia, air reconnaissance in the GDR, pilot and parachute training in Poland, and infantry in Hungary,[66] but most Third World personnel train in the USSR, which alone provided a comprehensive range of training facilities.

In recent years Soviet exports, though still absolutely large, have lost their initial momentum, both agreements and deliveries having fallen from previously achieved peak levels. In 1979, the Soviets signed 110 agreements with less developed countries, of which 65 per cent were for new weapons. In 1982, the number of new agreements fell to forty, and only 50 per cent were for new weapons. In 1984 the value of exports fell by almost 40 per cent to $2532m., from $4172m. the previous year, and in 1985 by a further 30 per cent.[67] This may possibly be due to market saturation as countries, having completed major procurement programmes, pause to assimilate the new weapons into their inventories. The more likely explanation is economic.[68] The fall in oil prices and Third World debt created a powerful constraint on demand. For Third World countries as a whole, arms related debts account for up to 25 per cent of the accumulated total.[69]

More significant perhaps is the declining Soviet share of the declining total. What was described as a commercial duopoly in which the USA and the USSR accounted for over 70 per cent of world trade, has become a more complex polypolistic market.[70] In 1980 the USA and the USSR accounted for 80 per cent of world sales. By 1984 this had fallen to 62 per cent. New producers, induced by the possibility of high sales in expanding markets in an otherwise faltering trading economy, having invested in production facilities, sought to maximise return by aggressive export sales. Not only traditional exporters such as France and Czechoslovakia, but intermediate level countries such as Spain and Israel and Third World producers themselves, such as Brazil and India, have all emerged as armaments exporters of growing importance. An increase in the number of producers would of itself lead to a statistical expectation that the market shares of the two leading oligopolists would fall, and the Soviet share has declined very substantially, from 50 per cent in 1980, to 24 per cent in 1985.[71]

It is possible that Soviet customers have completed procurement cycles, and its major markets are temporarily saturated, which appears to be the case with Libya, for instance. It is a cost of the high degree of export dependence on a small number of countries which has been the Soviet pattern, that stocking or procurement decisions by a few countries will have a disproportionate cyclical impact on export flows. If this is the case, the decline may be temporary, and in the meantime, the Soviet Union has sought to diversify its market by seeking new customers, for instance the $300 m. agreement with Kuwait in 1986.

However, the decline from $41 bn to $25 bn is far greater than may reasonably be explained as a procurement cycle, and probably reflects a more fundamental restructuring of the international armaments trade. Soviet arms are generally of a lower technical quality than those produced by the USA, and may therefore be more vulnerable to competition from the second echelon of exporters. French Mirage fighters are obviously perceived as offering a similar range of performance parameters to Soviet MIG's in Iran, India, and possibly other countries, and if the second-level producers seek to increase their market shares by initiating Soviet tactics of aggressive marketing, the new competition may be at the expense of the USSR.[72] It is unlikely that the smaller producers can compete with the two giants in R&D or the most advanced weapons, and the changing pattern of international competition will tend to push the Soviet Union at the margin to compete more aggressively at the high technology end of the arms spectrum, which might bring it into more direct competition with the USA, and in which it has a comparative disadvantage. Evidence from the war in Lebanon has led to some speculation that advanced Soviet equipment may be inferior to that from the USA, though comparison of battle effectiveness cannot exclude personnel performance, etc. The real explanation is probably a complex admixture of each, and the picture is in any case not a consistent one, for the export ratios of some important weapons categories have increased.

It is also the case that with few exceptions the Soviets have been unwilling to export military technology. Third World countries are demanding a greater share of the economic benefits of military production in the form of commercial and industrial offset agreements[73] and Soviet sensitivity to technology transfer may have to be modified if it is to regain its share of the world market.

Despite its comparative lack of industrialisation, Russia had, before the First World War, established a wide ranging armaments industry which provided the physical and human capital base for expansion in the 1920s and 1930s. Nevertheless, in military as in industrial terms, the Soviet Union lagged technologically behind the advanced Western nations, and chose to pursue a perfectly rational policy of substituting foreign arms and technology for basic research to supplement its own burgeoning industry. Although imports made an immediate contribution to its military capability, the Soviet objective from the outset was to use foreign technology as a means of reducing the economic costs of establishing its own indigenous technological capacity.[74] In the long-run the Soviet Union aimed to make itself as independent as possible of countries which were often unsympathetic to its very existence. The utility of Western assistance varied with the level of weapon sophistication, generally greater in the technologically more advanced armaments such as aero-engines,[75] where domestic engineers had particular difficulty in designing and building weapons to match those available to Western armies.

Soviet strategic precepts differed from those then fashionable in the West, requiring large quantities of comparatively simple but sturdy weapons. Western weapons or licences when acquired were "Sovietised" to reduce or simplify the operating parameters and make them compatible with the philosophy of evolutionary design, the stock of indigenous weapons and the skill level of the armed forces. Western technological assistance made valuable contributions to Soviet military progress, especially in reducing the cost of the most advanced weapons, and the speed with which they were deployed. Even in this period it should not be overstated, for indigenous designers and engineers made genuine contributions to Soviet military technology.

During the Cold War, the military relations between East and West became altogether simpler, for no country deliberately seeks to increase the military potential of its enemy. The American Export Administration Act prohibited sale of equipment which added to the military and economic potential of the enemy, and Western policy on export of military sensitive material was coordinated internationally via the Paris based Coordinating Committee (COCOM).

As the technological follower, the Soviet Union would have most to gain from international trade and it is a matter of some importance to establish how far the Soviet Union has been able to circumvent the embargo, and as a consequence the contribution which Western military technology made to the Soviet build up in the post-war period. Spokesmen for the American defence community argue that both have been and remain substantial. The Soviet Union has been able to import technology for every major industry engaged in research, development and production of weapon systems.[76] Academic economists tend to be on the whole more sceptical about the utility of the technology to the Soviet Union.[77]

Since the early 1930s, the Soviet Union has financed a large legal and clandestine programme to acquire Western technology. Several thousand technology collection officers, under the guise of diplomats, jounalists, etc., are coordinated by the State Committee for Science and Technology constantly to seek out militarily useful technologies to import by legal, semi-legal and wholly clandestine means into the USSR.[78] Since 1972 the programme has been stepped up and reorganized under the political guidance of a Central Committee secretary. So effective has the programme been[79] that American officials claim that up to 70 per cent of militarily useful or related technologies obtained from the West have been acquired by Soviet and East European intelligence agencies, dummy corporations etc., using clandestine collection techniques, leading to what some claim to be a 'haemorrhage' of American technology.[80] Soviet agencies are alleged to have bought, piece by piece over a three to four year period, an entire electronic integrated circuit manufacturing line, which had a primarily military function,[81] and they have acquired prescribed technology in the fields of computers, microelectronics, signal processing lasers etc.[82]

Assesing the contribution of such imports to Soviet military capability is however more difficult. The most notorious instance of alleged direct military assistance usually singled out by those who seek to tighten export restrictions, was the legal purchase in 1972 of 164 precision ball-bearing grinders from the Bryant Grinder Corporation. The Soviets had for ten years sought to buy bearing grinders with a higher degree of precision than available from domestic producers. In that year, following looser export control guidelines, the machines were eventually sold to the Soviet Union, and within a few years the Soviet Union began deploying a new generation of ICBMs up to ten times as accurate as their predecessors and capable of carrying multiple warheads. American security officials have implied that the imported grinders alone could have provided the precision inertial navigation systems which led directly to the deployment of the MIRV.[83] A careful analysis suggests that the imported American machines were not crucial for the development of Soviet MIRV missiles. They probably arrived too late to be decisive,[84] for the military research cycle, especially of weapons systems that show such dramatic improvements, is far longer than the few years which elapsed between procurement and deployment of the MIRV's. More advanced grinders were in any case available from Japan and Europe, and domestic manufacturers who produced lower quality but serviceable bearings could have produced higher precision bearings if they were so crucial to MIRV development. Imported machines obviously did contribute to Soviet military progress, mainly by economising on time and resources, but were unlikely to be decisive.

It is in any case highly unlikely that Soviet military planners would allow themselves to become dependent on imports of foreign technology in such a vital area of East–West competition, where legal trade is ever threatened by embargo, and the results of clandestine procedures so unpredictable. The defence industry is well funded and well staffed, though perhaps less innovative because of systemic inhibitions, and has shown itself to be capable of first rate scientific and engineering work. It is also likely that since, by and large, Soviet forces are, partly by design, technologically less well equipped than their American counterparts, importation of a single advanced piece of equipment, licence or know-how, legally or otherwise, will not be decisive. Modern weapons systems draw from a large array of scientific and engineering building blocks and it is the coordination of different inputs that provides the real basis for technological advance, especially since the Soviet Union usually 'Sovietises' Western equipment to its own operating parameters, a process which in itself suggests a high degree of indigenous skill and know-how. Soviet scientists and engineers are well able to design and produce one-off prototype machines of the highest quality. The bigger problem for planners is to improve the rate of diffusion throughout the appropriate branches.[85]

More useful than high profile examples, such as the Bryant grinders, is the slow and gradual accretion of information, often from sources such as scientific or trade journals, exchange visits by scientists, etc. This is especially the case in dual use technology where the distinction between civilian and military employment becomes less valid, and which makes it more difficult to forecast the likely military usefulness of technological progress which originates in the civilian sector. American defence officials argue that there are no military significant technologies which do not also have a peaceful use and are therefore more difficult to proscribe. The Soviet Union has been able to exploit Western difference on the appropriate degree of embargo, the benefits of which are applied first in the defence sector.

Soviet security precepts have always been predicated on the assumption that industrial strength, is a necessary prerequisite for military might. Policies to increase one must necessarily impinge on the other. In the early post-war period, the American Export Administration Act prohibited the export of goods and technology which added to the military and economic potential of the enemy. In 1969, the Act was modified to prohibit exports which added only to the military potential of the enemy, a narrower form of control, and by its very nature, more difficult to ascertain.

All imports add to the economic and hence, if only indirectly, the military potential of the country, for as Khrushchev remarked, 'imported buttons can be used to hold up soldiers' trousers'.[86] It is probably the case, however, that imports most likely to be immediately useful are those of machinery and equipment.

Following the narrower interpretation of prohibited exports after 1969, imports of machinery and equipment into the Soviet Union grew rapidly, at an annual average rate of 17 per cent, to a peak of $7200m. in 1981.[87] Even when, in absolute terms, they were largest, they failed to account for more than a small proportion of domestic investment, and never exceeded 10 per cent of total imports. Moreover, a high proportion was allocated to sectors where their military potential was almost certainly low. During the 1970s most foreign capital was invested in the chemical, timber and energy industries, and though military application of, for instance, synthetic rubber was not insubstantial, the objective was most likely to increase the domestic capital base and the nation's exporting capacity. Imports destined for the automotive industry are more borderline. Trucks have military as well as civilian functions, and though technical specifications differ, it is not difficult to substitute one function for another.

It has been alleged in support of firmer controls on economic exports that trucks made at the Kama River plant produced partly by Western capital have been used in the Afghanistan War.[88]

Even though the absolute quantity of imports each year was comparatively small, their marginal contribution to economic potential might still transcend their absolute value, if they were concentrated in particular products where the indigenous lag was especially severe, such as the electronics and computer industries, to relieve bottle-necks, or to complement domestic resources which might otherwise be underemployed. Given the Soviet Union's inability to compete effectively in international civilian manufactured goods markets, imports of civilian machinery and equipment releases industrial machinery for the manufacture of weapons in the export of which the Soviet Union is competitive. Machine imports, therefore, facilitate a degree of industrial specialisation which does increase economic and military potential.[89] Comparison of the marginal efficiency of Western imports and domestic capital depend as always on the nature of the assumptions and on the economic model. A reasoned assessment of the data suggests that even though foreign capital tends to be less effectively utilised in the Soviet Union than in the country of origin, it does add more to economic potential than an equivalent quantity of indigenous capital.[90] It is also likely that since the barriers to innovation are lower in the military sector, the technology embodied in Western imports will be more effectively used than in the civilian branches. Foreign capital has made an important supplementary contribution to Soviet economic, and hence military, potential, but is unlikely to have been decisive.

In 1559 King Sigismund Augustus of Poland wrote to Queen Elizabeth I of England that 'the Muscovite, enemy to all liberty under the sun daily grow[s] mightier by the increase of such things as be brought to the Narve, not only wares but also arts . . . by means whereof he makes himself strong to vanquish all others. . . . We seemed hithertoo to vanquish him only in this, that he was rude of arts. If be that this navigation continue what shall be unknown to him . . . We do foresee the Muscovite made more perfect in warlike affairs with engines of war . . . will make assault this way on Christendom to slay or bound all that shall withstand him.' Little, it seems, has changed.[91]

7 Conclusion and Speculation

Michail Gorbachev has characterised the current decade as critical for Soviet economic develpment,[1] an assessment with which most Western[2] and at least some Soviet[3] economists would concur. (It is, of course, a crude approximation to label economists as being either Western or Soviet, but it is, however, acceptable to the task at hand.) There is also a degree of agreement that the underlying cause of the long-term trend in the growth indices is the increasing inappropriateness of the extensive growth strategy to an economy constrained by factor scarcity and low productivity, and a society seeking a range of qualitative and often conflicting objectives.[4] Such agreement as exists, however, breaks down over what each side perceives to be the appropriate solutions, and the likely outcome of the array of policy measures which may be conveniently described as the Gorbachev modernisation programme, and which delineate the broad outlines of the Soviet response to the economic crisis.

The official Soviet view, not unexpectedly, is that the planning model in being since the 1930s is sufficiently flexible, especially if motivated by a vigorous political leadership, to achieve the degree of intensification which alone can resolve the economic contradictions.[5] The Draft Guidelines for 1990 and beyond reflect this optimism, and though growth indices are modest compared with the high rates achieved in earlier plan periods, the leadership is confident of attaining the major civilian and military objectives. Western economists are less sanguine about the appropriateness of the policy and the eventual outcome. The underlying structural and systemic obstacles to higher growth remain in place,[6] and energetic leadership exemplified by the current government is of itself unlikely to make the fundamental breakthrough to higher growth and productivity.

The disagreement between East and West also extends to the contribution of high defence spending to the economic record. Soviet leaders are certainly not unaware of the adverse consequences to economic welfare of the voracious demands of what Khrushchev called the steel eaters, and in his defence of the 18 per cent decrease in budgetary military spending in 1985, the Finance Minister argued that reduced military spending would release resources which could be used for the collective good of the people.[7] Nevertheless, there exists in the public domain no systematic analysis of the economic consequences, adverse or otherwise, of the sustained material and organisational investment in the military base and of the precise nature and degree of benefit which would accrue if it were held in check.

In most Western assessments of recent Soviet economic history there is a general belief that 'the growth of defence is one of the most important reasons why Soviet economic growth has declined in the last decade'.[8] Therefore, the distribution of the now more constrained economic resources between military and civilian investment and consumption assumes great importance for Western economists, and is one of the most critical policy choices facing Soviet leaders.[9] Economic outcomes cannot be adequately assessed independently of the military allocation, but by the same token military outcomes can no longer be considered independently of the economic environment. In February 1983, the USSR Deputy Minister of Defence for Armaments argued that the strengthening of the country's defence capabilities could be achieved 'only on the basis of a highly developed economy'.[10]

Econometric investigation of the defence burden points up the quantitative trade-off between the civilian and the military objectives, given appropriate assumptions,[11] the essential nature of which are likely to remain into the foreseeable future. The convergence of economic constraints during the eleventh Five Year Plan make it clear that though one variable may always be increased at the expense of the other, the simultaneous attainment of both civilian and military objectives will be more difficult than in the 1970s.[12] Growth over time is, of course, not independent of the allocation at a point in time, but since Soviet leaders have only bounded freedom, leadership choices in the short period are severely circumscribed. Based on production capacity already in place and known plans for Soviet force expansion and modernisation, military spending is predicted to increase by around 3 per cent p. a.[13] Long-term economic growth has also been forecasted to expand at about the same rate.[14] Although economic forecasting is always hazardous and hedged about with uncertainty, these projections show the economy to be finely poised between crisis and comfort. The ultimate outcome will depend on the objective environment and on the subjective evaluation by planners and leaders of alternative policy and resource options.

Conclusion and Speculation

During the 1970s the labour supply grew at an annual rate of 6.5 per cent, giving a net decade increment of 19 million to the labour force. During the current decade the labour supply will grow at only 0.6 per cent, yielding a ten-year increase of only 1 million.[15] In the absence of endogenously embodied technological progress, such a slow rate of labour increase must reduce the efficiency of capital investment. Investment in the Draft Guidelines is planned to increase at a surprisingly modest 3 to 4 per cent p.a. and if Soviet targets are to be attained, productivity must increase to more than compensate for adverse factor trends. Factor productivity is not only low but fell throughout the last decade,[16] reflecting the systemic and structurally determined inefficiencies in the economic system, aggravated by the declining vigour of the last years of Brezhnev. Soviet projections are based on the assumption that productivity can and will be improved to equalise the world's best indices.[17] Higher productivity has a twofold effect on economic activity: it increases the effective supply of labour, and makes profitable a larger quantity of investment than might otherwise have been the case.

Recent productivity performance has been mixed. The attempt by the authorities to regain control of investment associated with the reduction in its rate of expansion in 1976 has been at best modestly successful. Capital construction remains inefficient by the most advanced standards. The ratio of unfinished capital construction has at best improved only marginally, and may even have declined. Retirement rates and the depreciation ratio have not increased to any substantial degree and the average age of the capital stock has not fallen significantly.[18] Although the percentage of world standard goods has increased, a high proportion of these are little more than cosmetic improvements, and the introduction of real improvements has fallen below the rate attained in the last decade.[19] Finally, despite the exhortation of planners, the economy's energy intensity has worsened rather than improved in the wake of adverse price and cost movements. Oil production has peaked and despite the Food Programme agricultural output in the last ten years has not increased.

On the other hand, there have been some improvements to encourage the Soviet planners. Specific bottle-necks, which were partly responsible for the exceptionally poor performance at the turn of the decade, have been overcome. Coal production, which had fallen each year since 1976 showed a turnaround of 22m. tons in 1983, has been sustained since. Similarly, freight turnover has been particularly responsive to the disciplinary campaigns, and has shown improved figures of 2.9 per cent growth p.a. since 1982. Soviet official statistics indicate that 93 per cent of the increased output in the economy in 1985 was obtained by higher labour productivity, which in 1984 grew by around 3.8 per cent[20] in excess of that obtained in the earlier plan periods, and the Draft Guidelines plan for all the increase in output to 1990 to be obtained from this source. The eventual productivity outcome will have a decisive effect on economic potential, the overall pace of expansion, the rate at which civilian can be exchanged for military goods, and the subjective evaluation by Soviet leadership of the different potential arrays of civilian and military final outputs.

The discipline campaign which was begun by Andropov has been even more vigorously pursued by Gorbachev, who has assembled a team of like-minded officials such as Aliev, Shevernadze and Ligachev, who established their reputation by clearing corruption in their own Republics, and who seem intent in pursuing the discipline campaign with vigour. The outcome so far has been favourable. Production and productivity in a number of sectors has increased in direct consequence of the campaigns. The favourable consequences of discipline campaigns are generally short-lived however,[21] and they do not alone provide an appropriate basis for economic resurgence. For Gorbachev, the key to his objective of shifting the economy to higher growth is the intensification of production.[22] Improvement of the economic mechanism, and possible easement of the labour constraint by fairly modest reforms of the Shchekino type should not be underestimated. Productivity levels in Soviet industry at the moment are about 50 per cent of those achieved in American industry, which though indicative of low efficiency, also offers a high potential for improvement if they can be released through proper motivation.

The centrepiece of the Gorbachev programme is the modernisation of the economy, which means reducing the average age and increasing the overall quality of the capital stock.[23] Special emphasis is given to machine building and to the machine tool branches of the economy, which have replaced energy and agriculture as the key resource claimant.[24] Recent statistics show extraordinary growth in the machine building and machine tool industries, far surpassing that achieved in the economy. In 1984, production of machines increased by an average rate of 29 per cent p.a. The quantity of machine production is an inadequate index, however, for the Soviet Union already has the world's largest machine inventory. Qualitative indices are equally important. Expansion of the top quality machine tools, those which are mechanically controlled and capable of working at

Conclusion and Speculation 183

more than two axes increased by fully 28 per cent.[25] Nor is this pace predicted to slack, at least for the short period, for the 1986 plan called for an enormous 30 per cent increase in machine production, though that rate is unlikely to be sustained to the end of the decade. The draft programme identifies machine building for top priority development, especially the technologically most advanced machines such as computers, instrument building, electrical and electronic output.[26] High quality machinery cannot be expanded independently of material and human inputs. The plan for the MBMW sector also requires a corresponding increase in high quality steel which, however remains in short supply. It will also require skilled workmen to produce and operate the machinery. One Soviet report argues that skilled machinists capable of working to the necessary fine tolerances are already 50 per cent below the machine stock.

In view of the importance of investment for improved productivity, it is somewhat surprising that, despite the enormous demands made by the metal-working and energy branches, total investment is to increase over the plan period by only 3.5 to 4 per cent p.a. The bulk of the increased productivity presumably is to be disembodied via improvements in the economic mechanism or improved discipline, a most optimistic assumption in view of previous performance.

The comparatively low rate of investment is not a matter of choice but is partly a consequence of low growth in previous periods and also of competing demands for resources. If intensive production is to be achieved, an adequate supply of consumption goods must be available to induce higher productivity. The high incidence of absenteeism, labour turnover and drunkenness on the job, plus the large overhang of personal savings, give some circumstantial support to the view that the quality of living standards have a detrimental effect on output.[27] High productivity countries are normally characterised by high wages and living standards. Soviet planners have acknowledged this by allocating a growing proportion of the nation's income to improving economic welfare. The Draft Guidelines proclaim the improvement in the material living conditions as top priority, and plan category B consumer goods to increase faster, though marginally, than category A goods. Although Gorbachev has warned Soviet citizens that the fruits of the current programmes cannot be enjoyed until the 1990s, the planners clearly cannot take too many resources away from meeting consumer expectations without undermining the entire intensification strategy even though recent performance has been disappointing.

A key area of competition for resources between the civilian and military sectors is for the output of the capital MBMW sector. One disputed[28] source estimates that at the margin 60 per cent of the new machinery may be allocated for defence purposes,[29] but a figure of 40 per cent or so has a wider degree of credence. The modernisation programme must intensify that competition, the conflicting demands of which have not been fully resolved. On the one hand, civilian machinery is planned to increase by fully 30 per cent in 1985–6; on the other hand, the pattern of machine production is such as to suggest continuing priority for military purposes.

Current data show that in 1985 between 15 and 17 per cent of the nation's resources is directly allocated for military production. The revised CIA estimates, which showed a static trend in procurement since 1976, with which the DIA partly agrees, casts doubt on the hypothesis of more or less automatic access to whatever resources the defence sector wanted. This was ever an exaggeration,[30] but the sustained slowdown in military growth requires a reassessment of the sector's relative importance in the hierarchy of Soviet objectives. CIA analysts had anticipated a slowdown around 1976 or so following a completed procurement cycle. Normally a cycle of low procurement growth lasts a few years, to be followed by a period of higher than average growth, for the Soviet principle of the follow-on is designed to ensure continuous use of the fixed and human capital. Thus, though the secular trend may not have begun till 1980 or so, a ten-year down-phase of the procurement cycle clearly represents a new phase in civilian–military economic relations.

A possible explanation may be found in the exact timing of the trend, and in the distribution of contracting and expanding weapons systems, for, though on average the trend was steady, production of some weapons increased, while others decreased. This relative tendency cannot be simply explained as stretch-outs of technologically advanced projects, for some of the weapons, production of which did increase over the period, were quite as sophisticated as others which were decreased.[31] The combination of timing plus distribution may reflect deliberate policy decisions by Soviet leaders. Information on deployment of new weapons into the armed forces offers useful supplementary evidence to that of production, a high but variable and imprecisely known proportion of which is destined for stock and for exports. Western analysts know little about the quantitative parameters of the Soviet research, production and deployment cycle, but if it is assumed not to depart too far from the American pattern, it takes on average about ten years or so to bring a major weapons system to the stage of force deployment. On the one hand, the period may be shorter because the Soviets employ at each stage more resources than the Americans, and tend to produce weapons incorporating smaller design and engineering progression. On the other hand, they produce a larger array of weapons, they are in general lower on the learning curve, and as the overall complexity of new weapons increases exponentially the technological constraint may be more binding. If the cycle is indeed about that length of time, decisions on the production of the weapons deployed in the mid 1970s might have been made about 1970 or so, possibly in conjunction with the ninth five Year Plan. Analysis of deployment patterns shows that by far the greatest reductions were concentrated in strategic nuclear weapons. The Soviets had completed by the end of the 1960s a major deployment of strategic nuclear missiles, to be followed by a programme of investment in defensive and theatre weapons. Although the dates do not exactly coincide, it is possible that the decision on the deployment of strategic missiles coincided with a change in emphasis in Soviet strategic thinking. The evidence is inferential and not publicly available till later, but it is likely that the internal debate will have been completed before the Brezhnev speech in 1977, which argued that the Soviet emphasis must switch to preventing war by increasing the deployment of high technology conventional weapons.[32] This strategic view, associated with the then Chief of the General Staff, Ogarkoff, reduces the relative importance of strategic offensive weapons in the Soviet armoury. In this case, the slowdown in military growth was a strategic policy-induced decision. It was this which made the Soviet Union amenable to arms limitation agreements with the USA, and the procurement slowdown is largely concentrated in those weapons systems which were within SALT I and II guidelines.[33] The Pentagon however does not agree with this analysis of a policy determined de-emphasis of strategic offensive weapons.[34]

A change in emphasis between theatre and strategic weapons in any case only explains relative distribution; it does not of itself explain why total procurement growth was so considerably reduced after 1976. Deployed weapons fell in some instances by as much as 54 per cent below the ceilings agreed at SALT.[35] Our understanding of the Soviet military leadership does not suggest that it would voluntarily accede to a level of deployment lower than that allowable by military or political factors,[36] and it might have been anticipated that lower spending on strategic weapons might have been compensated by higher spending elsewhere. Retooling for a different production mix might have explained a temporary down-phase of the procurement cycle, but not one lasting ten years or so. Voluntary reduction on the scale indicated is also inconsistent with known trends in other components of military spending, such as military construction, operations and maintenance, and military R&D. Thus, while the voluntary element may not have been entirely absent, it is most likely that the reduction in procurement was forced upon the leadership by technological or economic problems which had mounted during the tenth Five Year Plan.

The slowdown in the quantity of nuclear weapons deployed was offset to a (unquantifiable) degree by a comprehensive programme of weapons modernisation. Despite the traditional Soviet policy of evolutionary progress, which keeps technological change within the ambit of intellectual competence, the range of its modernisation programme after 1972 which gave a high profile to expanding automated control systems, computerisation and enhanced use of more sophisticated structural materials and signal reducing technology stretched Soviet technological resources to the limit. New weapons, incorporating more advanced technology, included bomber and fighter aircraft, helicopters, missile systems, surface ships and submarines, and AWACS type early warning system.[37] Advanced weapons cannot be produced without also upgrading plant and machinery. Soviet problems are not that they technologically cannot produce the most advanced weapons; history shows that not to be the case, but that they do not possess the array of scientific and economic resources to research, develop and to produce over the entire range of existing, modified and new in principle weapons. To accommodate the strain, procurement cycles were stretched out, with deployment of some weapons systems being postponed. The new battle tank and large surface ships, incorporating the most advanced weaponry and electronics, appear to be behind schedule.[38] If more resources were available, the stretch-outs could have been reduced, for military producers can always trade time against cost. It is also possible that, because of reduced American spending in the Ford and Carter administrations, military planners were more sanguine about the security implications of the stretch-outs.[39]

Part of the explanation, however, is economic, for shortages in the military sector were matched by an equally tight resource constraint in the civilian economy at large. The coincidence of military and

Table 7.1 Soviet GNP and defence growth rate in real terms

	1966–76	1976–81
GNP growth	3.9	2.2
Total defence activities	4.5	2.0

Source: *Soviet Defence Trends*: A Staff Study prepared for the Subcommittee on International Trade, Finance and Security Economics, Joint Economic Committee of the Congress of the US, 1983 (Washington, DC.) p. 19.

civilian slowdown during the tenth Five Year Plan is unlikely to have been accidental. Lower growth was in all likelihood forced upon the military as a political solution to economic shortage, which was initially anticipated to be temporary but in fact became extended. The long relationship between the military and economic growth is reflected in Table 7.1.

In addition to chronic systemic and structural deficiencies, 1976–82 was characterised by specific bottle-necks which had a directly adverse impact on procurement. Shortages of high quality steels held back production of machines, and transportation bottle-necks reduced freight turnover. New priority sectors such as gas and agriculture absorbed much of the additional resources. The continuing essentially static trend of procurement after the bottle-necks were overcome suggests a more deep-rooted political problem of matching slow growing supply to a more insistent demand.

If indeed the slowdown was not one of choice, but imposed by technological or economic factors inside and outside the defence sector, the consequence may be more than a readjustment of the short-run military balance, important though that may be. If the delay was essentially technological in origin, it indicates that the Soviet Union is less able to insulate the defence sector from the inefficiencies of the civilian economy than might once have been imagined. The insulating devices have always been partial, but as protean science becomes a more all-embracing input into military production, the barriers between the civilian and military technological sectors become more inhibiting to both. Even this might have been accommodated, however, if the defence industries had been able to claim resources to compensate for the technological shortcomings. The fact that they have been unable to do so, or at least to compensate sufficiently, and that they have been obliged to bear a proportionate share of the burden suggests that the status of the military may not be as inviolable to economic constraint as has been generally considered.[40] The Brezhnev style of consensus required the burden of low growth to be shouldered more or less equitably between the competing sectors.[41] In a widely reported speech to army officers, he reassured them that the military would obtain the resources it needed, the implication being that need would be interpreted by the political, rather than the military, leadership.[42] Such a political solution was feasible in the short run only, for a number of factors, barely under control, makes this an unlikely permanent solution. The utility of defence spending depends not only on the quantity and the evaluation of domestic consumption foregone, but also on the absolute degree of security a given array of military goods provides. It is not independent of the size, growth and quality of the stock of weapons deployed by the USA in particular or NATO in general. It is also affected by the pace of technological progress in the USA, for the Soviet Union cannot lag too far behind the USA. A political compromise within a slow-growing total could leave the Soviet Union vulnerable to an absolute weapons gap which its leaders may eventually find intolerable.

Increasing domestic economic constraints have coincided with a more forbidding external environment. After a period of slow growth during the 1970s defence spending under the Reagan administration attained a high priority once more in the USA, and since 1980 spending has grown at 8 per cent p.a., though down from the 12 per cent of the first Administration. Since this coincided with the comparative decline in the growth of Soviet military spending, the defence ratio between the two countries has become adverse to the Soviet Union.[43] A comparison of NATO with the Warsaw Pact makes the ratios even more unfavourable. Moreover, up to 25 per cent of Soviet defence expenditure is for the Chinese front, though all weapons are ultimately mobile. American military competition has shifted to high technology areas, where the Soviet Union has the greatest comparative disadvantage. The introduction into Europe of intermediate range nuclear systems poses especial problems for Soviet defensive deployment. Western armies have upgraded the performance characteristics of a number of weapons, and American research on the Strategic Defence Initiative clearly worries Soviet leaders that they may be pushed to a new technological race they prefer to avoid. Though it is also the case that if they were provoked to match the American research effort, the Soviet style, conducive to managing large programmes, gives a higher probability of successful outcome than the USA.[44]

Conclusion and Speculation

The Reagan administration has also made a determined effort to increase the cost to the USSR of obtaining from the West machines and equipment which may directly or indirectly assist the military effort.[45] This is an area of East West relation over which there exists a degree of disagreement between the USA and its Western allies. Certainly President Reagan and his defence and intelligence officials have campaigned mightily to tighten COCOM procedures and to a degree have succeeded, even at the cost of diplomatic rifts with America's allies.

The more hostile external military environment coincided with an equally adverse international economic environment. The Soviet Union remains disproportionately dependent on exports of energy and raw material for its hard currency earning. Gold prices fluctuate in response to the state of international monetary confidence, but has, in general held its price, and in 1981 brought in 2.7 billion dollars of export revenue.[46] The price of raw materials such as timber products have been affected by the long period of relative stagnation in the capitalist world but the most volatile commodity has been that of petroleum, which was for a number of years kept high by a combination of economic circumstances and restrictive practices. In 1986, however, the OPEC cartel lost its control of the oil market and prices fell to, at one time, below 10 dollars a barrel. Falling oil prices are estimated to have cost the Soviet Union over 3.5 billion dollars in hard currency in 1984.[47] The decline in oil earnings coincided with the fall in arms exports by around 30 per cent. In view of the comparatively small role which international trade, especially with the capitalist nations, plays in the wealth creating process, the external sector is unlikely to be decisive, but it is far from incidental. Restrictions on imports due to currency constraints will be increasingly costly if the Soviet Union fails to meet its targets to produce the crucial high quality machinery. The balance of payments will also be affected by the amount of foreign currency required for food inputs, and the quantity and the terms of its East European trade.

In 1985, the US Department of Defence predicted a surge of military procurement, but the evidence is insufficient to indicate whether it is the start of another procurement cycle or a new long-term trend. Even though procurement has slowed since 1976, the other components of defence spending continue to grow at long-term trend rates; R&D growing at an annual average rate of 4 to 5 per cent, and Operations and Maintenance by 4 per cent p.a. The expansion of military construction and investment at around 3 per cent p.a. means that much of the plant and machinery required for the next upward phase of the procurement cycle is already in place,[48] and competition for construction and metal-working machinery with the civilian branches will be eased. That for raw materials and for skilled manpower remains intense, and within a few years investment for the next upward phase of the cycle for the generation of weapons which will be brought into service in the 1990s must once again intensify competition.[49] The modernisation programme may already be compromised if Soviet planners keep to the target of increasing investment at only 3.5 to 4 per cent p.a., for flexibility in reducing *per capita* consumption growth is limited if the leadership is to avoid political instability.[50] Gorbachev has emphasised the need for higher pay, but without quality goods in regular supply, that may serve to reduce rather than increase economic incentive and morale.

In the absence of major unforeseen circumstances, the current balance of forces is likely to remain much as it is. On the one hand, the comprehensive modernisation of its strategic and its defensive forces, by the 1990s, will sustain a high demand for investment in construction, equipment and R&D. On the other hand, there are strong reasons why the defence share is unlikely to increase very significantly. It is already large by world standards and the room for additional squeeze on the civilian community is limited. Moreover the representatives of the civilian sectors are better placed to resist military claims and to press their own than has traditionally been the case. Gorbachev's programme to modernise the economy gives the key civilian sectors a political clout they have long lacked. The military defence establishment has traditionally been uniquely placed to maximise its claims to economic resources via non-Ministerial organisations with direct access to the highest decision-making organs of Party and State. This was not accidental, but reflected the priority traditionally accorded to defence production. A more complex pattern of military civilian priorities has been marked by organisational changes in the key civilian sectors which appear to have been deliberately designed to replicate the Military Defence Council.[51] The creation of special commissions under the aegis of the Council of Ministers, at the apex of government, should constrain the privileged status of the military as the civilians compete more effectively for State and Party backing. In 1981, a Commission on the West Siberian Oil and Gas complex was created under the USSR Council of Ministers Presidium, and an associated inter-agency regional Commission located in Tyumen has been established under GOSPLAN. In 1985, the Politburo gave its approval to the creation of a super ministry in the machine tool industry – the Coordinating Bureau for Machine Tools, which has been given wide-ranging powers to coordinate planning in this key branch. In 1986, the Central Committee announced the creation of a Union-Republic Agro-Industrial Committee (GOSAGROPROM), which has taken over the entire responsibilities of six agricultural ministries, in addition to some of those not completely in the agricultural sector. The Agro-Industrial Committee is to carry out its duties under the immediate direction of the Council of Ministers, the chairman being a Vice-Chairman of the USSR Council of Ministers.

Administrative reorganisation does not, of itself, give political power, but it is unlikely that the Soviets would have departed from the traditional model without good reason, and it cannot be accidental that the first super-ministries are located in the energy, agriculture and machine tool branches. The new industrial strategy was worked out under the direction of Mr Nikolai Rhyzkov, who has since been promoted to Chairman of the Council of Ministers and thus well placed to ensure that the super-ministries perform the tasks for which they were created. New organisations create new opportunities for political alliances especially amongst a generation of managers and officials, who have progressed outside the traditional heavy industry track, and who may identify less with the defence establishment than has customarily been the case.[52] The new organisations' political alignments will make it more difficult for Military-Industrial chiefs to assume priority as a matter of course. Though it is unlikely that resources will be transferred to the civilian sectors, it is equally unlikely, in the short run at least, that the military can easily expropriate resources from the civilian branches.

Military output can grow at rates roughly equivalent to the long-term norm, only if productivity is improved in the defence sector itself.[53] Intensification is as relevant to military as it is for civilian producers,[54] and potential improvement is considerable. Military output is large, and is very demanding of key economic sectors such as R&D and machine building. Although military efficiency exceeds that in the civilian branches, it is on average sufficiently far behind American best practice to offer the prospect of considerable resource savings. Western analysts have identified many practices which reduce military economic efficiency, and Soviet planners have themselves sought to introduce optimising techniques to improve weapons selection. Reforms of military production and decision-making, useful though they may be, can take the military planners only so far, however, and as the distinction between military and civilian related R&D loses its operational significance, economic reform in one sector, to the exclusion of the other, offers only partial advance.

The military industrial sector has been perhaps the greatest beneficiary of the traditional allocation model. Soviet military might has always been based on economic strength, a relationship which defence chiefs continue to emphasise. The relevant conception of economic strength has, however, changed from that appropriate for the 1930s, when quantitative parameters provided crude but effective enough criteria, to more qualitative criteria. Though the Soviet Union has the largest stock of machines in the world, fully 30 per cent of those currently produced incorporate obsolescent technical parameters.[55] Military chiefs are having to face up to the reality of choice between short- and long-term horizons and between quantitative and qualitative performance criteria. If they oppose fundamental reform, they retain a strong though perhaps diminishing political influence on economic outcomes in a slow growing and increasingly cumbersome economy, where current levels of output may be bought at the expense of diminishing potential at some future date. Some Soviet officers therefore argue that the military sector has most to gain from a fundamental reform of the economic mechanism.

If they do support the constituency for the type of basic reform which most Western observers believe necessary to resolve the contradictions of modern Soviet society, the defence chiefs may have to accept a more fundamental erosion of their traditional status as prior claimant, but in exchange for an uncertain, not immediate but potentially large improvement in economic, and hence military, potential.

Defence chiefs have so far supported the Gorbachev modernisation programme because it offers the possibility of more resources and better weapons in the future[56] for despite the rhetoric, Gorbachev's proposals for reform and reorganisation have by and large been cautious and conservative. When the full implications of military-civilian resource competition and economic reform become clear the choices which the military-economic leaders make on the various issues will in all probability have a profound impact on the welfare of Soviet citizens and on the state of international relations into the next century.

Notes and References

1 Estimating the Scale of Defence Expenditures

1. *Allocation of Resources in the Soviet Union and China, 1983*. Hearings before the Subcommittee on International Trade, Finance and Security Economics of the Joint Economic Committee, Congress of the US (Washington, DC, 1984) p. 81.
2. M. Brzoska and T. Ohlson, 'The Trade in Major Conventional Weapons'. *World Armaments and Disarmament*, SIPRI Yearbook 1985 (London: Taylor & Francis, 1985) p. 346.
3. R. Hutchings, 'Soviet Defence Spending: Towards a Reconciliation of Different Approaches', *Jahrbuch der Wirtschaft Osteuropa*, vol. 9, 1981, p. 211.
4. V. Garbuzov, *Pravda*, 18 November 1984.
5. R. Leggett and S. Rabin, 'A Note on the Meaning of the Soviet Defence Budget', *Soviet Studies*, vol. XXX, no. 4, 1978, p. 566.
6. R. Hutchings, *The Soviet Budget* (London: Macmillan, 1983) p. 128.
7. Ibid., p. 131.
8. A. Becker. *The Meaning and Measure of Soviet Military Expenditure. The Soviet Economy in a Time of Change*, Part One. A Compendium of Papers Submitted to the Joint Economic Committee, Congress of the United States (Washington, DC, 1979) p. 354.
9. A. Becker, *CIA Estimates of Soviet Military Expenditure*. Statement prepared for the Subcommittee on Oversight of the House Permanent Select Committee on Intelligence, August 1980 (Washington, DC) p. 7.
10. National Foreign Assessment Center, *A Dollar Cost Comparison of Soviet and US Defence Activities 1967–1977*. SR78 – 10002 (Washington, DC, 1980) p. 2.
11. P. Odeen, 'In Defense of the Defense Budget', *Foreign Policy*, No. 16 Fall 1974, p. 99.
12. A. Marshall, 'Estimating Soviet Defence Spending', *Survival*, vol. XVIII, no. 2, March/April 1976, p. 74.
13. National Foreign Assessment Center (1980), *A Dollar Cost Comparison*, p. 3.
14. A. Becker (1979), *The Meaning and Measure of Soviet Military Expenditure*, p. 352.
15. W. Lee, 'Soviet Defence Expenditures in the 10th FYP', *Osteuropa Wirtschaft*, volume 2, 1977, p. 274.
16. W. Lee, Evidence, in R. Huffstatter, *CIA Estimates of Soviet Defence Spending*, Hearings before the Sub-Committee on Oversight of the Permanent Select Committee on Intelligence, House of Representatives, Washington, DC, 1980, p. 22.
17. R. Hutchings (1981), 'Soviet Defence Spending', p. 225.

18. R. Legget and S. Rabin (1978), 'A Note on the Meaning of Soviet Defence Budget'.
19. D. Bond and H. Levine, *The Soviet Machinery Balance and Military Durables in the SOVMOD. Soviet Economy in the 1980s – Problems and Prospects*, Part One. Selected Papers Submitted to the Joint Economic Committee, Congress of the US (Washington, DC, 1982) p. 298.
20. M. Kaser, 'Economic Policy', in A. Brown and M. Kaser (eds) *Soviet Policy for the 1980s* (London, 1982) p. 202.
21. P. Wiles and M. Efrat, *The Economics of Soviet Arms*. Suntory International Center for Economics and Related Disciplines, London School of Economics, London, 1981.
22. P. Cockle, 'Analysing Soviet Defence Spending: The Debate in Perspective', *Survival*, vol. XX, no. 5, Sept/Oct. 1978, p. 214.
23. National Foreign Assessment Center (1980), *A Dollar Cost Comparison*, p. 1.
24. S. Rosefielde, Evidence in R. Hufstatter (1980), *CIA Estimates of Soviet Defence Spending*, p. 13.
25. *The Soviet Economy Under a New Leader*, A Report Presented to the Sub-Committee on Economic Progress, Competitiveness and Security Economics of the Joint Economic Committee, by the CIA and the DIA, 16 March 1986, Washington, DC.
26. National Foreign Assessment Center, *Soviet and US Defence Activities 1970–1979, A $ Cost Comparison*, SR-80-10005, January 1980, p. 1.
27. National Foreign Assessment Center, *Estimated Soviet Defence Spending: Trends and Prospects*, June 1978, SR-78-10121, p. 1.
28. Ibid., p. 2.
29. Ibid., p. 1.
30. Ibid., p. 3.
31. N. Nimitz, *The Structure of Soviet Outlays on R&D in 1960 and 1968*. Rand R-1207 (Santa Monica, 1974) p. vii.
32. M. Leitenberg, 'The Counterpart of Defence Industry Conversion in the United States. The USSR Economy, Defense Industry and Military Expenditure', *Journal of Peace Research*, vol. XVI, no. 3, 1979, p. 266.
33. National Foreign Assessment Center SR-80-10005 (1980) p. 4.
34. W. Lee, in R. Hufstatter (1980), *CIA Estimates of Soviet Defence Spending*, p. 22.
35. D. Burton, 'Estimating Soviet Defence Spending', *Problems of Communism*, vol. XXXII, March/April 1983, p. 87.
36. National Foreign Assessment Center SR-80-10005 (1980), p. 8. *Soviet and US Defence Activities, 1970–9*.
37. A. Becker, *Sitting on Bayonets: The Soviet Defence Burden and Moscow's Economic Dilemma*, Rand P-6908 (Santa Monica, 1983) p. 11.
38. National Foreign Assessment Center SR-80-10005 (1980), p. 2. *Soviet and US Defence Activities, 1970–9*.
39. National Foreign Assessment Center SR-78-10002 (1978) p. 5. *op. cit.*
40. C. Weinberger, Secretary of Defense, Annual Report to the Congress, Fiscal Year 1987, 5 Feb 1986, Washington, DC, p. 17.
41. National Foreign Assessment Center, *Soviet and US Defense Activities SR80–10005 1980*, p. 2.

42. C. Weinberger (1986) Annual Report to Congress, p. 18.
43. S. Rosefielde 'Economic Foundations of Soviet National Security Strategy' *Orbis*, Summer 1986, p. 320.
44. S. Rosefielde (1980), *CIA Estimates of Soviet Defence Spending*, p. 12.
45. L. Freedman, *US Intelligence and the Soviet Strategic Threat* (London: Macmillan, 1986) p. 184.
46. S. Rosefielde 'On the Interpretation of Soviet Arms Procurement. Expenditure under Conditions of Rapid Technological Progress', *Osteuropa Wirtschaft*, vol. 25, March 1980, pp. 43–4.
47. D. Jones, *Soviet Armed Forces Review Annual*. Academic International Gulf Breeze, 1982, p. 48.
48. M. Boretsky, 'Growth of Soviet Arms Technology', *Survival*, vol. XIV, no. 4, July/August, 1972.
49. P. Hanson, Review of W. Lee, *The Estimation of Soviet Defence Expenditure 1955–1975: An Unconventional Approach* (New York: Praeger, 1977) in *Soviet Studies*, vol. XXX, no. 3, 1978, p. 402.
50. *World Armaments and Disarmament*, SIPRI Year Book, 1974, (London: Taylor & Francis, 1974) pp. 191–9.
51. F. Holzman, Evidence in R. Hufstatter (1980) *CIA Estimates of Soviet Defence Spending*, p. 45.
52. F. Holzman, 'Are the Soviets Really Outspending the US on Defense?' *International Security*, vol. 4, no. 4, 1980, p. 94.
53. A. Becker (1980), *CIA Estimates*, p. 12.
54. F. Holzman (1980) 'Are the Soviets Really Outspending the US', p. 94.
55. Ibid., p. 101.
56. S. Rosefielde (1980), 'On the Interpretation of Soviet Arms Procurement', p. 44.
57. S. Rosefielde, 'Are Soviet Industrial Production Statistics Significantly Distorted by Hidden Inflation', *Journal of Comparative Economics*, vol. 5, no. 2, 1981.
58. D. Burton (1983), 'Estimating Soviet Defence Spending', p. 89.
59. Ibid., p. 89.
60. *Allocation of Resources in the Soviet Union and China*, 1983, p. 19.
61. L. Freedman (1986) *US Intelligence and the Soviet Strategic Threat*, p. 25.
62. R. Kaufman, *Soviet Defence Trends*. A Staff Study prepared for the Use of the Subcommittee on International Trade, Finance and Security Economics of the Joint Economic Committee (Washington, DC, 1983) p. 6.
63. Ibid., p. 8.
64. Ibid., p. 13.
65. A. Becker (1980), *CIA Estimates*, p. 16.
66. *Allocation of Resources in the Soviet Union and China, 1984*, Hearings Before the Sub-Committee on International Trade, Finance and Security Economics of the Joint Economic Committee, Congress of the United States, Nov 1984, Jan 1985, Washington, DC, p. 8, 135.
67. *The Soviet Economy Under a New Leader*, p. 35.
68. Ibid., p. 8.
69. F. Holzman, Evidence in R. Hufstatter, *CIA Estimates of Soviet Defence Spending*, p. 43.

70. M. Thee, 'Dynamics of the Arms Race: R&D and Disarmament', *International Social Science Journal*, vol. XXX, no. 4, 1978, p. 910.
71. C. Jacobson, 'The Soviet Military Re-appraised', *Current History*, vol. 80, no. 468, 1981, p. 308.
72. S. Rosefielde (1980), 'On the Interpretation of Soviet Arms Procurement', p. 44.
73. *Allocation of Resources in the Soviet Union and China/1984*, p. 19.
74. Ibid., p. 70.

2 Explaining Soviet Defence Spending

1. M. Harrison, *Soviet Planning in Peace and War, 1938–45*, (Cambridge: Cambridge University Press, 1985) p. 46.
2. D. Holloway, *The Soviet Union and the Arms Race* 2nd edn (New Haven, Conn.: Yale University Press, 1985) p. 7.
3. F. Blackaby et al., 'World Military Expenditures and Arms Production', *World Armaments and Disarmament*, SIPRI Year Book 1982 (London: Taylor & Francis, 1982) p. 100.
4. F. Rubin, 'The Theory and Concept of National Security in the Warsaw Pact Countries', *International Affairs*, vol. 58, no. 4, 1978, p. 653.
5. L. Richardson, 'Arms and Insecurity', in N. Rashensky and F. Truco (eds) *A Mathematical Study of The Causes and Origins of War* (Pittsburg: Boxwood Press, 1960).
6. P. Baran and P. Sweezy, 'Monopoly Capital' (London: Penguin Books, 1966) chap. 7.
7. C. Ostrom. 'Evaluating Alternative Foreign Policy Decision-Making Models: An Empirical Test Between an Arms Race Model and an Organisation Politics Model', *Journal of Conflict Resolution*, vol. XXI, no. 2, 1977, p. 242.
8. Ibid., p. 257.
9. L. Hollist, 'An Analysis of the Arms Process in the USA and the Soviet Union', *International Studies Quarterly*, vol. 21, no. 3, 1977, p. 517.
10. S. Majeski and D. Jones, 'Arms Race Modelling: Causality Analysis and Model Specification' *Journal of Conflict Resolution*, vol. 25, no. 2, 1981.
11. P. Strauss, 'An Adaptive Expectations Model of the East West Arms Race'. *Peace Research Society*. The XIX Ann Arbor Conference 1971, Paper, vol. XIX, 1972.
12. R. Hamblin, et al., 'Arms Races: A Test of Two Models', *American Sociological Review*, vol. 32, 1977.
13. W. Saris and C. Middendorp, 'Arms Races: External Security or Domestic Pressure?' *British Journal of Political Science*, vol. 10, part 1, 1980, p. 126.
14. R. Nincic, *The Arms Race: The Political Economy of Military Growth* (New York: Praeger Special Studies, 1982) p. 72.
15. P. Gregory, 'Economic Growth, US Defense Expenditures and the Soviet Defence Budget: A Suggested Model', *Soviet Studies*, vol. XXVI, no. 1, 1974, p. 78.
16. R. Hutchings, *The Soviet Budget* (London: Macmillan, 1985) p. 142.
17. M. Nincic, 'Fluctuations in Soviet Defence Spending', *Journal of Conflict Resolution*, vol. 27, no. 4, 1983.

18. A. Warner, *The Military in Contemporary Soviet Politics* (New York: Praeger Special Studies, 1977) p. 5.
19. M. Nincic (1983) 'Fluctuations in Soviet Defence Spending.'
20. A. Alexander, *Decision Making in Soviet Weapons Procurement*, Adelphi Papers 147/148, International Institute for Strategic Studies, Winter 1978–9, p. 41.
21. A. Warner (1977) *The Military in Contemporary Soviet Politics*.
22. P. Jackson, *The Political Economy of Bureaucracy* (Oxford: Philip Allan, 1982) ch. 5.
23. H. Rattinger, 'Armaments, Detente and Bureaucracy: The Case of the Arms Race in Europe', *Journal of Conflict Resolution*, vol. XIX, no. 4, 1975.
24. N. Jasny, *Soviet Industrialization, 1928–1952* (Chicago: University of Chicago Press, 1960) p. 4.
25. M. Harrison (1985) *Soviet Planning in Peace and War, 1938–45*, p. 8.
26. Ibid., p. 8.
27. A. Erlich, *The Soviet Industrialization Debate 1924–1928* (Cambridge, Mass.: Harvard University Press, 1960) p. 29.
28. J. Cooper, *Defence Production and The Soviet Economy 1929–1941*. CREES Discussion Paper, Soviet Industrialization Project Series, No. 3 (University of Birmingham) 1976, pp. 5–9.
29. J. Hough, 'The Historical Legacy in Soviet Weapons Development' in J. Valenta and W. Potter (eds), *Soviet Decision Making for National Security* (London: Allen & Unwin, 1984) p. 90.
30. M. Harrison (1985) *Soviet Planning in Peace and War*, p. 47.
31. D. Holloway, 'Innovation in the Defence Sector', in R. Amann and J. Cooper, *Industrial Innovation in the Soviet Union*, (New Haven, Conn.: Yale University Press, 1982) p. 281.
32. J. Cooper, 'Western Technology and the Soviet Defense Industry', in B. Parrot (ed.) *Trade Technology and Soviet American Relations* (Bloomington: Indiana University Press, 1985–) p. 170.
33. H. Scott and W. Scott, *The Armed Forces of the Soviet Union* (Boulder, Col.: Westview Press, 1979) p. 288.
34. J. Cooper (1985), 'Western Technology and the Soviet Defense Industry', p. 3.
35. D. Holloway (1982), 'Innovation in the Defence Sector', p. 311.
36. J. McDonnell, 'The Defence Industry as a Pressure Group', in M. MccGwire, K. Booth and J. McDonnell (eds), *Soviet Naval Policy: Objectives and Constraints*, (New York: Praeger Special Studies, 1975) p. 87.
37. D. Holloway (1982) 'Innovation in the Defence Sector', p. 150.
38. D. Holloway, ibid., p. 111.
39. J. Hough (1984) 'The Historical Legacy', p. 106.
40. E. Jones, 'Defense R&D. Policymaking in the USSR', in J. Valenta and W. Potter (eds) (1984) *Soviet Decision Making*, p. 130.
41. A. Alexander (1978/79) *Decision Making in Soviet Weapons Procurement*.
42. D. Holloway, 'Doctrine and Technology in Soviet Armaments Policy', in D. Leebart (ed.), *Soviet Military Thinking* (London: Allen & Unwin, 1981).

43. M. Nincic (1983) 'Fluctuations in Soviet Defence Spending'.
44. D. Holloway (1985), *The Soviet Union and the Arms Race*, p. 127.
45. J. Cooper, (1985), 'Western Technology and the Soviet Defense Industry', p. 188.
46. J. Hough, 'Soviet Decision Making on Defense', *Bulletin of the Atomic Scientist*, vol. 41, no. 7, August 1985, p. 87.
47. G. Offer, *The Opportunity Cost of the Non Monetary Advantages of the Soviet Military R&D Effort*, Rand. R-1741-DDRE (Santa Monica, 1975) p. 7.
48. M. Checinski, 'The Costs of Armaments Production and the Profitability of Armaments Exports in COMECON Countries', *Osteuropa Wirtschaft*, vol. 20, no. 2, 1975, p. 127.
49. J. Cooper, 'The Civilian Production of the Soviet Defense Industry', in R. Aman and J. Cooper (eds), *Technical Progress and Soviet Economic Development* (Oxford: Blackwell, 1986) p. 44.
50. M. Checinski, 'The Cost of Armaments Production and the Profitability of Armament Experts in COMECON Countries', *Osteropa Wirtschaft*, vol. 20, no. 2, 1975, p. 118.
51. H. Scott and W. Scott (1979) *The Armed Forces of the Soviet Union*, p. 297.
52. D. Holloway (1982) 'Innovation in the Defence Sector', p. 312.
53. 'How to Strengthen Interaction', *Pravda*, 26 April 1982, *Current Digest of the Soviet Press*, vol. XXXIV, no. 17. p. 6.
54. K. Spielman, 'Defense Industrialists and the USSR Problems of Communism', vol. XXV, no. 5, September–October 1976, p. 57.
55. J. McDonnell (1975), 'The Defence Industry as a Pressure Group', p. 106.
56. E. Jahn, 'The Role of the Armaments Complex in Soviet Society (Is There a Soviet Military Industrial Complex)', *Journal of Peace Research*, vol. XII, no. 3, 1975.
57. K. Spielman (1976) 'Defence Industrialists and the USSR', pp. 59–60.
58. A Perlmutter and W. Leogrande, 'The Party in Uniform. Towards a Theory of Civil Military Relations in Communist Political Systems', *American Political Science Review*, vol. 76, no. 4, 1982, p. 782.
59. F. Long, 'Advancing Military Technology: Recipe for an Arms Race', *Current History*, vol. 82, no. 484, 1983, p. 215.
60. D. Holloway, 'Innovation in the Defence Sector' in R. Aman and J. Cooper (ed.) *Industrial Innovation in the Soviet Union* (New Haven, Conn.: Yale University Press, 1982) p. 276.
61. M. Thee, *Military Technology, Military Strategy and the Arms Race* (London: Croom Helm, 1986) p. 14.
62. R.D. DeLauer, *The FY 1985*, Department of Defence Programme for Research, Development and Acquisition, (Washington, DC) February 1984, pp. 11–13.
63. R. Nelson, 'Aggregate Production Functions and Medium Range Growth Projections', *American Economic Review*, vol. 54, 1964, p. 575.
64. N. Rosenberg, 'Science, Inventions and Economic Growth', *Economic Journal*, vol. 84, no. 333, 1974.
65. M. Acland-Hood, 'Military Research and Development: Some Aspects of Its Resource Use in the USA and the USSR'. *World Armaments and Disarmament*, SIPRI Yearbook, 1983, p. 214.

66. A. Warner (1977) *The Military in Contemporary Soviet Politics*, p. 172.
67. M. Acland-Hood (1983) *Military Research and Development*, p. 215.
68. H. York and A. Greb, 'Military R&D: A Post War History', *Bulletin of the Atomic Scientist*, Jan 1972, p. 276.
69. L. Nolting, M. Feshback, *R&D Employment in the USSR, Definitions, Statistics and Comparisons. Soviet Economy in a Time of Change*. A Compendium of Papers submitted to the Joint Economic Committee, Congress of the United States (Washington, DC, 1979) p. 739.
70. M. Acland-Hood (1983) *Military Research and Development*, pp. 228–37.
71. W. Lee, *CIA Estimates of Soviet Defence Spending*. Hearings before the Subcommittee on Intelligence, House of Representatives (Washington, DC, 1980) p. 70.
72. D. Holloway (1982) 'Innovation in the Defence Sector', p. 278.
73. R. Smith, 'Soviets Drop Further Back in Weapons Technology', *Science*, 16 March, vol. 223, no. 4641, 1984.
74. D. Holloway (1982) 'Innovation in the Defence Sector', p. 137.
75. M. Kaldor (1987) *The Baroque Arsenal Abacus*, (London 1982) p. 81.
76. R. Amann, 'Industrial Innovation in the Soviet Union: Methodological Perspectives and Conclusion', in R. Amann and J. Cooper (eds) *Industrial Innovation in the Soviet Union*, chap.1.
77. N. Clarke, *The Political Economy of Science and Technology* (Oxford: Blackwell, 1985) p. 117.
78. N. Nimitz, *The Structure of Soviet Outlays on R&D in 1960 and 1968*, Rand R-1207-DDRE (Santa Monica, 1974) p. 7.
79. 'Around the Machine Tool'. Ekonomika i organizatsia promyshlennovo proizvodstva, no. 1, January, 1982, *Current Digest of the Soviet Press*, vol. XXXIV, no. 18, p. 7.
80. R.D. Delauer (1984) *The FY 1985*, pp. 11–16.
81. J. Cooper (1985) 'Western Technology and the Soviet Defense Industry', p. 182.
82. R. Head (1978) 'Technology and the Military Balance', p. 548.
83. U. Albrecht, 'Military R&D Communities', *International Social Science Journal*, vol. XXXV, 1983, p. 19.
84. E. Jones (1981) 'Defense R&D Policy Making in the USSR', p. 126.
85. A. Alexander (1978/79) *Decision Making in Soviet Weapons Procurement*, p. 25.
86. M. Brzoska *et al.*, 'World Military Expenditures and Arms Production'. *World Armaments and Disarmament*, SIPRI Yearbook 1985 (London: Taylor & Francis, 1985) p. 252.
87. A. Yarmolinsky, *The Military Establishment: Its Impact on American Society* (New York: Harper Colophon, 1971) p. 129.
88. J. Gansler, *The Defense Industry* (Cambridge, Mass.: MIT Press, 1980) p. 83.
89. U. Albrecht, 'Military R&D Communities', *International Social Science Journal*, vol. XXXV, 1983, p. 19.
90. G. Offer (1975) *The Opportunity Cost*, p. 36.
91. L. Nolting and M. Feshback (1979) *R&D Employment in the USSR*, p. 731.
92. N. Nimitz (1974) *The Structure of Soviet Outlays*, p. 43.
93. Ibid., p. 55.

94. G. Offer (1975) *The Opportunity Cost*, p. 32.
95. *The Soviet Economy Under a New Leader*, A Report Presented to the Sub-Committee of Economic Resources, Competitiveness and Security Economics of the Joint Economic Committee by the CIA and the DIA, Washington, DC, 19 March 1986, p. 20.
96. M. Thee, 'The Dynamics of the Arms Race: Militiary R&D and Disarmament'. *International Social Science Journal*, vol. XXX, no. 4, 1918, p. 916.
97. D. Holloway (1974) *Technology and Political Decision*.
98. C. Rice, 'Defence and Security' in M. McCauley (ed.), *The Soviet Union under Gorbachev* (London: Macmillan, 1987) p. 198.
99. M. Thee (1986) *Military Technology, Military Strategy*, p. 73.

3 The Defence Burden

1. M. Checinski, 'An Estimate of Current Soviet Military Industrial Output and the Development of the Soviet Arms Industry in the 1980s', *Osteuropa Wirtschaft*, vol. 29, 1984, p. 142.
2. G. Hildebrandt. *The Dynamic Burden of Soviet Defence Spending. Soviet Economy in the 1980s: Problems and Prospects*, Part One. Selected Papers submitted to the Joint Economic Committee. Congress of the United States (Washington, DC, 1982) p. 334.
3. S. Cohn, *Declining Soviet Capital Productivity and the Soviet Military Industrial Complex*. US Arms Control and Disarmament Agency, World Military Expenditures and Arms Transfers, 1972–82 (Washington, DC, 1984) p. 111.
4. Ibid., p. 113.
5. F. Scott and W. Scott. *The Armed Forces of the USSR* (Boulder, Col.: Westview Press, 1979) p. 284.
6. A. Mosley, *The Arms Race: Economic and Social Consequences* (Lexington, Mass.: Lexington Books, 1985) p. 18.
7. G. Sen, 'The Economics of Defence, the Military Industrial Complex and New Marxist Theories', *Journal of International Studies*, vol. 15, no. 2, 1986, p. 193.
8. N. Spulber, *Soviet Strategy for Economic Growth* (Bloomington: Indiana University Press, 1964) p. 7.
9. A. Efremov, 'Effects of Disarmament on Employment in the USSR' *International Labour Review*, vol. 174, no. 4, 1985.
10. A. Marshall, 'Estimating Soviet Defence Spending', *Survival*, vol. XVIII, no. 2, March/April 1976, p. 73.
11. D. Holloway, 'Innovation in the Defence Sector', in R. Amann and J. Cooper (eds) *Industrial Innovation in the Soviet Union* (New Haven, Conn.: Yale University Press, 1982) p. 71.
12. G. Offer, *The Opportunity Cost of the Non-monetary Advantages of the Soviet Military R&D Effort* (Santa Monica: Rand R-1741-DDRE, 1975) p. 1.
13. A. Becker, *The Burden of Soviet Defence: A Political Economic Essay*, Rand R-2752 (Santa Monica, 1981) chap. 2.

14. N. Nimitz, *The Structure of Soviet Outlays on R&D in 1960 and 1968*, Rand R-1207-DDRE (Santa Monica, 1974) p. 43.
15. G. Offer, *The Opportunity Cost*, p. 20.
16. W. Lee, 'Soviet Defence Expenditures in the 10th FYP', *Osteuropa Wirtzchaft*, vol. 2, 1977, p. 279.
17. D. Holloway, *The Soviet Union and the Arms Race* 2 edn (New Haven, Conn.: Yale University, 1985) p. 146.
18. M. Agurski and H. Adomeit, 'The Soviet Military Industrial Complex', *Survey*, vol. 24, 1979, p. 106.
19. G. Becker, (1981) *The Burden of Soviet Defence*, p. 35.
20. H. Schaefer, *Soviet Power and Intentions: Military Economic Choices, Soviet Economy in a Time of Change*. A Compendium of Papers submitted to the Joint Economic Committee, Congress of the United States (Washington, DC, 1979) p. 341.
21. M. Agurski and H. Adomeit, 'The Soviet Military Industrial Complex'.
22. T. Colton, 'The Impact of the Military on Soviet Society', in S. Bialer (ed.), *The Domestic Context of Soviet Foreign Policy* (Boulder, Col.: Westview, 1981) p. 119.
23. W. Odom, 'The Militarization of Soviet Society', *Problems of Communism*, September–October, vol. XXV, no. 5, 1976.
24. T. Colton, 'The Impact of the Military on Soviet Society', p. 124.
25. E. Jones, 'Manning the Soviet Military', *International Security*, vol. 7, no. 1, 1982, p. 108.
26. R. Campbell, 'Management Spillovers from Soviet Space and Military Programmes', *Soviet Studies*, vol. 23, no. 4, 1971–2.
27. J. Bushell, 'The New Soviet Man Turns Pessimist', *Survey*, vol. 24, no. 2, 1979.
28. V. Vardys, 'Modernization and Baltic Nationalism', *Problems of Communism*, vol. XXIV, no. 5, September–October 1975.
29. A. Bennington, 'Mullahs, Mujahidin and Soviet Muslims', *Problems of Communism*, vol. XXXIV, no. 6, November–December, 1984.
30. A. Ulam, 'Russian Nationalism', in S. Bialer (ed.) *The Domestic Context of Soviet Foreign Policy*, p. 14.
31. E. Jones, 'Manning the Soviet Military', p. 107.
32. S. Bialer, 'Soviet Foreign Policy: Sources, Perceptions, Trends', in S. Bialer (ed.) *The Domestic Context of Soviet Foreign Policy*, p. 421.
33. M. Slovin, *The Epic of Russian Literature*, (New York, Oxford University Press, 1964).
34. F. Rubin, 'The Theory and Concept of National Interest in the Warsaw Pact Countries', *International Affairs*, vol. 58, no. 4, 1982, p. 655.
35. V.H. Garbuzov, *Pravda*, 28 November, 1984.
36. F. Griffiths, 'Ideological Development and Foreign Policy', in S. Bialer (ed.) *The Domestic Context of Soviet Foreign Policy*, p. 24.
37. D. Jones, 'Russian Tradition and Soviet Military Policy', *Current History*, vol. 82, 1983, p. 198.
38. *Allocation of Resources in the Soviet Union and China 1983*, Hearings before the Subcommittee on International Trade Finance and Security Economics of the Joint Economic Committee, Congress of the United States (Washington, DC, 1985) p. 49.

39. C. Rice, 'Defence and Security' in M. McCauley (ed.), *The Soviet Union under Gorbachev* (London: Macmillan, 1987) p. 192.
40. M. Klare, '*The Global Reach of the Super Powers*', *South*, Aug. 1985, p. 17.
41. E. Gasparini, 'East–South Economic Relations: Warsaw Pact Shifts to Military Deals with the Developing World', *NATO Review*, vol. 33, no. 2, 1985.
42. M. Checinski (1984) 'An Estimate of Current Soviet Military Industrial Output', p. 117.
43. M. Rush, 'The Soviet Policy Favouring Arms over Invesment since 1975', JEC, Part One (1982).
44. J. Cooper, *Defence Production and the Soviet Economy 1929–1941*. CREES Discussion Paper, Soviet Industrialization Project Series, no. 3, University of Birmingham, 1976, p. 3.
45. Ibid., p. 34.
46. D. Holloway (1985) *The Soviet Union and the Arms Race*, pp. 280–1.
47. M. Kaldor, *The Baroque Arsenal* (London: Abacus, 1982) p. 93.
48. J. Cooper, *Defence Production and the Soviet Economy*, p. 4.
49. Ibid., p. 40.
50. E. Carr and R. Davies, *Foundations of a Planned Economy 1926–1929*, vol. 1, no. 1 (London: Macmillan, 1969) p. 426.
51. N. Jasny, *Soviet Industrialization 1928–1952* (Chicago: University of Chicago Press, 1960) p. 4.
52. N. Spulber, *Soviet Strategy for Economic Growth*, p. 116.
53. E. Zaleski, *Stalinist Planning for Economic Growth, 1933–1952* (London: Macmillan, 1980) p. 482.
54. A. Erlich, *The Soviet Industrialization Debate 1924–1928* (Cambridge, Mass.: Harvard University Press, 1960) pp. 164–5.
55. Ibid., p. 149.
56. N. Spulber, *Soviet Strategy for Economic Growth*, p. 20.
57. N. Jasny, *Soviet Industrialisation 1928–1952*, p. 4.
58. D. Holloway (1985), *The Soviet Union and the Arms Race*, p. 280.
59. E. Zaleski, *Stalinist Planning for Economic Growth*, p. xxx.
60. J. Thomas, 'Political Strategic Factors in Soviet Modernization: Continuity and Change', *JEC* (1979), p. 90.
61. G. Grossman, 'Scarce Capital and Soviet Doctrine', *Quarterly Journal of Economics*, vol. LXVII, no. 3, 1953, p. 313.
62. M. Harrison, *Soviet Planning in Peace and War* (Cambridge: Cambridge University Press, 1985) p. 3.
63. N. Spulber, *Soviet Strategy for Economic Growth*, p. 116.
64. E. Carr and R. Davies, *Foundations of a Planned Economy*, p. 426.
65. J. Cooper, 'Western Technology and the Soviet Defence Industry', in B. Parrott, *Trade, Technology and Soviet American Relations* (Bloomington: Indiana University Press, 1985).
66. D. Green and C. Higgins, *SOVMOD 1. A Macroeconometric Model of the Soviet Union* (New York: Academic Press, 1977) p. 71.
67. Ibid., p. 118.
68. *Allocation of Resources in the Soviet Union and China, 1984*, Hearings Before the Sub-Committee on International Trade, Finance and Security

Economics, Joint Economic Committee, Congress of the United States, Nov 1985, Jan 1985, Washington, DC, p. 65.
69. S. Cohn, *Declining Soviet Capital Productivity*, p. 114.
70. *Allocation of Resources in the Soviet Union and China*, p. 77.
71. J. Cooper, 'Western Technology and the Soviet Defense Industry' in B. Parrot (ed.) *Trade, Technology and Soviet American Relations* (Bloomington: Indiana University Press, 1985) p. 180.
72. S. Cohn, *Declining Soviet Capital Productivity*, p. 114.
73. *Allocation of Resources in the Soviet Union and China*, p. 78.
74. H. Levine, *Possible Causes of the Deterioration of Soviet Productivity Growth in the Period 1976–1980*. Soviet Economy in the 1980s: Problems and Prospects. Selected Papers Submitted to the Joint Economic Committeess, Congress of the United States (Washington, DC, 1982) p. 158.
75. D. Bond and H. Levine, 'An Overview', in A. Bergson and H. Levine (eds), *The Soviet Economy: Towards the Year 2000* (London: Allen & Unwin, 1983) pp. 18–19.
76. G. Hildebrandt, *The Dynamic Burden of Soviet Defence Spending*, pp. 336–341.
77. M. Hopkin and M. Kennedy, *Comparisons and Implications of Alternative Views of the Soviet Economy*. Rand R-3075-NA (Santa Monica, 1984) p. 10.
78. Ibid., p. 57.
79. G. Offer, *The Opportunity Cost*, p. 14.
80. K. Tasky, 'Soviet Technology Gap and Dependence on the West', *JEC* (1979), p. 512.
81. J. Martens and J. Young, 'Soviet Implementation of Domestic Inventions: First Results', *JEC* (1979), p. 488.
82. 'The Novosibirsk Report', *Survey*, vol. 28, no. 1, 1984.
83. B. Parrott, *Politics and Technology in the Soviet Union* (Cambridge, Mass.: MIT Press, 1985) pp. 271–2.
84. *Allocation of Resources in the USSR and China*, p. 38.
85. *The Soviet Economy under a New Leader*, A Report Presented to the Sub-Committee on Economic Resources, Competition and Security Economics of the Joint Economic Committee by the CIA and the DIA, Washington, DC, March 1986.
86. B. Parrott, 'Theory and Praxis of Soviet Economic Modernization', *Problems of Communism*, vol. XXXIII, September–October 1984, p. 105.

4 Economic Growth

1. For a proper account of these two revolutionary developments see, for instance, A. Nove, *An Economic History of the USSR* (London: Allen Lane, 1969).
2. E. Zaleski, *Stalinist Planning for Economic Growth 1933–1952* (London: Macmillan, 1980).
3. G. Grossman, 'Scarce Capital and Soviet Doctrine', *Quarterly Journal of Economics*, vol. LXVII, no. 3, 1953.

4. A. Nove, *The Soviet Economic System* (London: Allen & Unwin, 1977), p. 151.
5. W. Nutter, *Growth of Industrial Production in the Soviet Union* (Princeton: Princeton University Press, 1962).
6. R. Clarke, *Soviet Economic Facts, 1917–70* (London: Macmillan, 1972) p. 8.
7. R. Clarke, Ibid., p. 3.
8. A. Nove, *Communist Economic Strategy: Soviet Growth and Capabilities* (Washington, DC: National Planning Association, 1959) p. 16.
9. J. Cornwall, *Modern Capitalism: Its Growth and Transformation* (Oxford: Martin Robertson, 1979) chap. II.
10. N. Rosenberg, 'US Technological Leadership and Foreign Competition', in N. Rosenberg, *Inside the Black Box: Technology and Economics* (Cambridge: Cambridge University Press, 1982) p. 280.
11. A. Sutton, *Western Technology and Soviet Economic Development 1945–1965* (Stanford: Hoover Institution, 1973).
12. R. Clarke, *Soviet Economic Facts, 1917–70*, pp. 8, 9.
13. N. Spulber, *Soviet Strategy for Economic Growth* (Bloomington: Indiana University Press, 1964) p. 117.
14. F. Durgin 'More on the New Model of Soviet Growth', *The ACES Bulletin*, vol. XXV, no. 1, Spring 1983.
15. P. Hanson, 'Economic Constraints on Soviet Policies', *International Affairs*, vol. 57, no. 1, 1980–1, p. 22.
16. R. Hutchings, *Soviet Economic Development* (Oxford: Blackwell, 1971) p. 87.
17. S. Rapawy and G. Baldwin, *Demographic Trends in the Soviet Union, Soviet Economy in the 1980s. Problems and Prospects*, Part 2, Selected Papers submitted to the Joint Economic Committee, Congress of the United States (Washington, DC, 1982) p. 267.
18. M. Feshback and S. Rapawy. *Soviet Population and Manpower Trends. Soviet Economy in a New Perpective*. A Compendium of Papers submitted to the Joint Economic Committee, Congress of the US (Washington, DC, 1979) p. 132.
19. Ibid., p. 152.
20. R. Clarke, *Soviet Economic Facts*, p. 30.
21. Ibid., p. 12.
22. F. Durgin, 'More on the New Model of Soviet Growth', p. 39.
23. M. Weitzman, 'Industrial Production', in A. Bergson and H. Levine, *The Soviet Economy: Towards the Year 2000* (London: Allen & Unwin, 1983) p. 182.
24. A. Bergson, 'Technological Progress' in A. Bergson and H. Levine, ibid. p. 40.
25. Ibid., p. 37.
26. M. Weitzman, 'Soviet Post-War Growth and Capital Labour Substitution', *American Economic Review*, vol. LX, no. 4, 1970, p. 682.
27. M. Gorbachev, 'Report to the Plenary Session of the Central Committee of the CPSU', *Pravda*, 24 April 1985, *Current Digest of the Soviet Press*, vol. XXXVII, no. 17, 1985, p. 3.
28. M. Goldman, *USSR in Crisis: The Failure of an Economic System* (New

York: Norton, 1983) p. 33.
29. 'The Novosibirsk Report', *Survey*, vol. 28, no. 1, Spring 1984.
30. G. Schroeder, 'Soviet Economic Reform Decrees: New Steps on the Treadmill', *JEC* (1982).
31. N. Nimitz, 'Reform and Technological Innovation in the Five Year Plan', in S. Bialer and T. Gustafson, *Russia at the Crossroads* (London: Allen & Unwin, 1982).
32. N. Fedorenko, 'Mathematical Economic Models and Methods', *Ekonomicheskaya Gazeta*, no. 1, January 1985, *Current Digest of the Soviet Press*, vol. XXXVII, no. 6, 1985, p. 9.
33. R. Whitesell, 'The Influence of Central Planning on Economic Slowdown', *Economica*, May 1985, p. 139.
34. N. Cameron 'Economic Growth in USSR, Hungary and East Germany', *Journal of Comparative Economics*, vol. 5, no. 1, 1981.
35. M. Weitzman, 'Industrial Production'.
36. S. Gomulka, 'Slowdown in Soviet Industrial Growth, 1942–75, Reconsidered', *European Economic Review*, vol. 10, 1977.
37. P. Desai, 'Total Factor Productivity in Post-War Soviet Industry and Its Branches', *Journal of Comparative Economics*, vol. 9, no. 1, 1985, p. 12.
38. Ibid., p. 12.
39. A. Goodman and G. Scheifer, 'The Soviet Labour Market in the 1980s', *JEC* (1982), p. 324.
40. M. Feshback, 'Issues in Soviet Health Problems', *JEC* (1982), p. 206.
41. M. Feshback, 'Prospects for Outmigration from Central Asia and Kazakhstan in the Next Decade', *JEC* (1979).
42. 'Looking into Supply Bottlenecks', *Pravda*, 26 April 1982, *Current Digest of the Soviet Press*, vol. XXIV, no. 17, 1982, p. 7.
43. V. Belkin, 'The Commodity Money Balance', *Ekonomika i organizatsia promyshlenovo proizvodstva*, no. 2, February 1982, *Current Digest of the Soviet Press*, vol. XXXIV, no. 17, 1982, p. 4.
44. M. Lavigne, *The Socialist Economies of the Soviet Union and Eastern Europe* (London: Martin Robertson, 1974) p. 251.
45. M. Goldman, 'Economic Problems in the Soviet Union', *Current History*, vol. 82, no. 486, 1983, p. 324.
46. *The Guardian*, 24 June 1987.
47. G. Schroeder, 'The Slowdown in Soviet Industry, 1976–82', *Soviet Economy*, vol. 1 1985, p. 47.
48. S. Rosefielde, 'Are Soviet Industrial-Production Statistics Significantly Distorted by Hidden Inflation', *Journal of Comparative Economics*, vol. 5, no. 2, 1981.
49. S. Cohn, *Declining Soviet Capital Productivity and the Soviet Military Industrial Complex*. US Arms Control and Disarmament Agency, World Military Expenditures and Arms Transfers (Washington, DC, 1982) p. 111.
50. R. Leggett, 'Soviet Investment Policy in the 11th Five Year Plan', *JEC* (1982) p. 139.
51. S. Cohn, 'Sources of Low Productivity in Soviet Capital Investment', *JEC* (1982) p. 174.
52. P. Desai, 'Total Factor Productivity'.

53. R. Leggett, 'Soviet Investment Policy', p. 141.
54. J. Krammer, 'Prices and Conservation', *Soviet Studies*, vol. 24, no. 3, 1972–3.
55. S. Cohn (1982) 'Sources of Low Productivity in Soviet Capital Investment', p. 180.
56. H. Levine, 'Possible Causes of the Deterioration of Soviet Productivity Growth in the Period 1970–80', *JEC* (1982) p. 158.
57. S. Cohn, (1982) 'Sources of Low Productivity in Soviet Capital Investment', pp. 181–2.
58. H. Levine (1982) 'Possible Causes of the Deterioration of Soviet Productivity Growth', p. 159.
59. M. Feshback and G. Rapawvy, *Soviet Population and Manpower Trends*, p. 140.
60. R. Leggett, 'Soviet Investment Policy', p. 142.
61. S. Cohn (1982) 'Declining Soviet Capital Productivity', p. 114.
62. R. Leggett, p. 146.
63. M. Rush, 'The Soviet Policy Favouring Arms over Investment since 1975', *JEC* (1982).
64. 'Draft Basic Guidelines Policy for the Economic and Social Development of the USSR in 1986–1990 and the Period up to the Year 2000', *Pravda*, 9 November 1985, *Current Digest of the Soviet Press*, vol. XXXXVII, no. 46, 1985, p. 13.
65. M. Gorbachev, 'The Fundamental Question of the Party's Economic Policy', *Pravda*, 12 June 1985, *Current Digest of the Soviet Press*, vol. XXXVII, no. 23, 1985, p. 3.
66. D. Dyker, 'The Economy', in D. Jones, *Soviet Armed Forces Review*, Annual, vol. 7, 1982–3, Academic International, 1984, p. 275.
67. 'We will successfully complete the Five Year Plan. On Results of the Fulfilment of the *State* Plan for the Economic and Social Development of the USSR', *Pravda, 26 Jan. Current Digest of the Soviet Press*, vol. XXXVII, no. 4, 1985, p. 11.

5 Competing Claims

1. M. Goldman, *USSR in Crisis: The Failure of an Economic System* (New York: Norton, 1983) p. 36.
2. M. Gorbachev, 'The Acceleration of Scientific and Technical Progress is a Demand of Life', *Pravda*, 12 June 1985, *Current Digest of the Soviet Press*, vol. XXXVII, no. 23, p. 4.
3. G. Schroeder, 'The Slowdown in Soviet Industry 1976–1982', *Soviet Economy*, vol. 1, 1985, p. 52.
4. CIA, *Sluggish Soviet Steel Industry Holds Down Economic Growth. Soviet Economy in the 1980s, Problems and Prospects*, Part One, Selected Papers submitted to the Joint Economic Committee Congress of the US (Washington, DC, 1982) p. 204.
5. Ibid., p. 206.

6. 'Overhaul of Ferrous Metallurgy', *Izvestia*, 18 March 1985, *Current Digest of the Soviet Press*, vol. XXXVII, no. 11, p. 19.
7. *The Soviet Economy under a New Leader*, A Report Presented to the Sub Committee on Economic Resources, Competition and Security Economics of the Joint Economic Committee by the CIA and the DIA, Washington, DC, March 1986, p. 22.
8. B. Rumer, 'Structural Imbalance in the Soviet Economy', *Problems of Communism*, vol. XXXIII, July–August 1984, p. 28.
9. V. Zorkaltser, 'The Anatomy of Scarcity', *Economika i organizatsia promyshlennovo proizvodstva*, no. 2 February 1982, *Current Digest of the Soviet Press*, vol. XXXIV, no. 17, p. 5.
10. B. Rumer, 'Structural Imbalance in the Soviet Economy', p. 27.
11. 'Around the Machine Tools', *Ekonomica i organizatsia promyshlennovo proizvodstva*, no. 1, January 1982, *Current Digest of the Soviet Press*, vol. XXXIV, no. 18, p. 7.
12. J. Grant, *Soviet Machine Tools: Lagging Technology and Rising Imports. Soviet Economy in a Time of Change*. A Compendium of Papers submitted to the Joint Economic Committee Congress of the United States, vol. 1, (Washington, DC, 1979) p. 555.
13. 'Around the Machine Tools', *Current Digest of the Soviet Press*, vol. XXXIV, no. 18, p. 6.
14. J. Grant, *Soviet Machine Tools*, p. 557.
15. S. Kheinman, 'The Machinery's Production Apparatus and the Machine Tool Industry', *Economika i organizatsia promyshlennovo proizvodstva*, no. 1, January, *Current Digest of the Soviet Press*, vol. XXXIV, no. 18, 1982, p. 5.
16. G. Kulagin. 'At Crossroads of Opinion: The Roads that Choose', *Pravda*, 21 January 1985, *Current Digest of the Soviet Press*, vol. XXXVII, no. 3, 1985.
17. Ibid., p. 2.
18. M. Gorbachev, 'Initiative, Organization and Efficiency', *Pravda*, 12 April 1985, *Current Digest of the Soviet Press*, vol. XXXVII, no. 15, 1985.
19. '"We will successfully complete the Five Year Plan." On Results of the Fulfilment of the State Plan for the Economic and Social Development of the USSR in 1984', *Pravda*, 26 January 1985, *Current Digest of the Soviet Press*, vol. XXXIII, no. 4, 1984, p. 12.
20. 'Draft Basic Guidelines for the Economic and Social Development of the USSR, 1986–1990, and the Period up to the Year 2000, *Pravda*, 9 November 1985, *Current Digest of the Soviet Press*, vol. XXXVII, no. 45, 1985, p. 21.
21. 'On the Work of the Ministry of the Machine Tool and Tool Industry', *Pravda*, 13 December 1986, *Current Digest of the Soviet Press*, vol. XXXVII, no. 50, 8 January 1986, p. 10.
22. G. Schroeder, 'The Slowdown in Soviet Industry, 1976–82', p. 61.
23. V. Kontorovich, 'Discipline and Growth in the Soviet Economy', *Problems of Communism*, vol. XXXIV, November–December 1985.
24. H. Hunter and D. Kaple, 'Transport in Trouble', *JEC* (1982) p. 222.
25. R. Campbell, 'Energy', in A. Bergson and H. Levine (eds), *The Soviet*

Economy: Towards the Year 2000 (London: Allen & Unwin, 1983) p. 191.
26. L. Dienes, 'The Soviet Energy Policy', *JEC* (1979) p. 200.
27. R. Campbell, 'Energy', p. 193.
28. T. Gustafson, 'The Origins of the Soviet Oil Crisis 1970–85', *The Soviet Economy*, vol. 1, no. 2, 1985, p. 112.
29. *The Soviet Economy under a New Leader*, p. 40.
30. T. Gustafson, 'Soviet Energy Policy: From Big Coal to Big Gas', in S. Bialer and T. Gustafson, *Russia at the Crossroads: The 26th Congress of the CPSU* (London: Allen & Unwin, 1982) p. 123.
31. M. Styrikovich and V. Popov, 'The Coal Prospects', *Pravda*, 6 October 1984, *Current Digest of the Soviet Press*, vol. XXXL, no. 40, 1984, p. 11.
32. Ibid., p. 11.
33. Y. Ruzzulyayer, 'The Lessons of Ekibastuz', *Pravda*, 8 August 1984, *Current Digest of the Soviet Press*, vol. XXXVI, no. 32, 1984, p. 13.
34. M. Styrikovich and V. Popov, 'The Coal Prospects', p. 11.
35. T. Gustafson, 'Soviet Energy Policy', *JEC* (1982) p. 435.
36. Ibid., p. 435.
37. Ibid., p. 435.
38. G.A. Terentyev, 'Casinghead Gas: By-Product or Waste', *Ekonomika i organizatsia promyshlennova proizvodstva*, no. 10, October 1980, *Current Digest of the Soviet Press*, vol. XXXIII, no. 14, 1980, p. 18.
39. W. Kelly et al., 'The Economics of Nuclear Power in the Soviet Union', *Soviet Studies*, vol. XXVIV, no. 1, 1982, p. 44.
40. W. Kelly et al., Ibid., p. 43.
41. R. Maddock, 'Nuclear Energy in the Soviet Union', *Energy Policy*, vol. 11, no. 4, 1983, p. 326.
42. V. Shilov, 'Light from the Atom', *Pravda*, 4 August 1977, *Current Digest of the Soviet Press*, vol. XXIX, no. 31, 1977, p. 10.
43. R. Maddock, 'Nuclear Energy in the Soviet Union', p. 330.
44. M. Gorbachev, 'Report to 27th CPSU Congress, *Pravda*, 24 April 1985, *Current Digest of the Soviet Press*, vol. XXXVII, no. 17, 1985, p. 3.
45. M. Walker, 'Hard Men to Carry Moscow's New Image', *The Guardian*, 6 March 1986.
46. *The Soviet Economy under a New Leader*, p. 40.
47. M. Ellman, *Socialist Planning* (London: Cambridge University Press, 1979, p. 94–6.
48. J. Millar, 'The Prospect for Soviet Agriculture', *Problems of Communism*, May–June, vol. XXVI, 1977, p. 3.
49. K. Gray, 'Soviet Consumption of Food: Is the Bottle "Half Full", "Half Empty", "Half Water", "Too Expensive"', *The ACES Bulletin*, vol. XXIII, no. 2, Summer 1981, p. 31.
50. R. Ambroziak and D. Carey, 'Climate and Grain Production in the Soviet Union', *JEC* (1982), Part 2, p. 113.
51. K. Gray, 'Soviet Consumption of Food', p. 41–2.
52. M. Goldman, *USSR in Crisis*, p. 111.
53. Ibid., p. 66.
54. 'Communiqué on the Plenary Session of the Central Committee of the Communist Party of the Soviet Union', *Pravda*, 25 May 1982, *Current Digest of the Soviet Press*, vol. XXXIV, no. 21, 1982, p. 21.

55. D. Diamond, 'Soviet Agricultural Plans for 1981–85', in S. Bialer and T. Gustafson (eds) *Russia at the Crossroads: The 26th Congress of the CPSU* (London: Allen & Unwin, 1982) p. 108.
56. V. Treml, 'Subsidies in Soviet Agriculture: Record and Prospects', *JEC* (1982), Part 2, p. 178.
57. D. Johnson, 'Prospects for Soviet Agriculture in the 1980s', *JEC* (1982), Part 2, p. 13.
58. J. Millar, 'The Prospects for Soviet Agriculture', p. 11.
59. N. Gladkov and V. Somov, 'The Cotton Season is not for Children', *Pravda*, 6 March 1985, *Current Digest of the Soviet Press*, vol. XXXVII, no. 10, 1985.
60. Y. Markish and A. Malish, 'The Soviet Food Programme: Prospects for the 1980's, *The ACES Bulletin*, vol. XXV, no. 1. Spring 1983, p. 58.
61. A. Malish, 'The Food Programme: A New Policy or More Rhetoric', *JEC* (1982), Part 2, p. 47.
62. M. Goldman, *USSR in Crisis*, p. 81.
63. 'Communique on the Plenary Session of the CPSU', *Pravda*, 25 May 1982.
64. 'The USSR Food Programme for the Period up to 1990', *Pravda*, 27 May 1982, *Current Digest of the Soviet Press*, vol. XXXIV, no. 22, 1982.
65. M. Ellman, *Socialist Planning*, p. 154.
66. G. Schroeder, 'Soviet Living Standards, Achievements and Prospects', *JEC* (1982), Part 2, p. 368.
67. G. Schroeder, 'Consumption', in A. Bergson and H. Levine (eds), *The Soviet Economy: Towards the Year 2000* (London: Allen & Unwin, 1983) p. 322.
68. G. Schroeder (1982) 'Soviet Living Standards, Achievements and Prospects', p. 375.
69. G. Andrusz, *Soviet Housing Policy: The End of an Era*, Paper presented to the Annual Conference of NASEES, March 1985, p. 1.
70. Ibid., p. 2.
71. A. Katsenelinboigen, 'Coloured Markets in the Soviet Union', *Soviet Studies*, vol. XXIV, no. 1, 1977.
72. F. Durgin, 'More on the New Model of Soviet Growth', *The ACES Bulletin*, vol. XXV, no. 1, Spring 1983, p. 39.
73. L. Dienes, 'Regional Economic Development', in A. Bergson and H. Levine (eds), *The Soviet Economy: Towards the Year 2000*, p. 241.
74. B. Rumer and S. Sternheimer, 'The Soviet Economy: Going to Siberia', *Harvard Business Review*, vol. 60, no. 1, 1982, p. 30.

6 External Relations

1. T. Sandler, 'Economic Theory of Alliances', in C. Liske *et al.*, (eds) *Comparative Public Policy: Issues, Theories and Methods* (New York: Wiley, 1975).
2. M. Marrese and J. Vanous, 'Unconventional Gains from Trade', *Journal of Comparative Economics*, vol. 7, 1983.
3. R. Johnson, 'Has Eastern Europe Become a Liability to the Soviet

Union: The Military Aspect', in C. Gati (ed.). *The International Politics of Eastern Europe* (New York: Praeger, 1976) p. 51.
4. R. Starr, 'Soviet Policies in Eastern Europe', *Current History*, vol. 80, no. 468, 1981, p. 318.
5. T. Alton *et al.*, *Defence Expenditures in Eastern Europe, 1965–1975. East European Economies Post Helsinki*. A Compendium of Papers submitted to the Joint Economic Committee, Congress of the US 1977, p. 272.
6. J. Ericson, 'Military Management and Modernization within the Warsaw Pact', in R. Clawson and L. Kaplan (eds) *The Warsaw Pact: Political Purpose and Military Means* (Wilmington: Scholarly Resources, 1984) p. 217.
7. T. Clements, 'The Cost of Defense in the Non-Soviet Warsaw Pact: A Historical Perspective' in *East European Economies. Slow Growth in the 1980s, Vol. 1 Economic Performance and Policy*. Selected Papers Submitted to the Joint Economic Committee, Congress of the United States, Washington, DC, 1985, p. 452.
8. T. Alton *et al.*, 'East European Defense Expenditures 1965–82', in *East European Economies*, p. 80.
9. C. Rice, 'Defense Burden Sharing', in D. Holloway and J. Sharpe (eds) *The Warsaw Pact: Alliance in Transition* (London: Macmillan, 1984) p. 69.
10. T. Clement (1985) 'The Cost of Defense in the Non-Soviet Warsaw Pact', p. 452.
11. E. Moreton, 'Foreign Policy Goals', in D. Holloway and J. Sharpe (eds), *The Warsaw Pact*, chap. 7.
12. J. Ericson, 'Military Management and Modernization', p. 218.
13. M. Brzoska *et al.*, *World Military Expenditure and Arms Production: World Armaments and Disarmament*. SIPRI Yearbook 1985 (London: Taylor & Francis 1985).
14. M. Checinski, 'The Cost of Armament Production and the Profitability of Armament Exports in COMECON Countries', *Osteuropa Wirtschaft*, vol. 20, no. 2, 1975, p. 119.
15. J. Ericson, 'Military Management and Modernization', p. 214.
16. T. Callaghan, 'A Common Market for Atlantic Defense', *Survival*, vol. XVII, no. 3 May/June 1975.
17. C. Rice, 'Defense Burden Sharing', p. 60.
18. J. Ericson, 'Military Management and Modernization', p. 215.
19. M. Checinski, 'The Cost of Armament Production', p. 128.
20. C. Rice, 'Defense Burden Sharing', p. 70.
21. F. Holzman, *International Trade under Communism: Politics and Economics* (London: Macmillan, 1976) p. 67.
22. Ibid., p. 74.
23. P. Marer, 'Has Eastern Europe Become a Liability to the Soviet Union? The Economic Aspect', in C. Gati (ed.) *The International Politics of Eastern Europe*, p. 64.
24. F. Holzman, *International Trade under Communism*, p. 64.
25. P. Marer, 'Has Eastern Europe Become a Liability to the Soviet Union?' pp. 65–9.
26. E. Hewett, *Soviet Economic Relations with the CMEA Countries*. The

Soviet Economy After Brezhnev Colloquium 1984 (Brussels, 1984) p. 241.
27. J. Kramer, 'Soviet CMEA Energy Ties', *Problems of Communism*, July–August, vol. XXXIV, no. 4, 1985, p. 34.
28. R. Dietz, *Price Changes in Soviet Trade with CMEA and the Rest of the World since 1975*. Soviet Economy in a Time of Change. A Compendium of Papers submitted to the Joint Economic Committee Congress of the USA 1979 (Washington, DC, 1979) p. 267.
29. M. Lavigne, 'The Soviet Union Inside COMECON', *Soviet Studies*, vol. XXXV, no. 2, 1983, p. 139.
30. M. Lavigne, 'The Soviet Union Inside COMECON', p. 140.
31. J. Vanous, 'East European Economic Slowdown', *Problems of Communism*, July–August, vol. XXXI, no. 4, 1982, p. 8.
32. J. Zoeter, 'USSR Hard Currency Trade and Payments', *JEC* (1982) p. 490.
33. E. Hewett, *Soviet Economic Relations with the CMEA Countries*, p. 247.
34. P. Marer, 'Has Eastern Europe Become a Liability to the Soviet Union?' p. 23.
35. J. Vanous, 'East European Economic Slowdown', p. 7.
36. J. Brabant, 'USSR and Socialist Economic Integration', *Soviet Studies*, vol. XXXVI, no. 1, 1984, p. 130.
37. P. Summerscale, 'Is Eastern Europe a Liability to the USSR', *International Affairs*, vol. 97, no. 4, Autumn 1981, p. 58.
38. M. Marrese and J. Vanous, 'Unconventional Gains from Trade', p. 385.
39. M. Marrese, 'CMEA: Effective but Cumbersome Political Economy', *International Organisation*, vol. 40, no. 2, 1986.
40. M. Mackintosh, 'The Warsaw Treaty Organization: A History', in D. Holloway, and J. Sharpe (eds) *The Warsaw Pact*, p. 43.
41. V. Aspaturian, 'Has Eastern Europe Become a Liability to the Soviet Union? The Political Ideological Debate', in C. Gati (ed.) *The International Politics of Eastern Europe*.
42. C. Rice, 'Defense Burden Sharing', p. 77.
43. M. Kohn, 'Soviet East European Economic Relations 1975–1978', *JEC* (1979) p. 251.
44. E. Goldstein, 'Soviet Economic Assistance to Poland', *JEC* (1982) Part 2, p. 567.
45. C. Wolfe et al., *The Costs of the Soviet Empire*, Rand R-3073/1-NA (Santa Monica, 1983) p. 29.
46. Ibid., p. 45.
47. R. Pajak, 'Soviet Arms Transfer as an Instrument of Influence', *Survival*, vol. XXIII, no. 4, July–August 1981, p. 166.
48. R. Menon, 'The Soviet Union, the Arms Trade and the Third World', *Soviet Studies*, vol. XXXIV, no. 3, 1982, p. 381.
49. U. Albrech, 'Soviet Arms Exports', *World Armaments and Disarmament*, SIPRI, Yearbook 1983 (London: Taylor & Francis, 1983) p. 362.
50. M. Efrat, 'The Economics of Soviet Arms Transfers to the Third World', in P. Wiles and M. Efrat. *The Economics of Soviet Arms*, Suntory Toyota International Centre for Economics and Related Disciples, London School of Economics 1985, p. 10.
51. U. Albrech, *Soviet Arms Exports*, p. 361.

52. R. Pajak, 'Soviet Arms Transfer', p. 167.
53. R. Menon, 'The Soviet-Union, the Arms Trade and the Third World', p. 379.
54. M. Klare, 'The Global Reach of the Superpowers', *South*, Aug 1983, p. 17.
55. R. Pajak, 'Soviet Arms Transfer', p. 166.
56. S. Deger, *Soviet Arms Sales to LDC: The Economic Forces*. Birkbeck Discussion Paper, no. 152, Birkbeck College, London, p. 18.
57. R. Pajak, 'Soviet Arms Transfer', p. 167.
58. W. Lewis, 'Emerging Choices for the Soviets' in *Third World Arms Transfer Policy. US Arms Control and Disarmament Agency. World Military Expenditures and Arms Transfers, 1981*, Washington, DC, 1985, p. 30.
59. M. Brzoska and T. Ohlson, 'The Trade in Major Conventional Weapons' World Armaments and Disarmament. *SIPRI Yearbook 1985* (London: Taylor & Francis, 1985) p. 364.
60. T. Ohlson, 'The Trade in Major Conventional Weapons', *World Armaments and Disarmament*, SIPRI, Yearbook 1982 (London: Taylor & Francis, 1982) p. 186.
61. J. Krause, 'Soviet Military Aid to the Third World', *Aussen Politik*, vol. 3, no. 4, 1983, p. 395.
62. E. Gasparini, 'East–South Economic Relations: Warsaw Pact, Shifts to Military Deals with Developing World', *NATO Review*, vol. 33, no. 2, 1985, p. 30.
63. S. Deger, *Soviet Arms Sales to LDC*, p. 4.
64. J. Zoeter, *USSR: Hard Currency Trade and Payments. Soviet Economy in the 1980s: Problems and Prospects Part 2*, Selected Papers submitted to the Joint Economic Committee, Congress of the United States, Washington, DC, 1982, p. 490.
65. S. Deger, *Soviet Arms to LDC*, p. 7.
66. R. Pajak, 'Soviet Arms Transfer', p. 169.
67. *The Soviet Economy under a New Leader*, A Report Presented to the Sub-Committee on Economic Resources, Competition and Security Economics of the Joint Economic Committee by the CIA and DIA, Washington, DC, March 1986, p. 29.
68. M. Brzoska and T. Ohlson, 'The Trade in Major Conventional Weapons', *World Armaments and Disarmament*, SIPRI Yearbook 1985 (London: Taylor & Francis, 1985) p. 345.
69. M. Brzoska, 'The Military Related Debt of Third World Countries', *Journal of Peace Research*, vol. 20, no. 3, 1983, p. 275.
70. T. Ohlson and M. Brzoska, 'Trade in Major Conventional Weapons', *World Armaments and Disarmament*, SIPRI Yearbook, 1984 (London: Taylor & Francis, 1984) p. 175.
71. *World Armaments and Disarmament*, SIPRI Yearbook, 1985, p. 373.
72. W. Lewis, 'Emerging Choices for the Soviets', p. 32.
73. Ibid., p. 32.
74. J. Cooper, 'Westen Technology and the Soviet Defence Industry', in B. Parrott (ed.) *Trade, Technology and Soviet American Relations* (Bloomington: Indiana University Press, 1985).
75. Ibid., p. 172.
76. CIA, 'Soviet Acquisition of Western Technology' in G. Bertsch and J.

McIntyre (eds), *National Security and Technology Transfer: The Strategic Dimension of East–West Trade* (Boulder: Westview Press, 1983) p. 92.
77. T. Gustafson, *Selling the Russians the Rope? Soviet Technological Policy and US Export Controls* (Santa Monica: Rand R-2649-ARPA, 1981).
78. *The Extent of Technology Transfer from the West to the Soviet Union During the Past Decade and the Contributions Such Transfers Have Made to Strengthen the Soviet Military Industrial Base*. Hearings before the Sub-Committee on International Trade and Monetary Policy of the Committee on Banking, Housing and Urban Affairs (Washington, DC, 1982).
79. B. Inman, 'Control of Technology Transfer to the Soviet Union', in *US Arms Control and Disarmament Agency, World Military Expenditures and Arms Transfers* (Washington, DC, 1985) p. 26.
80. D. Holloway, *Western Technology and Soviet Military Power*, Paper prepared for the Millennium Conference on 'Technology Transfer and East West Relations in the 80s', 5 and 6 May 1983.
81. Hearings (1982); *The Extent of Technology Transfer*.
82. CIA, 'Soviet Acquisition of Western Technology', p. 100.
83. *The Extent of Technology Transfer from the West to the Soviet Union During the Last Decade and the Contribution such Transfers have made to Strengthen the Soviet Military Industrial Base*, Hearings Before the Sub-Committee on International Trade and Monetary Policy of the Committee of Banking, Housing and Urban Affairs (Washington, DC, April 1982).
84. T. Gustafson, *Selling the Russians the Rope? Soviet Technological Policy and US Export Controls*, Rand R- 2649-ARPA (Santa Monica, 1981).
85. M. Miller, 'Foreign Technology in Soviet Strategy', *Orbis*, Fall 1978, p. 562.
86. J. Cooper, 'Western Technology and the Soviet Defence Industry', p. 189.
87. G. Halliday, 'Western Technology Transfer'.
88. W. Baxter, 'Soviet Exploitation of Western Military Technology and Military Art', *Military Review*, vol. 2, 1983.
89. D. Bond and H. Levine, 'The Soviet Machinery Balance and Military Durables in SOVMOD', *JEC* (1982) Part One, p. 306.
90. P. Hanson, *Trade and Technology in Soviet Western Relations* (London: Macmillan, 1981) chap. 7.
91. L. Kochan, *The Making of Modern Russia* (London: Penguin 1962), p. 52.

7 Conclusion and Speculation

1. M. Gorbachev, 'Initiative, Organization and Efficiency', *Pravda*, 12 April 1985, *Current Digest of the Soviet Press*, vol. XXXVII, no. 14, 1985, p. 1.
2. M. Goldman, *USSR in Crisis: Failure of an Economic System* (New York: Norton, 1983).
3. The Novosibirsk Report, *Survey*, vol. 28, no. 1, 1984.

4. T. Zaslavskaya, 'The Choice of Strategy', *Izvestia*, 1 June 1985, *Current Digest of the Soviet Press*, vol. XXXVII, no. 22, 1985, p. 7.
5. E. Denton, *Soviet Perceptions of Economic Prospects*, Soviet Economy in the 1980s: Problems and Prospects, Part One, Selected Papers submitted to the Soviet Economic Committee Congress of the US (Washington, DC, 1982) p. 42.
6. G. Schroeder, The Slowdown in Soviet Industry 1976–1982, *Soviet Economy*, vol. 1, 1985, p. 69.
7. V. Garbuzov, Budget Speech, *Pravda*, 28 November 1984.
8. W. Lee, *CIA Estimates of Soviet Defense Spending*. Hearings before the Subcommittee on Oversight of the Permanent Select Committee on Intelligence, House of Representatives (Washington, DC, 1980) p. 22.
9. B. Parrott, 'Theory and Praxis of Soviet Economic Modernization', *Problems of Communism*, vol. XXIII, September–October, 1984, p. 105.
10. *Allocation of Resources in the Soviet Union and China, 1983*. Hearings before the Subcommittee on International Trade, Finance and Security Economics of the Joint Economic Committee, Congress of the US (Washington, 1984) p. 38.
11. G. Hildebrandt, 'The Dynamic Burden of Soviet Defence Spending' *Soviet Economy in the 1980s*, Part One, Selected Papers submitted to the JEC, 1982.
12. M. Hopkins and M. Kennedy, *Comparisons and Implications of Alternative Views of the Soviet Economy*, Rand R-3075-NA (Santa Monica, 1984) p. 10.
13. *Allocation of Resources in the Soviet Union and China, 1983*, p. 19.
14. P. Hanson, 'Economic Constraints on Soviet Politics', *International Affairs*, Winter 1980–1, p. 23.
15. A. Goodman and G. Schliefer, 'The Soviet Labour Market in the 1980s' *Soviet Economy in the 1980s*, 1982, p. 324.
16. A. Bergson, 'Technological Progress', in A. Bergson and H. Levine, *The Soviet Economy: Towards the Year 2000* (London: Allen & Unwin, 1983).
17. 'Draft Basic Guidelines for the Economic and Social Development of the USSR in 1986–1990, and in the Period up to the Year 2000', *Pravda*, 9 November 1986, *Current Digest of the Soviet Press*, vol. XXXVII, no. 45, 1986, p. 11.
18. R. Leggett, '*Soviet Investment Policy in the 11th Five Year Plan*', *The Soviet Economy in the 1980s*, Part One, p. 135.
19. B. Rumer, 'Structural Imbalance in the Soviet Economy', *Problems of Communism*, vol. XXXIII, no. 4, July–August, 1984, p. 24.
20. '"We will successfully complete the Five Year Plan." On the Results of the Fulfilment of the State Plan for the Economic and Social Development of the USSR in 1984', *Pravda*, 26 January 1985, *Current Digest of the Soviet Press*, 1985, p. 11.
21. Y. Antosenkov, 'Why is Wage Levelling So Tenacious?' *Izvetia*, 26 April 1985, *Current Digest of the Soviet Press*, vol. XXXVII, no. 17, 1985, p. 21.
22. M. Gorbachev, 'Initiative, Organization and Efficiency', p. 3.

23. *The Soviet Economy under a New Leader*, A Report Presented to the Sub-Committee on Economic Resources, Competition and Security Economics of the Joint Economic Committee by the CIA and the DIA, Washington, DC, March 1986, p. 1.
24. M. Gorbachev, 'The Acceleration of Scientific and Technical Progress is a Demand of Life', *Pravda*, 12 June 1985, *Current Digest of the Soviet Press*, vol. XXXVII, no. 23, 1985, p. 4.
25. Report on 1984 Fulfilment Plan, *op. cit.* p. 12.
26. Draft Basic Guidelines for 1986–1990, *op. cit.* p. 21.
27. V. Belkin, 'The Commodity Money Imbalance and its Role in the Supply Problem', *Ekonomika i organizatsia promyshlenovo proizvodstva*, no. 2, 19 February 1985, *Current Digest of the Soviet Press*, vol. XXXIV, no. 17, p. 4.
28. J. Cooper, 'Western Technology and the Soviet Defense Industry', in B. Parrott (ed.) *Trade, Technology and Soviet–American Relations* (Bloomington: Indiana University Press, 1985) p. 180.
29. *Allocation of Resources in the Soviet Union and China, 1983*, p. 7.
30. G. Offer, *The Opportunity Cost of the Non Monetary Advantages of the Soviet Military R&D Effort*. Rand R-1741-DDRE (Santa Monica, 1975) p. 38.
31. R. Kaufman, 'Causes of the Slowdown in Soviet Defense', *Soviet Economy*, January–March 1985, vol. 1, no. 1, p. 16.
32. D. Holloway, 'Comment on R. Kaufman's Article', *Soviet Economy*, Ibid., p. 38.
33. J. Steinbruner, 'Comment', ibid., p. 34.
34. *Allocation of Resources in the Soviet Union and China 1984*, Hearings Before the Sub-Committee on International Trade, Finance and Security Economics, Joint Economic Committee Congress of the United States, Nov 1984, Jan 1985, Washington, DC, 1985, p. 234.
35. J. Steinbruner, 'Comment', p. 35.
36. N. Nimitz, *The Structure of Soviet Outlays on R&D in 1960 and 1968*. Rand, R-1207-DDRE (Santa Monica, 1974) p. 55.
37. Department of Defence, *Soviet Military Power 1985*, (Washington, DC, 1985).
38. M. Brzoska *et al.*, *World Military Expenditure and Arms Production: World Armaments and Disarmament*, SIPRI, Yearbook, 1985 (London: Taylor & Francis, 1985) pp. 252–4.
39. *Allocation of Resources 1984*, p. 55.
40. R. Kaufman, 'Causes of the Slowdown in Soviet Defense', p. 15.
41. B. Parrott, 'Theory and Practice of Soviet Economic Modernization', p. 106.
42. E. Moreton, 'Comrade Colossus: The Impact of Soviet Military Industry on the Soviet Economy', in C. Keeble (ed.), *The Soviet State: The Domestic Roots of Soviet Foreign Policy* (London: Gower, 1985) p. 133.
43. C. Weinberger, Secretary of Defense, *Annual Report to the Congress, Fiscal Year 1987*, Washington, DC, 1987, pp. 14–18.
44. J. Kiser, 'How the Arms Race Really Helps Moscow', *Foreign Policy*, no. 60, Fall 1985.
45. *East–West Technology Transfer: A Congressional Dialog with the Reagan

Administration, A Dialog Prepared for the Use of the Joint Economic Committee, Congress of the United States, Washington, DC, 1984.
46. J. Zoetler, 'USSR Hard Currency Trade and Payment', *JEC* (1982) p. 488.
47. *The Soviet Economy under a New Leader*, p. 28.
48. Ibid., p. 21.
49. Ibid., p. 24.
50. B. Kaplan, 'The Soviet Economy: The Political Options', *The Banker*, vol. 131, no. 663, May 1981, p. 41.
51. P. Cocks, 'Administrative Reform and Soviet Politics', *JEC* (1982) p. 49.
52. S. Bialer, 'The Harsh Decade', *Foreign Affairs*, vol. 59, 1980–1, p. 106.
53. M. Checinski, 'An Estimate of Current Military Industrial Output', p. 148.
54. M. Gorbachev (1985) 'Initiative, Organization and Efficiency', pp. 1–2.
55. M. Checinski, 'An Estimate of Current Military Industrial Output', p. 151.
56. *The Soviet Economy under a New Leader*, p. 24.

Index

Abenbegyan, A. 122
absenteeism 183
Academy of Sciences, undertakes
  military research 56
action–reaction models 28–32
aeroengines, imports 174
Afghanistan 165, 178
aggregate production function 102
agriculture 137–43
  declining productivity 139, 142
  growth 97, 138
  labour trends 140–1
  lack of investment 141
  neglected by Stalin 137
  output 181
  consumption 138
  post-Stalin 137–8
  residual claimant 99
  undercapitalised 137
  variable output 106, 139
  waste 141–2
Agro-Industrial Committee
  (GOSAGROPROM) 191
agro-industrial sector 142
Air Force 15–16
All Union Institute of Interbranch
  Information 42, 72
Algeria 168
Aliev, G. 182
alliances
  benefit to USSR 162
  theory 146
allocative efficiency ignored 96
American pay, exaggerates Soviet
  military spending 13–14
Andropov, Y. 119, 125
Anti-Parasite Laws 104
Armed Forces
  size 1
  structure 15–16
arms trade 166–74
  Chief Engineering Directorate 166
  easy terms 167
  economic motivation 169–70
  estimating value 165
  exports 160
  hard currency 169
  oil 169
  soft currencies 167
  political motivation 165, 167

regional distribution 167
market 172
refuses to export technology 174
Army
  politicising function 73
  Russification 74
ATOMASH 135
austere technological style 62
autarchy 62, 85, 99, 153
autocorrelation 33

'B' Team 25
Baku 126
balance of payments 189
Baltic States 109
BAM Railway 74, 125
Bolsheviks
  reject market 79, 82, 84–5
  view of capitalist dynamic 26
Brazil 173
Brezhnev, L. 119, 136, 181, 188
Bryant Grinder Corporation 175
buffer capacity 38, 43
building-block technique
  critique 17
  estimates 12–13, 43
Bukharin, N. 80
Bulgaria 158
bureaucratic model 33–5
Burton, D. 22

Canada 139
capital
  contribution to growth 95, 101,
    105–6, 107, 111–17
  construction unfinished 116, 118,
    181
  depreciation rate 181
  distribution 116
  formation in 1930s 98
  growth 105, 111, 117, 183, 190
  importance to growth 95
  labour ratio 107
  productivity 98, 99
  repair 115
  retirement rates 114, 181
capitalism
  counterrevolutionary 75
  tendency to war 75
Carter, J. 186

Index

Category 'A' and 'B' Goods 137, 183
catching up with the West 79
Central Asian Republics
  labour abundant 109, 110, 145
  migration 145
  productivity 145
Central Intelligence Agency 12, 14,
    15, 19–24, 87, 165, 184
  asymmetric function 25
  building block 12–13, 17, 20
  confidence in 12
  criticisms of 17–22
  hybrid 12
  manipulated 21, 22
  overstates 22
  revised 15, 23
  Sovietised 12–13
central planning
  ad hoc 82
  Empirical 85
  instrument of mobilisation 81
  military major beneficiary 39, 93
  physical 84
  as propaganda 83
  quantitative 84
chemicals 177
Chernobyl 135, 136
China 16, 27, 34, 165, 188
Chief Engineering Directorate 166
civilian military experts 42
clothing 143
coal 103, 107, 113, 121, 126, 130–1
  exhaustion 128, 130
  investment 130–1
  production 120, 131, 181
  transport costs 130
COCOM 175, 189
Cohn, S. 111, 115
collective farms 125, 140, 141, 142
collective goods, defence as 148
collectivisation 81, 82, 95
coloured markets 144–5
Commissariat of Heavy Industry 38
Commission on West Siberian Oil &
    Gas 190
Committee of Defence 38
commonality of weapons 57
Communist Party Plenum 63, 64, 96
computers 183
Congo 168
consumption
  increasing 143
  residual claimant 99
  squeezed 86

consumption goods 118, 143–5
  growth 137, 143
  organisation 144
  produced in military plants 43, 144
  sacrificed 81
construction
  investment 116
  military 189
  troops 74
Coordinating Bureau for Machine
    Tools 124
copper 97
correlation of forces 27, 75
correlation of variance between civilian
    and military expenditure 33
cost of new weapons 46–7
Council of Ministers 41, 42, 44, 124,
    190, 191
Council of Mutual Economic
    Assistance 153–64
  Agreed Plan for Multilateral
    Measures 161
  bilateral clearing 159
  Bucharest Principle 155
  critical decade 179
  East European investment in the
    USSR 161
  irrational prices 145
  Moscow Principle 158
  reparation payments 153–4
  Socialist Integration 156
  Soviet: export surplus 159; oil
    exports 157–60; subsidy 157–60
  terms of trade 156, 158
Cuba 163
Czechoslovakia 132, 151, 154, 157,
    164, 172, 173

decolonisation 164
defence
  budget 1, 8–10, 34, 76
  as collective good 148
  Council 38, 41
  industry 37, 38, 40, 44, 57, 93
  industry produces civilian goods 38
  influences economic outcomes 76,
    77
  less efficient 71
  more efficient 69
  sector less able to insulate 187
Defense Intelligence Agency
  data 23, 24
  disagreement with CIA 24
  distorts data 23

Index

methodology 23
DeLauer, R. 54
Dienes, L. 134
discipline campaign 125, 182
doctrine
 and weapons selection 57
 quantitative 27, 71
 reject western 27
Dolgikh, V. 136
dollar estimates
 American prices 12
 criticism of 15–22
 exaggerates Soviet expenditure 6
 methodology 12–14
 revised 15, 23–4, 184–7
 value 4, 15
Donbas 102, 113, 121, 128, 131
Draft Guidelines to 1990 122, 126, 137, 145, 179, 181, 182, 183
Dyker, D. 106

Eastern Europe
 energy deficit 157
 growth strategy 159
 incomplete identification with USSR 150
 investment in USSR 156–7, 161
 military expenditures: burden 149; conversion problems 150; data problems 147; definition 148; dollar estimates 148; export market for USSR 150–1; index number problem 148; military contribution 148–50; R&D excluded 148; subsidised by the USSR 156–7, 159–60
econometric tests of civilian–military trade-off 88–92
economic
 ageing 113
 aid 164, 167
 debate in the 1920s 80, 82, 190–1
 growth: 1930–39 97, 98; 1950–60 100; 1960–82 102; accounting techniques 100–1; benefit of youth 98, 108; cf. capitalistic countries 101; correlation with industrial growth 98; extensive 27, 96, 107, 116, 143, 179; forecasts 180; main objective 83; military dimension of 26, 27; post-Stalin 99–100; slowdown 102, 106, 108; technology in 101; unbalanced 98

obsolescence 114
 prospects 118–19
 reform 93, 107
 warfare 154
economy
 as one firm 96
 richly endowed 97
education 105
Egypt 164, 165, 167
employment in military industries 88
energy 96, 126–37, 177
 Commission on West Siberian Oil & Gas 190
 Contract Brigades 132
 expansion 127
 imbalance 127, 133, 134
 inefficient 133
 inflexible 127
 intensity 181
 ministers sacked 181
 output elasticity 126–33
 westward movement 134
Ekibastuz 131
excessive preoccupation with security 28
exchange rate conversion 20, 21
exports
 arms 165–73
 industrial goods 170, 178
 oil 157–8
extended reproduction 95
Export Administration Act 175, 177

ferrous metals 103
Five Year Plans
 1st 26, 81, 99
 5th 103
 6th 103
 8th 104
 9th 108
 10th 111, 116, 120, 128, 129, 141, 185, 186, 187
 11th 131, 132, 135, 142, 180
Five Year Plan For Defence 26, 37
follow-on principle 49, 60
food
 central problem of the decade 142
 consumption 138
 diet 138
 imports 140
 investment 143
 prices 140
 programme 142–3
 queues 140

riots 140
subsidies 140
wasted 141–2
Ford, President G. 186
foreign advisers 171
foreign technology 85, 174–8
France 173
Friendship (Druzba) Pipeline 157
frontal aviation 16
full employment 68

General Purpose Forces 16
General Staff 42, 57, 62, 72
German Democratic Republic 150, 151, 154, 157, 158, 162, 172
Germany 153
Glavmetall 37
gold 189
goods
  famine 80
  not neutral 7
Gorbachev, M. 63, 65, 93, 106, 111, 118, 119, 120, 122, 124, 136, 179, 183, 190, 192
Gorki 140
GOSPLAN 38, 40, 190
GOSSNAB 40, 41, 44
grain 125
Great Patriotic War 99
Greater Russia 74
gross industrial output 98
ground forces 16
Gu Guan Fe 167
Guinea 167, 168

Hanson, P. 102
hardware, residual 11
Holloway, D. 40
Holzman, F. 21, 22
Hungary 152, 157, 158, 172

imports
  aeroengines 174
  food 140
  machine tools 123
  technology 174
incremental capital output ratios 112, 116, 117
index number problem 18–19
India 166, 169, 173
industrial
  bottlenecks 117
  output 97

in-house production 44, 61, 123
institutional pluralism 34
intensification of production 117, 133, 182
investment
  competitive with military expenditure 87
  contribution to economic growth 101
  crisis rate 111
  distribution 116
  and intensification of production 181, 182, 183
  and productivity 183
  planned 181
  ratio 98
Iran 167, 173
Iraq 168
iron ore 97, 120, 121
Israel 166

Japan 101, 102, 113, 176

Kama River Truck Plant 178
Kansk–Achinsk basin 130
Khazakstan 103
khozraschet 9
Khrushchev, N. 27, 100, 103, 164, 179
Kulaks 82
Kuzbas 120, 122, 131
Kuwait 173

labour
  auxiliary jobs 50
  birth rate 109
  Central Asia 109–10
  contribution to economic growth 101
  death rate 109
  discipline 119
  discipline campaigns 182
  force 104
  participation rates 104
  supply 103–5, 180–1
  inefficiently used 110
  migration 98, 108–9
  regional imbalance 108
  RSFSR 109
Laspeyres index 18, 19
Lee, W. 15, 49, 51
leftist views 80
Lenin, V. I 95
Libya 168, 169, 173

Ligachev, Y. 182
lignite 130
living standards 143
long land borders 74

Machine Building and Metal Working Branch 11, 20, 87, 89, 183, 184
machine tools 81, 84, 86, 96, 115, 122–4
  growth 124, 182
  imports 123
  industry criticised 124
  in-house production 123
  lack of skilled labour 124
  lag with West 122
  paramount attention to 124
machinery 122–4
  imports 178
  inflation in 22
'mad momentum' 49
Magnitogorsk 122
Mali 168
market rejected by Bolsheviks 79, 82, 84–5
Marx, K. 95
Marxian value 96
Marxism-Leninism 36, 75, 164
  role of armed forces 73
  warring camps 74
  ideology 74
  guide and justification 95
migration 95, 105
military
  academies 38
  assistance 75, 164, 167
  borrowing 174
  budget 1, 2, 3, 34
  capital, specific 69
  civilian trade-offs 79, 86, 180
  construction 189
  Defence Council 190
  doctrine 27, 45, 57, 71
  Economic Analysis Center 22
  education 73
  estimates: analytic tool 3; deliberately manipulated 21; dollar 4, 5, 15; fixed price 6; hardware, residual 11; ideological 25; misused 25; parametric cost-estimating techniques 22; personnel costs overstated 21; political purpose 12; residual 8–10; Rubles 4, 5, 15

expenditure 4, 9, 15, 17, 24, 78; in 1930 8, 9; in 1940 9; in 1986 24; propaganda 1; R&D 50–1; summary measures 3
force potential 8, 32
goods: as ends 82; high status 7, 10
greatest beneficiary of central planning 93, 192
industrial commission 38, 41, 192
industrial complex 44, 45, 191
inspectors 39, 43, 44, 71
organisation in 1930s 37
operations and maintenance 13, 189
plants produce civilian goods 43, 69
power and the economic base 93
as powerful customer 71
priority 39, 43; source of inefficiency 77
procurement 16, 20, 22
production: 1930s 36; 1940 174; buffer capacity 38, 43, 168; overheads 7; postpones socialism 36; justifies central planning 82; shielded 39, 70; usefulness to Soviet leaders 72–6
R&D: avoids 'mad momentum' 49; effective 52; estimating expenditure 49–50; evolutionary 57; follow-on 49, 60; national style 57–8; organisation 56–7; user philosophy 57
vocational training 73
worth 3
Ministry of Defence 57, 74
  undertakes R&D 41, 42
  of medium machine building 37, 40
  of general machine building 37
  of radio industry 37
mobilisation of resources 96
modernisation programme 46, 63, 64, 93, 179, 182, 190
  intensification 182
  supported by defence chiefs 192

National Air Defence 16
NATO 28, 34, 45, 165, 188
natural gas 126, 131–3
  contract brigades 132
  growth 131
  pipeline system 132
  reserves 131
  transportation costs 132

Index

natural resources 114
Navy 16
net material product 97
New Economic Policy 79
Nimitz, N. 14, 51, 69, 70
nuclear energy 134–6
　Chernobyl 135, 136
　fast breeder reactors 135
　growth 134–5
　resource saving 135–6
　shortfall 135

Ob 128
obedinenie 37
Ogarkov, N. 63
OPEC 189
operations and maintenance 13, 189
Orenburg 125, 161
output elasticity of substitution 108

Paasche index 18, 19
Pakistan 166, 167
parametric estimating techniques 22
participation rates 104
patents 92
'peace' electricity grid 157
Pentagon 58, 64, 185
personnel costs overstated 21
personal savings 183
petroleum 97, 107, 126–30
　cheap 126
　exhaustion 128
　expansion 127
　exports 127, 157–60
　falling prices 163
　inefficient pricing 128
　pipelines 126, 127, 189
　production 181
　shortfall 128
　trusts 114
　water injection methods 128
planning in depth 38
Poland 150, 154, 157, 162, 172
political leaders empathise with
　　military 41
Politburo 38, 62, 63, 190
　active in weapons selection 41
population 98, 103
post-Stalinist growth strategy 99–100
Preobrazhenski, Y. 80
prices
　accounting function 96
　exclude rent and interest 69
　not equal opportunity cost 6, 10

rejected by Bolsheviks 84
　temporary 7
procurement 16, 20, 22
　cycles 190
　declining trend 24, 185, 186
　stretch-outs 186
productivity 117
　in agriculture 139, 141
　in APF analysis 102
　capital 99, 108, 112
　and civil–military trade-off 91
　contribution to growth 101
　factor 113, 181
　labour 105, 107, 111
　performance 102, 181
purchasing power parity 20

rail 125
rate of interest 84–5, 96
Reagan, R. 171, 188, 189
Red Army 26
reform of military planning 37
regional distribution 145–6
rent 96
R&D 13, 14, 22, 41, 45–8, 51, 65, 99,
　　186, 189, 190, 192
　by Academy of Science 56
　by armed services 56
　autonomy 56–7
　burden 63
　civilian 54–5
　countries compete against
　　themselves 48
　conversion ratios 13
　cycle 48
　and doctrine 57
　employment in 59, 89, 92
　estimating expenditure on 49–50
　excluded from budget 9
　finance of 59
　and follow-on principle 49, 60
　military: demand on 191; more
　　effective than civil 52; percentage
　　of total 49; priority 42
　by Ministry of Defence 56
　non-monetary opportunity cost 60
　organisation of 56–7
　patents 92
　percentage of military budget 14
　quantitative targets 56
　Soviet monopoly in Warsaw
　　Pact 152
　user philosophy 57
research cycle 184

Index

residual method 8–10
resource exhaustion 114
Rhyzkov, N. 191
Richardson models 28–32
rightist views 80
Rosefielde, S. 17, 22
RSFSR 109, 145
ruble estimates 4, 15
Rumania 156, 157
Russian
  nationalism 74
  preoccupation with defence 74
  sole language of instruction 74

SALT I & II 185
satisficing in bureaucratic models 35
Samotlar Oil Field 129
science
  budget 14
  catalyst in East–West balance 62
SDI 64, 188
secrecy 62, 72
Shanin, L. 36, 80
Shchekino 182
Siberia 103, 109, 130, 131, 132, 134, 136, 146
simple reproduction 95
SIPRI 23
Somalia 168
social and cultural measures 10
Socialism in One Country 29
socialists and a standing army 26
soldiers cheap in the USSR 18
Soviet Empire 163
'Sovietising' weapons 21, 99, 176
SS 10 SAMS 64
Stalin 45, 72, 81, 100, 137, 164
  crushes opposition 81
  military goods as ends 82
  prohibits economic debate 85
  suppresses living standards 143
  unrealistic growth targets 83
State Committee
  on Labour and Social Questions 108
  for Science and Technology 55, 175
State Farms 125, 140, 141, 142
static defence burden 66
superpower status based on military might 75
steel 81, 84, 86, 96, 107
  eaters 179
  failure to modernise 120
  low quality 121
  output 120

shortage 120, 187
  as symbol 120
strategic forces 16
sugar 163
superindustrialists 82, 190–1
supply constraints 34
Supreme Council of National Economy 37
synthetic rubber 177
Syria 165, 168

T-72 Tank 57
technological
  change: avoid 'mad momentum' 49; contribution to economic growth 101; embodied 99, 107; quantitative 56
  follower 46, 49
  imports: aeroengines 174; benefit to follower country 99; Bryant Grinder Co. 175; covert 175; and MIRV capacity 176; 'Sovietised' 174, 176; value 177
  level (cf. USA) 52–3, 69
  progress in military sector 49
  style 57, 64; austere 62; consistent with doctrine 58
teleological view 84, 97
Third World
  debt 172
  as recipient of Soviet arms 165–9
  welcomes USSR 164
timber 103, 113, 177
Togliatti 140
transportation 124–6
  bottlenecks 125, 187
  cost of coal prohibitive 130–1
  eastwards expansion 125
  of natural gas 132
  Minister of Railways sacked 125
  rail 125
Troitsk 134
Tuymen 131, 132, 133, 136, 190

unbalanced growth 98
Ukraine 109
Urals 103, 113, 127, 134, 145
urban population 98
Urengoi 131, 132
USA 28, 30, 32, 34, 45, 49, 50, 52, 64, 120, 122, 137, 166, 188
Ust Ilim 161

Virgin Lands 103

Volgodonsk 135
Voyenpred 43, 44
Voznesenski 38

war
  not fatalistically inevitable 27
  the decisive phase 26
weapons
  cost of new 46–7
  evolutionary design 57
  modernisation 186
  performance characteristics 47
  stock 8
Warsaw Pact 147, 153, 155, 188
  Eastern Europe: buffer zone 162; economic cost to USSR 158–60; exhorted to increase military expenditure 151; export market for Soviet weapons 150–1; military expenditures 147, 148, 149; produce Soviet weapons under licence 152
  Joint Technical Committee 151
  military: benefit to USSR 162; integration 151; modernisation 152
  Political Consultative Commission 151
  USSR: dominates 147; monopoly of R&D 152; pays disproportionate share 147; prevents indigenous weapons development 152; subsidy 162
  weapons standardisation 52, 57, 151
wastage
  capital 116
  natural resources 114
  food 141–2

X-inefficiency 70

Yamburg 132
Yakutia 132

Zambia 169